GW00360845

Russian Journal of
Lady Londonderry
1836–7

Russian Journal of
Lady Londonderry

1836–7

Edited by *W. A. L. Seaman*
and *J. R. Sewell*

JOHN MURRAY

Editorial © W. A. L. Seaman
and J. R. Sewell 1973

Printed in Great Britain at
The Pitman Press Bath
0 7195 2851 8

Contents

Illustrations

Notes on the Text

THE PRESENT CHAPTER I comprises material from the first three chapters of the original manuscript. These have not been printed in full as they contain a certain amount of repetitious detail concerning the outward journey, but any omission is indicated by the use of three dots . . . Later chapters have been renumbered accordingly and the text is then complete with the exception of the seldom apposite poetical quotations at the beginning of each chapter. Spelling and punctuation have been modernized and the opportunity has been taken to correct a number of obvious errors in passages in French.

Place names have been modernized with the exception of such well-known names as St. Petersburg and Tsarskoe Seloe. Where the modern name differs significantly from that in the original manuscript, the latter appears in round brackets after the modern name. The spelling of personal names has been standardized throughout and several transcriptional mistakes have also been corrected, e.g. "Broki" in error for "Brahe".

Words in square brackets correct or explain the term or terms which they follow or, occasionally, complete the text itself. Gaps in the manuscript are indicated by angle brackets ⟨ ⟩ and words appearing in angle brackets represent editorial conjectures for matter omitted in the original. The footnotes have been used to provide a certain amount of explanatory and illustrative material intended to supplement the narrative.

Introduction

FRANCES ANNE EMILY VANE-TEMPEST was the only child of Sir Henry Vane-Tempest and his wife, Anne Catherine, Countess of Antrim. She was born at Lord Lichfield's house in St. James's Square, London, on 16th January, 1800. Her paternal grandfather, the Rev. Sir Henry Vane, was Rector of Long Newton which lies midway between Stockton and Darlington in the south-east of the County of Durham. He was also a prebend of Durham and Treasurer of Durham Cathedral. In 1768 he married Frances, daughter of John Tempest of Sherburn, and through her inherited extensive estates, including Wynyard, which was later to become the principal seat of the Londonderrys in the North of England.

His son, Sir Henry Vane-Tempest, the father of Frances Anne, was born in 1771. He was reputedly both handsome and dissolute and is reported to have rushed into every kind of costly extravagance. He sat in Parliament as Member for Durham City from 1796 to 1800 and he represented the County from 1807 until his death in 1813 at the early age of forty-two. He married in April 1799 and his only child, a daughter, was born early in the following year.

She appears to have had an insecure and unhappy childhood being committed to the care of a succession of indifferent and repressive governesses. "A Miss Webb was found", wrote Frances Anne in later life, "who stayed with me six months, during which time she did little but box my ears and rap my knuckles."* Her childhood was further marred by illness. As an infant she nearly died of smallpox and at the age of ten she suffered a severe attack of scarlet fever. Following her father's death in 1813, Frances Anne was made a ward of Chancery for, despite Sir Henry's extravagant way of living, she was heiress to a very substantial fortune.

Frances Anne first met her future husband, Lord Stewart, later the third Marquess of Londonderry, at her mother's house in

* Edith, Marchioness of Londonderry, *Frances Anne* (London, 1958), p. 14, hereafter cited as *Frances Anne*.

Bruton Street, London, early in 1818. Her initial reactions were not very favourable. "When my mother asked what I thought of him", she wrote afterwards, "I said not much, that he seemed finniken and looked as if he had false teeth."* At this time, Stewart, who was twenty-two years older than Frances Anne, already had a distinguished military and diplomatic career behind him although his activities were always overshadowed by those of his more renowned half-brother, Castlereagh.

The Stewarts were of Irish extraction having settled at Mount Stewart, County Down, in the seventeenth century. Robert Stewart, born in 1739, had sat in the old Irish Parliament. He was created a baron in 1789 and became the first Marquess of Londonderry in 1816. His only son by his first marriage was Robert, Viscount Castlereagh, who held various political appointments and served as Foreign Secretary from 1812 until his death in 1822. By his second marriage the first Marquess had several children but only one son, Charles, later Lord Stewart, born in 1778.

Stewart entered the army at the age of sixteen and served both in the Netherlands and with the Austrians on the Rhine and the Upper Danube. In 1808 he commanded a brigade of hussars in the Peninsula under Sir John Moore and was later Adjutant General to Wellington there. He sat in the House of Commons for County Derry from 1800 to 1814 and for a time was Under Secretary for War. In 1813 he was sent as Minister to Berlin charged specifically with "the military superintendence, so far as Great Britain is concerned, of the Prussian and Swedish armies."† This appointment brought him into close contact with both the Russian Emperor Alexander I and also with Bernadotte, a former marshal of Napoleon, and then Prince Royal and heir to the throne of Sweden. Relations between Stewart and Bernadotte were often strained. A letter written to Frances Anne in December 1860 by Sir James Reynett, aide de camp to Queen Victoria, recalled that at the time Stewart had

"acquitted himself with marked ability. This was particularly shewn in his negociations with Bernadotte, then the Crown Prince of Sweden—a man of great duplicity and chicane. *He*

* *Frances Anne*, p. 31.
† Sir A. Alison, *Lives of Lord Castlereagh and Sir Charles Stewart* (Edinburgh and London, 1861) vol. I, p. 546*n*., hereafter cited as Sir A. Alison, *Lives*.

2

then commanded a numerous & detached corps d'Armée of not less than 70,000 men. His bias & inclinations were very naturally supposed to be wholly French, tho' he had sufficient talent & ability to discover that their Side was become the losing game [*sic*]. Lord Londonderry appreciated the Character & sentiments of this remarkable Individual & foiled him with great talent & ability—the great difficulty was to get him to act as he was bent upon temporising—but Lord L. was determined to hold him to his political obligations—This was at length determined upon, after a most stormy discussion at a very remarkable interview between the Prince Royal & Sir Charles [Stewart] & which ended by the Prince admitting that he must give way adding 'J'avoue, Général, que vous m'avez vaincu'."*

Shortly afterwards, in August 1814, Stewart was appointed Ambassador at Vienna, a post which he retained until after the death of Castlereagh in 1822. In this capacity he attended the various congresses held by the major powers during the post-Napoleonic period to determine the political structure of Europe.

Stewart's first marriage, to Lady Catherine Bligh, daughter of the third Earl of Darnley, took place in August 1804. By her he had one son, Frederick, who was later to become the fourth Marquess of Londonderry. Lady Catherine died in 1812.

His second marriage, in 1819, to Lady Frances Anne Vane-Tempest, was only achieved in the face of considerable opposition and recourse to litigation. Frances Anne's joint guardians were her mother, the Countess of Antrim, and her aunt, Mrs. Taylor, wife of Michael Angelo Taylor, who represented the City of Durham in the House of Commons between 1800 and 1802 and again from 1818 until 1831. The Countess and Mrs. Taylor were rarely in agreement on any matter and it appears that while the mother was ready to support Lord Stewart's suit for her daughter's hand, the aunt was irrevocably opposed to the proposal. Moreover, as Frances Anne was at this time a ward of Chancery Mrs. Taylor was in a position to create difficulties. This she proceeded to do by applying to the Lord Chancellor to restrain the Countess of Antrim "from having communication with her daughter, except in the presence

---

* D/Lo/C 178. References in this form are to documents among the Londonderry Papers in the Durham County Record Office.

of her governess; because without application to the Court, and without the consent of Mrs. Taylor, the Countess of Antrim had promoted a marriage between her daughter and Lord Stewart."* The case, which was heard before Lord Chancellor Eldon, dragged on for three months and terminated in a judgement, albeit somewhat reluctantly given, allowing the marriage. The ceremony took place at Lady Antrim's London house on 3rd April, 1819. In July of the same year Stewart and his young wife set out for Vienna travelling by leisurely stages and spending some time in Paris on the way. They arrived on 10th October, 1819.

It is clear that Frances Anne greatly enjoyed her travels and her newly acquired sense of freedom. Equally, she entered with zest into the social life of Vienna though her lack of maturity, especially in personal relationships, sometimes caused offence. Martha Wilmot, wife of the Rev. William Bradford who was chaplain at the Vienna Embassy, wrote to Lady Ennismore on 8th December, 1819 " . . . 'tis plain she is not free from caprice, and 'tis equally plain that she is a compleat spoilt child . . . "† Relations between the two women seem to have deteriorated rapidly. By the summer of 1821 Martha Wilmot was writing to Lady Bloomfield about the Stewarts in the following terms:

"I declare that their united Vanity and Selfishness amounts almost to madness and their *wish* of keeping in the back ground, as Domestic animals, those connected with them is only to be exceeded by the *Regal Airs* which they assume in their own persons . . . Their pride renders their very kindness an insult. For example when they give an entertainment if you think they mean to give pleasure you are mistaken. No, no, 'tis an ostentatious display of their superiour riches and grandeur. She, decked out like the Queen of Golconda seated on a Sofa, receives you with *freezing* pomp and the atmosphere which surrounds her is *awful* and *chilling*. He is her most humble slave and casts on all besides such looks of condescending *protection* that one involuntarily bursts out laughing at the suppress'd pride of the creature."‡

* *Frances Anne*, p. 38.
† Edith, Marchioness of Londonderry & H. M. Hyde, *More Letters from Martha Wilmot* (London, 1935), p. 35.
‡ *Ibid.*, pp. 108–109.

4

In a letter to her mother-in-law a week later, Mrs. Bradford described the christening in London of Frances Anne's eldest son, the future Lord Seaham, as "superb" adding, " . . . so well do both Lord and Lady Stewart understand effect that they ought to have been managers of Drury Lane!!!!"* Princess Lieven, who was also present on this occasion, wrote in a letter to Metternich:

"Lord Stewart's child was christened yesterday with a great deal of vulgar ostentation. I was there; it took nearly the whole day. The famous bed, surmounted by a coronet and supported by the gilt figures of Hercules . . . was transformed into an altar before dinner and a sideboard after, and back into a bed at the end of the festivities. The whole town came to see the farce."†

After the death of Castlereagh in 1822 and the appointment of his rival Canning as Foreign Secretary, Stewart (or Londonderry as he had become) resigned from the Vienna Embassy and returned home to administer and exploit his family's large and potentially profitable estates.

In addition to his own inheritance and the property which had come to him by marriage, Stewart had purchased the Seaham estate of Sir Ralph Milbanke in 1821 for £63,000. This was subsequently developed by the building of Seaham Harbour, an outstanding engineering feat of its time, which provided an outlet for the export of coal from Lord Londonderry's Durham collieries and which avoided the need for a roundabout and costly journey through the port of Sunderland. At the same time, substantial improvements were made in the family's domestic arrangements. The Tempest residence at Wynyard described as "a large, old house in the Flemish style of rural architecture"‡ was demolished to make way for a neo-classical mansion designed by Philip Wyatt and built at a cost of £102,000. A further £27,000 was spent on furnishings and £18,000 on landscaping and pleasure grounds. When on 19th February, 1841, the still uncompleted building was damaged by fire, rebuilding commenced at once under the direction of

* *Ibid.*, p. 115.
† Peter Quenell (ed.), *The Private Letters of Princess Lieven to Prince Metternich, 1820–26* (London, 1948), p. 139.
‡ Sir A. Alison, *Lives*, III, p. 241.

5

Ignatius Bonomi and a further £40,000 was spent on making the house "the most splendid 19th century mansion in the county."*

But building and the development of their estates did not interfere with the social activities of the Londonderrys. Parties, receptions, balls, banquets and house parties followed each other with almost monotonous regularity. In 1824, on a visit to the Doncaster Races, they encountered Thomas Creevey, the Whig M.P. and diarist, who in his most vitriolic style wrote of Frances Anne, "—Such a dumpy, rum-shaped and rum-faced article as Lady Londonderry one can rarely see."†

Nevertheless, despite the time and energy given over to the development of his family estates and to social activities, Lord Londonderry still kept up his political connections and his correspondence shows quite clearly his desire for public office. The nearest he ever came to attaining it was during the short-lived minority government of Sir Robert Peel in 1834–35 when he was named as Ambassador to St. Petersburg. The appointment produced a storm of criticism both in Parliament and in the press. On 2nd January, 1835, *The Times* reported, "We notice, merely to discountenance, an absurd report that Lord Londonderry has been, or is to be, named Ambassador to St. Petersburg. The rumour is a sorry joke." Sorry joke it may have been but the rumour was not without foundation. Frances Mary Gascoyne-Cecil wrote in her diary what may have been a rather fanciful account of a dinner which she attended on 20th February, 1835. Also present on that occasion was Peel who:

"went on telling *me*, to my infinite entertainment, of the successful flattery he had employed in the various transactions and negotiations about offices. 'I used to scribble off these letters at once. I had not time to consider . . . But I never yet found the amount of flattery too large for any man to swallow. To Lord Londonderry I made the offer of the Mastership of the Buck-hounds *or* of the Embassy to Russia. I laugh when I think of my impudence in proposing both to the same man, but I told him that few people possessed that extent of acquirement and

---

* N. Pevsner, *The Buildings of England: County Durham* (London, 1953), p. 246.
† *Frances Anne*, p. 135.

6

variety of talent which could have justified me in offering him at once two situations so different'."*

There was considerable scepticism concerning Lord Londonderry's "acquirement" and "talent", however, and this was forcibly expressed in the course of a debate in the House of Commons on 13th March, and three days later in *The Times* where it was reported somewhat ponderously:

". . . speaking of him as a politician, there is in our opinion ample reason for the fullest concern on the part of Lord Londonderry's friends, and of strong disapprobation throughout the country generally, arising out of so ill-judged, unsuitable, and unpopular an appointment . . . we quite agree with those who think, that for a trust at once so difficult and so distinguished, the noble Marquis has disqualified himself as much by his want of sympathy with the known feelings of Englishmen in favour of the oppressed liberties and trampled rights of Poland, as nature and education have incapacitated him for the complex and arduous duties of Minister at the most subtle and insidious Court of Europe . . .".

In view of the government's precarious position and the widespread opposition to the appointment itself, Lord Londonderry reluctantly felt compelled to decline Peel's offer.

However, the fleeting prospect of the Russian Embassy had stimulated a desire for travel and the Londonderrys determined to undertake a "grand tour" of northern Europe, visiting Russia as private individuals. Five months after the birth of her third son on 29th February, 1836, Frances Anne and her husband along with their eldest son, Lord Seaham, set out on their journey. They left London on 3rd August, 1836, taking the short crossing from Dover to Calais because of Frances Anne's "horror of a long sea".† From there they travelled by way of Brussels, Rotterdam (where they were met by a retinue of servants and the heavy carriages), Bremen and Hamburg to Copenhagen. Crossing into Sweden they travelled on

* Carola Oman, *The Gascoyne Heiress. The Life and Diaries of Frances Mary Gascoyne-Cecil*, 1802–39, London, 1968, p. 152.
† See p. 1 of the manuscript *Journal*.

to Stockholm by way of Göteborg. It had been intended to proceed from there to St. Petersburg by way of Turku (Åbo) and overland across Southern Finland but the arrival during their stay in Stockholm of Count Potocki, the new Russian Ambassador, aboard the Imperial yacht *Ischora* led to a change of plan. The new envoy placed the yacht at the disposal of the Londonderrys for the remainder of their outward journey and the offer was accepted with alacrity despite Frances Anne's previous "horror of a long sea". Sacrifices in favour of status, not to mention comfort, no doubt provided more than adequate recompense.

The Londonderrys arrived in St. Petersburg on 17th September, 1836, a little more than six weeks after their departure from England. They were received informally by the Tsar and other members of the Imperial family on many occasions; they attended Court and social functions; they saw art collections, churches and museums; they visited theatres and military establishments; they were present at parades and reviews; they inspected palaces, prisons, hospitals, monasteries and educational institutions. In fact, they were indefatigable in their determination to see and do everything. They also made journeys from St. Petersburg travelling as far south as Moscow which greatly impressed them both. "Petersburg", wrote Frances Anne, "is a magnificent town and on a colossal scale, but it can never be the capital of Russia. Moscow is Russia with an Asiatic colouring."*

At the time of their visit the vast Russian Empire was ruled by the autocratic Tsar Nicholas I. He had been born on 6th July, 1796, the third son of Tsar Paul who was assassinated when Nicholas was four years old. Unlike his two elder brothers Alexander and Constantine, Nicholas was not subjected to the influence of the Empress Catherine II who died in the year of his birth, and he was placed under the tutelage of a succession of foreign women, Miss Lyon, a Scottish nurse, the governess Julie Adlerberg and Madame de Lieven, daughter of a Westphalian noble who had joined the Russian army. In his early years he spent little time with other members of his family and he was educated by General de Lambsdorff, Director of the Corps of Cadets, a man who inspired fear and from whom he may have acquired his great love of military discipline, a passion he shared with his younger brother Michael. Nicholas learned to

8

speak French, German, and English, as well as Russian, and studied Latin and Greek, but it was in the science of warfare that he excelled, becoming an enthusiastic and exacting drill-master. He spent most of his youth at Gatchina or, in summer, at Pavlovsk and he remained at some distance from the centre of Court life at St. Petersburg and Tsarskoe-Seloe.

Nicholas married Princess Charlotte of Prussia on 13th July, 1817, and his bride then adopted the Russian names Alexandra Fedorovna. She was aged nineteen at the time, the daughter of King Frederick William III of Prussia, and, by all accounts, she and her husband made an attractive couple. Both were tall and Nicholas had the reputation of being one of the handsomest men in Europe. By Russian standards, he was a faithful and devoted husband (although the names of at least two mistresses are known) and he had seven children by his wife. Their eldest son, the future Alexander II, was born in April 1818 and he was followed by three daughters, Marie in 1819, Olga in 1822 and Alexandra in 1825. The second son, Constantine, was born in 1827 and two other sons, Nicholas and Michael, arrived after Nicholas had ascended the throne.

The education of the Tsarevich or *Héritier*, as he is called by Lady Londonderry, was entrusted to the poet and humanist Basil Joukovsky. A headstrong youth, he caused his parents much anxiety which culminated in his desire to marry a Polish maid of honour named Olga Kalinovsky in 1839. This was prevented and in 1841 he married Marie, daughter of Louis II, Grand Duke of Hesse, a marriage which provoked a certain amount of criticism since there was some doubt concerning her legitimacy. Nicholas's second son, Constantine, chose a naval career while the younger brothers, Nicholas and Michael, were later employed in military office, the former acting as commander-in-chief during the Russo-Turkish War of 1877-78, the latter becoming Inspector General of Russian Artillery. The eldest daughter, Marie, married Duke Maximilian of Leuchtenberg in 1839, while Olga, the second daughter, married Charles, the Prince Royal of Württemberg in 1846. The youngest, Alexandra, who was generally regarded as the living image of her mother, married Prince Frederick of Hesse-Cassel but died a year later in 1844.

Brief reference should be made also to the Tsar's brothers and sisters. His eldest brother, Tsar Alexander I, was born in 1777 and succeeded to the throne in 1801. His implication in the conspiracy which led to the assassination of his father, Tsar Paul, gave rise to feelings of guilt which troubled him for the remainder of his days and may help to explain his pious obsessions. Towards the end of his life there were numerous conspiracies of which he was well aware but he failed to take any action to avert them. Still more surprising was Alexander's handling of the succession. He had no legitimate children and his next brother Constantine, born in 1779, was the obvious heir to the Imperial throne. However, Constantine had renounced his claims in an official proclamation of 1823 but this was not published and Nicholas may well have been unaware of its precise terms. An additional complication was that the enactment which determined the succession on the principle of male primogeniture was of recent origin, and these circumstances combined to produce a period of confusion when news of Alexander's death reached St. Petersburg in December 1825. Nicholas immediately swore allegiance to Constantine who was in Warsaw and who, unaware of this, swore allegiance to Nicholas. It was not until after the exchange of numerous despatches between the two capitals that Nicholas claimed the throne and by that time a serious situation had developed. The first battalion of the Moscow Regiment mutinied but the revolt of the Decembrists, as the rebels were known, was put down and Nicholas became Tsar. Constantine died in 1831.

Nicholas's younger brother, Michael, was born in 1798 and was widely regarded as his living caricature although he lacked the charm of the Tsar. He married in 1824 Charlotte, daughter of Prince Paul of Württemberg, who was henceforth known as the Grand Duchess Hélène. A complete contrast to her husband whose only interest was soldiering, she was a person of great intelligence whose knowledge tended to astonish everyone. She was responsible for the foundation of the St. Petersburg Conservatory. Both Nicholas's surviving sisters had married and no longer lived in Russia by the time of the Londonderrys' visit. Marie, born in 1786, was the wife of the Grand Duke Frederick of Saxe-Weimar, while Anna Paulovna born in 1795 was the wife of Prince William of Orange, the son of King William I of the Netherlands, who acceded to the throne on his father's abdication in 1840.

The trials of the Decembrists were to overshadow Nicholas's reign by permanently alienating those members of the Russian nobility who sympathized with the desire for institutional change. The suppression of the Polish revolt in 1831 had an equally serious effect on Western European views of Russia and, in London and Paris in particular, public opinion was fiercely pro-Polish. Poland was perhaps the only matter on which Frances Anne was critical of Russia although she was shrewd enough to observe "Poland is to Russia very much what Ireland is to England, a conquered country, a subdued kingdom that can never forget it was once independent but is always internally agitating and bringing down misery and forging for itself fresh chains".* The "Organic Statute" of 26th February, 1832, which abolished the Diet, the Polish army and the independent administration, reinforced the suspicion that complete assimilation was the intention of Russian policy. This was the view of many western travellers at the time.†

Although he led an austere and simple daily life, Nicholas shared the Russian love for lavish entertainments. The Marquis de Custine in his book *Russia in 1839* commented: "I saw the Congress of Vienna but cannot remember one assembly which can equal those of the Winter Palace in wealth of jewels, costumes, variety of uniforms and their luxury and in the splendour of the arrangements."‡ The men were usually dressed in uniform while the ladies wore a robe of white silk with a bodice of red velvet and a long embroidered train, and a head-dress ornamented with real or artificial jewels. One of the most important events in Court life was the fête to celebrate the New Year when the Winter Palace was opened to all ranks of Russian society. Some forty thousand were allowed inside and those who failed to gain admission filled the courtyard of the Palace. Dr. Robert Lyall, who spent several years in Russia after 1812, contrasted the different impressions formed by noblemen and other travellers of lesser rank. The titled "everywhere find open tables, cheerful and pleasant society, all kinds of

* See pp. 147-8.
† George F. Kennan, *The Marquis de Custine and his 'Russia in 1839'* (London, 1972), p. 87.
‡ Quoted by Constantin de Grunwald, *Tsar Nicholas I* (London, 1954), p. 148.

amusements, evening parties, *conversaziones*, balls, masquerades. The same round of pleasures meets them wherever they sojourn", while "Other travellers, without rank or introductions, find everything gloomy and are startled with difficulties and disagreeables at every step. At length they get introduced to the secondary circles of the nobility and are disgusted with their customs and manners."* Certainly little will be found about the poorer classes of Russian society in this *Journal*.

By European standards Russia was a backward country. The building of the road from Moscow to St. Petersburg on which Frances Anne commented so favourably was commenced in 1816 but it was not completed until 1834. The first railway was an experimental line from St. Petersburg to Tsarskoe Seloe but a decision to undertake the building of the first important railway between Moscow and St. Petersburg was not taken until 1842 and the line was not opened until ten years later.

Educational reforms had been initiated during the first ten years of the reign of Alexander I and the Empress Maria had been the founder of a variety of educational and benevolent institutions. Large foundling homes were maintained in St. Petersburg, Gatchina and Moscow which had accommodation for many orphans. St. Petersburg was the centre of technological and scientific training but a remarkable feature was the organization of the institutes on military lines. Emphasis on military training was a general feature of Russian life and even the great fêtes often took on the aspect of military parades. The Tsar treated his Empire as a vast military command and this prompted his frequent journeys to distant parts of the country.

Travelling in Russia was a hazardous affair as the pages of this *Journal* make clear. The Londonderrys, who arrived at St. Petersburg in the Imperial yacht, did not experience any of the difficulties which they had encountered elsewhere at frontier posts, but other travellers including the Marquis de Custine complained about the customs and immigration authorities. Relays of post-horses were used to transport travellers of means who were thus moved over the eight miles or so which separated one post-station from another. Robert Ker Porter in his *Travelling Sketches in Russia and Sweden*

* Francesca Wilson (ed.), *Muscovy: Russia Through Foreign Eyes* 1553–1900 (London, 1970), p. 191.

(1809) gives a graphic description of a typical post-house: "One room is the habitation of all the inmates. Here they eat, sleep, and perform all the functions of life. One quarter of it is occupied by a large stove . . . on which many of them take their nocturnal rest; and during the day lull over its baking warmth, for hours, by threes and fours together, in a huddle, not more decent than disgusting. . . . A bed with dirty curtains filled one corner of the room; a few benches and a table, completed the furniture."* Nearly all travellers remarked on the vermin to be found in even the best houses and the inn in Moscow run by Madame Howard, an English woman, had the reputation of being the only clean hostelry in Russia.

One of the most hated of the Tsar's officials was the courier known as the *feldjaeger*, one of whom accompanied the Londonderrys as far as Berlin on their return from Russia. Frances Anne was flattered by the attention and appreciated his organizational capacity during the rigours of the journey, but more astute observers regarded the *feldjaeger* with disdain as a spy of the Emperor. Custine called him "the man of power . . . the word of the master . . . a living telegraph line".†

From Moscow the Londonderrys returned to St. Petersburg where they remained throughout the early part of the winter before setting out again for England on 9th February, 1837. This time they travelled overland, under the most appalling conditions, by way of Riga, Warsaw and Breslau to Berlin where they arrived on the evening of 5th March. In the course of their journey their path crossed that of another traveller J. G. Kohl who, in 1842, published an account of his Russian experiences which refers to a near-meeting with the Londonderrys while passing through Estonia.

"We found the proud Marquis of Londonderry, with his wife, his son, and the tutor of the latter, fast asleep at the second station from Dorpat where that thorough going English Tory, a *rara avis* on these snowy plains, had taken up his quarters for the night on his return to England. The postmaster, as he smoked his pipe with us at breakfast, related to us how his lordship's first

* Anthony Cross (ed.), *Russia under Western Eyes* 1517–1825 (London, 1971), pp. 286–287.
† Quoted by Kennan, *op. cit.*, p. 29*n*.

command, on entering the house, had been that during his stay no one should smoke . . . I asked whether the marquis had made any inquiries respecting the character of a country so new to him, and so replete with interest; whether he had conversed with any of the inhabitants. The postmaster said he had done neither; that the whole company had sat till seven o'clock, employed in silent and devout consumption of their tea and toast; the ladies and children had then retired, but his lordship had continued to sit in silent solitude till twelve o'clock, when he went to bed. I had not the good fortune to meet the great man, for he was still in bed when we left the station."*

The Londonderrys remained in Berlin for almost a month recovering from the rigours of their journey and seeing something of social life in the Prussian capital. Leaving Berlin on 1st April they journeyed south, first to Dresden and then on to Frankfurt where Frances Anne was "taken very ill with spasms and remained for above a week in wretched suffering".† This was hardly surprising in view of the stamina and sheer physical endurance which must have been required to make such a journey in the worst part of the winter.

It had been intended originally to complete the return trip by steamer down the Rhine to Rotterdam returning to England from there by packet. However, in view of Frances Anne's uncertain health, it was decided to travel on in easy stages by way of Metz to Paris. There they remained for a month while Frances Anne recuperated. In the French capital she only ventured into society twice, once to dine with the King and Queen at the Tuileries, and once to a reception given by the Russian Ambassador. Many years later Lord Augustus Loftus recalled the former occasion in his *Diplomatic Reminiscences*:

"I was present at a dinner given by the King [Louis Philippe] to the late Marquis and Marchioness of Londonderry on their arrival from St. Petersburg *en route* to London", he wrote. "It was in May, 1837, and after the 1st of May, by the etiquette of the Court, all the guests appear *en frac*, and the ladies in demi-toilette. Lord and Lady Londonderry, not being aware of this

* J. G. Kohl, *Russia* (London, 1842), pp. 348–349.
† See p. 161.

14

Court regulation, appeared in full dress—the Marquis in his handsome Hussar uniform covered with decorations, the Marchioness a blaze of diamonds . . . Nothing could exceed the attentions both of the King and Queen to Lord and Lady Londonderry, to which the Marquis was duly entitled by his distinguished services."*

At the end of May she and her husband returned to England after an absence of almost ten months.

There are two other sources which supplement the account of the tour contained in Frances Anne's *Journal*. The first of these is a small collection of letters written by her to Henry Thomas Liddell, a neighbouring Durham landowner, who later became the first Earl of Ravensworth.† Liddell was three years older than Frances Anne and he sat in Parliament at various times as Member for Northumberland, Durham and Liverpool. He also translated the Odes of Horace into English lyric verse.

The first letter, written from the Hague on 9th August, 1836, commented on the weather and the luxuriance of the crops. "The cleanliness, neatness and exactitude of the people is wonderful", continued the account, "every morsel of every town is washed and scrubbed every day—each person doing their own bit!" However, these estimable qualities were counterbalanced to some extent by the fact that the milk was ". . . full of dust and fleas . . ."

The second letter, dated 24th September, was written from St. Petersburg and described the remainder of the outward journey: ". . . how we toiled through Dutch swamps", wrote Frances Anne, "how I survived for twenty-two hours in a small dirty Danish steam boat from Kiel to Copenhagen where I found grass growing in the street." Sweden, on the other hand, made an unexpectedly pleasing impression despite earlier forebodings. "I was charmed with Stockholm", she wrote, "spent twelve days there—beautiful situation, lovely islands—the poor Swedes were so amiable and civil and hospitable and all treated us like Celestial Visitants. I fell in love with Charles Jean [King Charles XIV, formerly Bernadotte], so agreeable and such an extraordinary man . . . Then by the

* *The Diplomatic Reminiscences of Lord Augustus Loftus* (London, 1892), vol. I, p. 8.
† D/Lo/T 70.

strangest piece of good luck and favour we had the Emperor's own private steam yacht and came straight to Petersburg, four days and four nights."

The next letter, written from Moscow and dated simply "October 1836" reported: "This is the most singular and beautiful town that I ever saw . . . The immense extent, the gardens, the variety and the hundreds of gold domes and cupolas of every colour and shape and shade and pattern and the spires and crosses . . . and the glorious Kremlin." The superior qualities of the Russian people were also the subject of favourable comment:

". . . so different from the hollow French, the cheating Dutch, the slow Germans, the stupid Danes. The poor Swedes are too good to be abused though they are very inferior to the Russians who are so clever, intelligent, agreeable, candid, true, friendly and warm hearted—in short I should say Russia was Heaven and the Russians Angels—if it were not for the dirt, the bugs, the fleas, the filth, the vermin—this is beyond belief and really the fleas never leave one a moment's peace and you can't go into a shop or a church without bringing in whole regiments—and in the fur shops there are armies. I suffer *mort et martyre*."

Writing in the same month from St. Petersburg Frances Anne complained: "The greatest drawback here is the climate—the town is built on a bog and so damp and low and a westerly wind setting in strong with the water rising may overflow the town . . ."

In another letter from St. Petersburg dated 31st January, 1837, Frances Anne informed Liddell that ". . . We start [the return journey] in a week. The Emperor wishes us to see Warsaw and the wish is a command . . . it will be a fearful journey . . . hundreds of versts through howling wilderness . . . I am getting chilblains and hands like a housemaid . . . I'll write again if we get alive to Berlin . . . they say the wolves attack single travellers only and when they do they leave nothing but the boots with the toes in them! I said, 'Will the wolves stop our carriage?' 'Are you afraid they will take your jewels?' said Seaham."

In the circumstances Lady Londonderry's misgivings about the strains and rigours of the long, overland journey were only too well-founded. Short of being eaten alive by wolves the travellers

16

experienced every manner of misfortune. By the time they reached Dresden at the begining of April Frances Anne had become, in her own words, "a poor wretch and invalid".

The information contained in the *Journal* is further supplemented by the printed *Recollections of a Tour in the North of Europe in 1836–37* compiled by Lord Londonderry and published in 1838 by Richard Bentley of New Burlington Street, London. Dedicated to Sir Robert Peel, no doubt with an eye to future preferment, this volume contains a factual and rather pedestrian account of the journey together with a series of short essays on such diverse topics as the Russian Colonies in America, the Trade of Odessa, the Wool Trade, the Herring Fishery in the Black Sea, the Mines in Finland and the Blagodate Iron Mines, to mention only a few. Edith, Marchioness of Londonderry, writing about the *Recollections* in 1958 observed: "Though not without considerable interest, this account, being intended for publication is somewhat formal."*

Certainly, the *Journal* of Frances Anne, published now for the first time, is a much more lively work containing, as it does, graphic accounts of places, personalities and social life in the countries which she and her husband visited. Not least, it portrays vividly the degree of organization and sheer physical stamina required to undertake an extended journey of this kind and the measure of discomfort which travellers were compelled to endure.

Subsequently the Londonderrys made two other foreign tours. The first of these was in 1839 when they visited Portugal, Spain and North Africa. In the following year they undertook an even more ambitious journey down the Rhine and the Danube, through Central and Eastern Europe as far as Constantinople (where Frances Anne was received by the Sultan), on to Asia Minor, and back by way of Greece and Italy. Sir Archibald Alison in his three-volume *Lives of Lord Castlereagh and Sir Charles Stewart* published in 1861, mistakenly, and in the face of the written evidence at his disposal, compressed these three separate expeditions into one extended tour involving a journey by way of Berlin, Göteborg, Stockholm, St. Petersburg, Moscow, Odessa, Constantinople, Algiers and Carthage and returning to England through Spain—an itinerary which would surely have daunted even the intrepid Frances Anne.

* *Frances Anne*, p. 187.

Thereafter, the Londonderrys spent more of their time in supervising the development of their estates while still maintaining their social and political connections. Lord Londonderry had hoped to be offered the Paris Embassy after the Conservatives under Sir Robert Peel were returned to office in the general election of 1841. In this he was disappointed although he was offered once again the post of Ambassador in Vienna which he declined. He died in 1854. Frances Anne lived on for another eleven years and became increasingly preoccupied with the management of her estates and business concerns. In a letter written from Seaham Hall on 8th December, 1861, Disraeli remarked in his more romantic style:

"This is a remarkable place, and our hostess a remarkable woman. Twenty miles hence she has a vast palace [Wynyard] in a vast park . . . and all the splendid accessories of feudal life. But she prefers living in a hall on the shores of the German Ocean, surrounded by her collieries, and her blast furnaces, and her railroads, and unceasing telegraphs, with a port hewn of the solid rock, screw steamers and four thousand pitmen under her control . . . In the town of Seaham Harbour, a mile off, she has a regular office, a fine stone building with her name and arms in front, and her flag flying above; and here she transacts, with innumerable agents, immense business—and I remember her five-and-twenty years ago, a mere fine lady; nay, the finest in London! But one must find excitement, if one has brains . . ."*

Frances Anne died on 20th January, 1865, four days after her sixty-fifth birthday. In many respects she was, as Disraeli observed, a very remarkable woman and it may be appropriate to leave the last word about her to him. In 1874 he wrote in his capacity as Prime Minister: "I have given the [Order of] St. Patrick to Lord Londonderry, the son of the *grande dame* who was so kind to me in my youth though she was a tyrant in her way, but one remembers only the good in her."† The Lord Londonderry referred to by Disraeli was the fifth Marquess and Frances Anne's eldest son who, as Viscount Seaham, had accompanied his parents on their Russian

* W. F. Monypenny & G. E. Buckle, *The Life of Benjamin Disraeli, Earl of Beaconsfield* (London, 1929), vol II. p. 38.
† *Frances Anne*, p. 301.

18

tour almost forty years earlier. Unlike many of his family he took little active part in politics and public affairs although he had been despatched to St. Petersburg in 1867 to invest Tsar Alexander II with the Order of the Garter, on which occasion the Emperor conferred on him the Grand Cross of the Russian Order of St. Alexander Nevsky.

The *Journal* is written on paper bearing a watermark of 1839. It comprises 273 large pages of manuscript text bound in red velvet with an ornamental clasp and a red roan outer cover. It is written in a bold, clear hand copied from Frances Anne's original manuscript, and contains a number of transcriptional errors, as well as occasional corrections and additions in her own hand. There are also some gaps in the text. The volume contains a substantial number of enclosures and contemporary illustrations including a printed account of the great organ at Haarlem built by Christian Müller in 1738; letters and autographs of the Emperor Nicholas I of Russia, the King and Queen of Sweden, the King of Prussia, the Queen of Saxony and the Queen of Hanover; engravings and illustrations of places of interest on the journey including the Cloth Hall at Ypres and the Town Hall at Louvain as well as various views of St. Petersburg, Moscow and scenes of Russian life; a Polish bank note and theatre programme; a translation of Persian poetry, etc. Some of these have been included in this edition of the *Journal*.

The *Journal* itself forms part of the Londonderry family archives deposited in the Durham County Record Office. The editors wish to express their gratitude to Lord Londonderry for allowing them to edit and publish this volume. They would also like to record their appreciation for the help given by Mr. J. A. Bosmans of the *Mauritshuis*, The Hague; Mr. W. Kellaway of the Institute of Historical Research; Miss B. Masters of the Corporation of London Records Office; Mr. J. C. Maxwell of the English Faculty Library, Oxford; M. Bagrov, of the Lenin Library, Moscow, and I. F. Grigoryev, of the Saltykov-Shchedrin Library, Leningrad. Special thanks are due to Miss J. Sayer for help given in preparing the typescript for publication.

W. A. L. SEAMAN

J. R. SEWELL

CHAPTER I

Horror of a Long Sea

ON THE 3RD OF AUGUST, 1836, we sent our servants and heavy carriages by the Attwood steamer to Rotterdam but having a horror of a long sea we hired a little britska¹ to take us to Dover. This carriage, however, on trial proved so comfortable that we determined on taking it over and sending it back from Rotterdam . . .

The noise, the smell, the discomfort of Dover is, I believe, unrivalled and undisputed and we gladly availed ourselves of the first packet that sailed at six o'clock in the morning, the *Firefly*. We had a smooth passage of three hours but could not make Calais Harbour and were obliged to get into a very dirty French boat and be rowed in with the pleasing prospect of waiting five hours for the tide to permit of the landing of the carriage . . . At last our carriage came out of the vessel, our clothes out of the custom house and our passports out of the hands of the jacks in office who examine them . . .

On leaving Calais instead of following the well beaten and hideous road to Paris, we turned off to Gravelines, an old fortified French town. The passport was demanded, examined and snuffled over by some dirty looking military whose amusement during the idleness of peace seems to consist in plaguing travellers by their [*sic*] impertinent curiosity and officious importance. The same ceremony awaited us at Dunkirk the last French fortress on the Belgian frontier. The country from Gravelines is rich and fertile and very different from the plains on either side of the Paris road. Dunkirk is a large, fine, old town with handsome churches and a *place* or square . . . The journey from Gravelines to Ghent is like a drive through some beautiful park. The industry and extreme cleanliness of the peasantry is very remarkable. Nothing is neglected, wheat, barley, oats, potatoes, cabbages, all literally growing together, diversified by hop-gardens, luxuriant oak hedges and now and then some Dutch gentleman's house given to full view, its gardens *à l'Anglaise*, its box and yew trees cut into fantastic shapes and all this, instead of being as *chez nous* enclosed by a thick wall or impervious fence, has a broad ditch full of green water, equally protecting but not equally private . . .

Ypres is a fine town and the first Belgian fortification, with an old cathedral and a large, ancient and most beautiful building in the middle of the principal square. This Gothic pile has the appearance of a church having a lovely spire in the middle and immense square wings flanked by four towers[2] . . . We proceeded to Brussels where we arrived at three o'clock in the morning . . . Sir George Seymour called on us and having kindly lent us his carriage we drove over Brussels which I had not seen for fourteen years and had nearly forgotten.[3] It is a clean, sweet, gay, bright town; the shops and display of French things give it all the effect of Paris, while the broad streets, white houses and absence of bad smells render it in many respects superior to that capital. We saw some of the great *fabriques de dentelles* for which Brussels is so famous; one person told me she had nine hundred *ouvrières* in her establishment and the demand was so great that they could not work fast enough and that if she had three thousand she could occupy them all . . . Brussels, like most foreign towns, is ill-lighted, here and there a lantern slung in the middle of the street . . . The railway from Brussels to Antwerp is completed and I was anxious to go by it as the thirty miles are accomplished in an hour. We therefore sent our carriage round and, having ascertained that the departure was at six, we took our places. When I saw the assembled crowd and the contents of two omnibuses preparing for this same conveyance I found I should derive great amusement from the novelty of accompanying this motley group. Great then was my disappointment on finding our places taken in a stately solitary *berline* of which we had entire possession[4] . . .

Antwerp is the last Belgian fortress and has suffered most severely by the late revolution. Many persons were ruined and from being a most prosperous, busy place it has become dull and still. Its commerce no longer flourishes and the people are looking out and praying for any change that might bring back the *ancien régime* at Brussels. As far as we heard things seemed settled and feeling subsided there but at Antwerp there is much smothered discontent, and great devotion and affection to the Orange family.

We were assured that when Leopold entered Antwerp eight hundred merchants stood near where he passed and not one raised his hat while only little ragged boys paid by the police cried *"Vive le Roi"*. The same person expressed his conviction that if anything happened to Louis Philippe, Leopold's government would not last twice twenty-four hours[5] . . .

From Brussels the face of the country changed, no longer the same rich crops. From Antwerp the difference seemed still more striking, and we found the smell of flax poisonous . . .

Once out of Belgium we got on slowly but peaceably and un-molested . . . As the traveller penetrates farther into Holland the change in the face of the country strikes him; the flat, ugly marshes and the little dykes filled with green water. Peat is found in the morasses and is much burnt as in Scotland and Ireland. Rich and varied crops no longer strike the eye but on all sides flat, marshy pastures filled with cattle. I had heard so much of Dutch dairies that I was surprised not only at finding the milk there and the cheeses nasty but at the difficulty of procuring any cream. The bread in Holland is generally good. The people seem peaceable and civil saluting you as they pass. They are generally ugly, especially the women, both in form and feature. Indeed, as to the former, however much in early youth the mind may have associated the expression "Dutch built" with the idea of a squat, dumpy figure, still in reality they far surpass what the imagination had portrayed. A Dutch frow [*sic*] is absolutely like a large stuffed bag with a string tied round the middle. The wooden *sabots* worn by the peasants are noisy and ugly. The language is harsh and guttural resembling the worst German. The roads are narrow but excellent, flat and straight, with trees forming avenues and the grass turf neatly cut on each side. The greatest regularity pervades everything; the houses, the farms, the hedges, the gardens, etc. are all extremely neat. The cottages are generally of one floor built with small bricks and the painted shutter and Dutch signs give a peculiar character to the villages . . .

We remained only one day at Rotterdam and having found our servants and carriages waiting we proceeded to the Hague through a country of marshy pasture surrounded by dykes and covered with herds of cattle grazing or being milked. We passed long trains of carts filled with brass jugs like large pitchers full of milk . . .

The cleanliness and precision of these people, their houses and their towns, is very remarkable. The whole city [the Hague] is washed every Saturday each person being responsible for the pavement, posts, etc. before his own door and it is curious to see the maids scrubbing. In Rotterdam dogs are not allowed to be in the streets and mine was fined twice for appearing without a string . . . The day after our arrival at the Hague we dined at the British Minister's, Sir Edward Disbrowe, who was kind enough to send his carriage for us and we found a large diplomatic party[6]. . . . I was greatly interested by Count Stroganov, a clever Russian, who sat next me at dinner and conversed most agreeably the whole time. He was at the Hague for sea-bathing. His wife was a Portuguese and I found they had been two years out of Russia. He was most obliging promising to give us every assistance and protection at St. Petersburg where he was going in three weeks. He advised our being at Moscow for the Emperor's return to see the enthusiasm with which he is received, a feeling the expression of which is perhaps more controlled at St. Petersburg but there bursts forth unrestrained and is most gratifying to witness . . .

The second day of our *séjour* at the Hague . . . we went to see the museum[7] . . . The Indian and Japanese collections on the ground floor are extremely curious and interesting. The first object of attention is the large and minutely detailed model of a Dutch house made for Peter the Great, who, after all the pains and time bestowed on it, thought it too dear and refused to buy it.[8] Two thousand pounds was a large sum for a plaything but it was curiously and beautifully executed . . .

Upon the whole, I own, the Hague disappointed me. I expected a large city, fine buildings, etc. It is small and rather pretty, but without anything striking or magnificent. It must be a most monotonous residence . . .

All these Dutch towns are much alike but I think Amsterdam the largest and the busiest. The canals and avenues run through the principal streets as at Rotterdam. The dress of the sailors is picturesque: the red jacket, the coarse blue trousers and the bright colours give effect. The Dutch vessels are of a peculiar shape—broad, flat-bottomed, very glaringly painted, and highly varnished and, like everything in Holland, cleanliness itself. It is a curious sight and would be a good lesson to English maids if they could see the servant girls in Holland with their feet in wooden *sabots*, their tub in one hand and brush in the other, cleaning the pavements, doors, windows, post rails, etc. before their respective habitations . . . Here [Amsterdam] we shipped our heavy landau and footmen for Hamburg and proceeded to the same destination by land . . .

We proceeded to Osnabrück, one of the principal towns in Hanover . . . The approach to the town is through little gardens but the difference after Holland is striking; the people dirty, the cottages miserable, the crops poor, and wastes of heath and sand around. The roads are generally macadamized but there are none of the beautiful *allées*; a few mis-shapen birch struggle against the blast, peat is burned, half starved oxen much used, and the women doing the hardest work in the fields and as ostlers do . . .

From Osnabrück to Bremen is a long day through ugly country and great poverty. It is tedious, slow travelling, without interest . . .

[At Hamburg] I was tolerably satisfied . . . at having accomplished this portion of our journey in so short a time, exactly a fortnight from leaving England. Lord L. rather checked my exultation by observing that if we had had courage to go from London to Hamburg by sea this might have been performed in two days . . .

We consulted much and long as to our future journey, Lord L. being desirous to see Denmark and Sweden, and I only anxious to arrive in Russia. The Riga road, which I wanted to take, was rejected as long and tedious. The passage of four days' sea from Lübeck to St. Petersburg which we adopted for our heavy carrriages and servants was declined and, against my consent, the journey through Denmark and Sweden was determined on. The packets only sail once a week from Kiel to Copenhagen. We were therefore obliged to leave Hamburg at six o'clock the morning of the 20th to arrive in time to sail that evening . . .

We had not any trouble on entering Denmark either about passports or *douane*. In fact we were almost unconscious of the event. From Hamburg to Kiel is from ten to twelve hours of excellent macadamized road. The horses were generally ready without delay and the posts were performed at about six or seven English miles an hour. The postillions [were] dressed in long red coats lined and trimmed with yellow and, like the Hanoverians, they had a horn slung round. The country was flat and bleak, the crops poor, and generally a barren heath from which they get peat to burn. The

24

long basket-worked wagons with four or five rows of seats struck me as convenient and pretty. The female peasantry generally wear black hats, like the men. I remember observing the same custom in Wales. Here, however, from hard work, exposure to air and original plainness, there is nothing feminine in their appearance. The Danish cottages are very peculiar, only one storey, but large and immensely high, with pent-roofs which are not above ten or twelve feet from the ground at the bottom and perhaps thirty at the top. . . . There is uniformity and neatness in the villages formed by these buildings but plenty of dirt inside. There are also large barns into which you are driven while the horses are changed or fed. In Holland, Hanover, Denmark and Sweden they give them black bread. On arriving at Kiel we had another consultation as to whether we should go round by Holstein, Schleswig and the Belts or sail straight for Copenhagen . . . While we were debating, Baron Nicholay the Russian chargé d'affaires at Copenhagen came in having just arrived from that capital. He earnestly advised us to embark on board the *Frederik VI*. This turned the scale and decided us . . . At eight o'clock in the evening we deposited ourselves in this Danish steamer of about eighty horsepower, small, dirty beyond description and filled with all sorts of people from every country. I sat on deck for a couple of hours. However, it got cold and dark and at last I retreated and passed the night in the britska. I found it cold, dreary and disagreeable though I now and then forgot my sufferings in a short doze. My next neighbour—I believe, the cleanest and most *comme il faut* passenger on board—was an English racehorse going to Copenhagen to run for some famous stakes he was sure of winning . . .

I never saw a capital [Copenhagen] that so completely realized one's idea of the city in the *Arabian Nights* which was depopulated by the Queen having turned all the people into animals. It looked as if the plague had raged—large holes in the pavement, grass growing in the streets, walls crumbling, houses uninhabited, buildings falling into decay, not a sound heard or a soul seen . . . Here, however, we determined to rest two or three days . . .

CHAPTER II

The Poverty of Denmark and a
Desolate Journey to Stockholm

ON THE NEXT MORNING, the 23rd, our first visit was from the English Minister, Sir Henry Wynn,[1] who informed us of our singular ill luck in arriving at a moment of general distress and mourning, the old Queen having just lost her aged father of ninety two, who lay dead and as yet unburied. Consequently not even a theatre was open.[2] He had maintained that no one died on reaching a hundred unless he so willed, and that though he did not feel quite well he considered himself as safe. This old Landgrave was one of the *illuminés* of Germany and rational enough except on this subject when he became completely *tête montée*. He believed in the metempsychosis, fancied he had conversations with the Comet, declared his previous existence had been in the persons of King James II and his daughter Queen Mary. He and the Landgravine were descendants of George II and were united for sixty years.

Soon after, Lady Wynn called, accompanied by Monsieur and Madame Talleyrand, all in profound black.[3] They asked us to dinner at their country house six English miles from Copenhagen at half past five the next day. Our next visit was from Monsieur Krabbe-Carisius, the Prime Minister,[4] an agreeable, civil, little old man, who signified that the King would receive Lord L. the last day of our stay and explained the Queen's regrets at the impossibility of her having the pleasure of making my acquaintance, plunged as she was in affliction and mourning her father yet unburied. He told us that the King, who is a nephew of George III, had reigned ⟨twenty eight⟩ years and was popular, that as to radicalism *il y avait des amateurs partout*, but in general all was peaceable and went on smoothly, that no one was in town it being the season for the country and winter the gay moment for Copenhagen as in all other foreign capitals.[5] He then very kindly arranged our sight seeing which he settled should begin next morning with the Palace. After he had taken his leave we walked about the town and went into some of the shops in the principal streets but saw nothing to alter or improve our first impression of the dullness, misery and wretchedness of the place. The people are generally plain and ill dressed and the pavement worse than all the previous bad ones I had seen. We went into the Church of Our Lady. Thorwaldsen, the great sculptor, by birth a Dane, has made for this thirteen colossal statues, Our Saviour and the Twelve Apostles and these he designs as an offering to his native country.[6] They wait his arrival to place the statues where the casts now are in this church. We went next day, Wednesday 24th, to see *les antiquités du Nord*, found in Norway, Scandinavia, Denmark, etc.[7] I should think they began to date from the deluge. This is one of the most curious collections in the world and there are most interesting specimens of savage and primitive inventions. They would strike one as belonging to a still more distant date in a more civilized country and under a more southern sky but in this town, where everything still seems centuries behind all others, they appear part and parcel of the general and surrounding barbarism. This seems severe on the poor Danes but it is really true and I was the more impressed with their inferiority in walking through the *Exposition d'Arts et Métiers* at Charlottenborg, which is curious, and shows they are laudably struggling to imitate the manufactures of other countries.

The difference between the wealth of Holland and the poverty of Denmark is very striking and yet I prefer the simplicity and humility of the poor Danes to the grasping and avarice of the Dutch. The poverty is very great among the *noblesse* and frequently, at sales, curious and valuable things are to be bought for a mere nothing. At Charlottenborg I saw many casts of Thorwaldsen's works.[8] At the Castle of Christiansborg is an immense collection of pictures, many rooms on the floor above the *antiquités du Nord* and in so great a mass, of course, there are many bad ones. The Dutch school is the best. There are several Rubenses—his *Judgement of Solomon*, etc.—some Wouwermans, Tenierses, a Paul Potter (whom I never can admire) and a quantity of Danish daubs with high sounding titles. The collection is the private property of the King and is only momentarily placed here till the newly built *château* is ready to receive it.[9]

We saw the royal stables which are dirty and ill kept, filled with horses, but I was not struck with any except six white ones with long tails and manes that looked the realization of Wouwerman's beautiful ones.

The Castle of Christiansborg is a fine stone building of immense size and on the floor between the *rez de chaussée* where the *antiquités du Nord* are kept and the third storey where the pictures are, is the suite for the King, the Queen and the Princesses.[10] These are innumerable and very handsome, with satin *teintures*, lustres, etc., but though the enfilade is fine, taste is wanting. The rooms are all low and look heavy and there are not any pictures. The great ballroom, yet unfurnished, would have been very handsome if it had had height. The want of this entirely spoils the whole. It is one hundred and thirty six feet long, seventy two wide and thirty six high. Columns of white scagliola[11] gilt support a gallery. The room is to be finished with large mirrors and will be very beautiful, but my admiration of it was not free from regret at the fault which prevents its being perfect. There is a small chapel with a pretty ceiling and good proportions. Three immense silver lions round the altar are curious supporters of the Danish throne. The large chapel of the Palace I thought ugly.[12] We saw the ruins of the marble church destroyed by Nelson.[13]

We then went to the *Château de Rosenborg*, a most curious old place built by Christian IV.[14] There is a long gallery with a raised old ceiling where the Knights of the Elephant are made.[15] The walls are hung with tapestry covered with the battles by sea and land between the Swedes and the Danes. There are silver arm chairs. A little closet is partitioned off, filled with Venetian glasses of all shapes and sizes. We saw one of surprising height for champagne. The ground floor consists of a suite of small, old-fashioned rooms, filled with souvenirs of Christian. His walking stick of twisted ivory, an immense enamel top studded with rubies, containing his compasses, pencil, etc. would suit the fashion of the present day. His saddle and furniture of gold and pearls, his coat and dresses, are all preserved—gold boxes given him by Queen Anne and one which the goldsmiths of London presented to him.[16] There are quantities of armchairs, tripods, screens, tables, etc. of solid, old, embossed silver which it is impossible not to admire and covet. Altogether, this old castle with its small rooms, low ceilings, narrow stairs, dark passages and ancient reminiscences, is most curious and interesting.

We dined with Sir Henry Wynn at his villa about six miles from Copenhagen, close to the sea. The weather was wet and stormy and it was impossible to judge of its beauty. We met Monsieur and Madame Talleyrand, Monsieur Krabbe-Carisius, the Prime Minister, and the Swedish chargé d'affaires.

On Thursday 25th at eight o'clock in the evening we left Copenhagen and, after twenty five miles of dreadful road, we arrived at the Castle of Frederiksborg.[17] This most curious old fortress was the prison of Queen Matilda,[18] and truly of it might be said:

> "A double dungeon, wall and wave
> Have made and like a living grave"[19]

The exterior is very singular, built with red brick round two squares, with old figures in recesses. We were first shown a long old chapel where the Kings of Denmark are crowned; the ceiling is very fine, the floor and the pillars which support the gallery are marble. The altar piece is the most beautiful thing I ever beheld. It is like an immense embossed silver cabinet every part of which, on being touched, starts open and displays splendid reliefs on gold. This is of surprising magnificence as is also the pulpit which is of ebony and silver. In the gallery are the shields and stalls of the Knights of the Elephant and at the end, a small room with a curious ebony ceiling ornamented with ivory knobs and ornaments turned by Christian IV who built this castle as well as that of Rosenborg. We then went through endless small rooms and old passages interesting from their age (between two and three centuries), filled with strange old pictures and but little furniture. The room of Queen Matilda is distinguished by a line she wrote on one of the windows looking into the dreary moat below, "O keep me innocent, make others great". This castle is only used for coronations and sometimes the Crown Prince Christian comes to shoot here.[20] He will be the future King of Denmark as the present monarch, Frederick VI, has no children. At the end of all, and up some steps leading to the top of the castle, is a beautiful old gallery used for the Coronation feast. The floor is marble, the length one hundred and fifty feet, forty wide and

29

twenty high. [There are] huge black marble fireplaces once embossed with silver which had been picked off, but the extraordinary beauty of the ceiling is indescribable, and being like all old rooms low, it is easily examined. It is of wood, and one mass of fretted work so beautifully and finely carved, so richly gilt, so brightly painted in the most brilliant colours that I can only compare it to one glittering sheet of the finest old enamel, where, though each separate hue is vivid, all are mellowed and harmonized together. We then descended to a vault where the shields of the Knights are brought at their death from the stalls in the gallery of the chapel. The last placed was that of George IV of England.

We waited a long time for horses and then proceeded to Helsingör, passing another *château* of the King's. Helsingör is a miserable little place with a very small harbour and nothing worth a second glance except the picturesque exterior of the old fortress, the Castle of Kronenborg.[21] The shore is flat and the passage to Hälsingborg from twenty minutes to an hour. There is not a steamboat on the station and we were obliged to hire two little ricketty open sailing or fishing boats so small that but one carriage could go in each. The sea was not rough but I confess I was alarmed as well as sick with the motion of the boat and disappointed with all around me. When one forms a *beau idéal* of whatever is to be seen by fatigue and exertion, we are proportionably disgusted at all that falls short of our expectations. I fancied the Sound, like the Downs, covered with vessels of every size and class. I imagined the Danish and Swedish fortresses frowning on either side, magnificent harbours with all the stir and movement of populous commercial places, bold rocky shore and a fine outline of coast, but the flat beach and small red town of Hälsingborg presented a very different reality. Nevertheless, I was rejoiced to land and find myself in rather a clean, tidy inn. We were received at the water's edge by the *Commandant de la Ville* in full uniform. His fine dress, cocked hat and abundant yellow plumes ill suited the rude barbarism of the little harbour. There were several vessels riding at anchor. We then commenced our preparations for travelling which in Sweden is no slight undertaking. The first thing was to procure a carriage wagon for the couriers who must precede at least a day in order to prepare rooms, order horses, carry provisions, get bread baked, cows milked, etc. The second necessary arrangement is to purchase

30

harness, such as it is, and the third to engage coachmen, for the peasants only provide horses, or rather rough ponies which are tied with a string at the end of a post by the roadside. Nothing can be more inconvenient than the want of proper arrangement in posting and the delay of harnessing these beasts at every stage. Feeding them etc. is a great trial of patience.

The Swedish mile is about six English ones and is hardly accomplished under an hour. The houses are built of wood, the crops deplorable and the people a complete personification of squalid misery. The ugliness of the men, women and white haired children is striking. The roads are wonderfully good considering they are seldom repaired; no provision is made for this purpose and they are badly laid down, great part on rock with the steepest hills, sharpest pitches and shortest turnings, and one's progress is greatly impeded by the number of gates which recur every ten minutes, sometimes to divide the little property of each peasant. From Hälsingborg, after much trouble and delay and many attempts to impose upon us and much disputing, we went by Halmstad to Falkenberg, a most desolate journey through a bleak country, uninhabited, or at most thinly peopled. The little ponies, to do them justice, shuffled over the ground up hill and down dale at their best pace. Whatever may be the number they are harnessed abreast, and the only thing they appear to do in concert is pulling from the the pole and against all the cords that fetter them. The day was wild and stormy and the barren heaths, the brown rocks and flinty mountains appeared doubly dreary. The very milestones have a stamp of barbarism—rude heaps of stones with a pole. At Falkenberg we stopped, and a most miserable place we found it, abounding in fleas, dirt, etc. and as the baggage wagon with all our comforts had been delayed, we felt all this tenfold.

I have omitted to mention that nothing but light carriages can be used in Sweden, and even these must not be loaded heavily because in the first place the ponies could not move them, and in the second the tremendous pace and steep descents would render it very dangerous. The storm raged without and we were too thankful for the shelter of any roof, however desolate and bad, and at three o'clock in the morning I lay down on the cushions of the carriage to rest till six when we were to start for Göteborg, about the same distance and through a similar desolate country. We arrived on

Saturday and found some dirty rooms *au second*. The baggage had come up in the night and having learnt wisdom by experience, we took care not to let it lag behind again.

The peasants are very fond of their ponies and make a point of going the stage to feed and bring them back; nor will they suffer them to be hurried or overloaded. Our two coachmen, hussars in the Prince Royal's regiment, proved treasures—very careful, sober, steady men, speaking a little French. The Governor of Hälsingborg gave them to us and they drove the chariot and britska without a single accident the whole way to Stockholm. The other carriages were driven by peasants and frequently upset.

Göteborg is a large, old, populous town, principally built of wood, very dirty and wretched and certainly not a tempting *séjour*. We therefore went on next day to Trollhättan to see the wonderful falls said to equal Niagara. Great was my disappointment to find only a picturesque rapid, the descent of which is hardly equal to the falls of the Clyde or those of the Rhine at Schaffhausen, the only ones I have ever seen.[22] The inn was clean and we rested a day. The canal is most curious as a monument of Swedish patience, industry and perseverance. It is hewn out of the solid rock and must have required Herculean labour and much time to accomplish.[23] By this the steam boats go from Göteborg to Stockholm and back. We should have availed ourselves of this had we known the day of departure from the former place but this being only once a week we could not wait for it. There are great waterworks, sawmill, etc. here. Next day [the] 30th we went on to Mariestad, a small village, where we slept; from thence to Örebro where I expected a fine town as it was formerly the great rendezvous of the Swedish Diet. It is, however, a miserable village and, as usual, the houses wooden huts. Our third and worst inn was Enköping from whence we had a short day to Stockholm where we arrived the 2nd September, one month from England. It certainly is a most *pénible* journey from Hälsingborg for a woman from the absence of all comforts and the misery of the lodgings, and, as my French maid said, *"encore c'est superbe si la rue ne les partage pas"*, for often I had a room one side of a street and all the rest were on the other. The dreariness of the country, the misery and barbarism of the people and the difficulty of obtaining provisions etc. [were only too evident]. They only baked twice a year black bread which is cut with a hatchet and boiled.

However, I must say, when time was given they made good white bread.

The scenery is more picturesque by the canal. This road was only used at times and I was wearied of the long dark pine forests through which it passed. We had many advantages and I rejoice to have seen the interior of Sweden, but it is a journey more enjoyable in the retrospect than in the execution and I should not advise others to attempt it. I feel that nothing could induce me to repeat it.

CHAPTER III

The King and Queen of Sweden

STOCKHOLM is very striking as a capital presenting a singular combination of fine buildings and the movement of a large thriving town with every variation of the wild picturesque scenery of the forest. The park, which is close to the town and the fashionable drive, is as romantic as if it were a hundred miles removed from the haunts of men. There is also a cheerful hum and busy stir in the aspect of the place, very different from the silent and deserted streets of Copenhagen. The town is beautifully situated in the midst of rocks, wood and water and a variety of little islands that render the scene extremely picturesque. We found the first floor of a fine hotel in the principal street secured for our reception, and really our lodging would have been as comfortable as it was magnificent had not the whole suite been a passage, and those alone who have existed through such a trial of patience can understand how much is required to endure the continual bursting in and tramping through your bedroom to arrive at a waiting room one hundred yards off. However it was clean and to us, in our circumstances, a palace.

Mr. Bloomfield, the chargé d'affaires, came to see us in the evening, and next day, September 3rd, we went first to the porphyry manufacture.[1] This is a royal one by name though certainly not in appearance. The work is handsome but extremely dear; very hard to cut though it takes a high polish; of various colours but little taste or variety in shape or form. I bought some little specimens for souvenirs and then went to the stables which are much like those of the King of Denmark and like a long wide street. The only difference was that the horses were larger, with extraordinary ancient Scandinavian names over each stall where, as in most foreign stables, was no straw. We were shown eight white horses kept for state purposes and one duty they perform is when a new foreign chargé d'affaires arrives the Prime Minister goes to fetch him to be presented to the

King, and these horses drag the state carriage that contains these gentlemen—a pageantry defrayed by the newcomer and, in the instance of our country, not repaid to him. Some large black horses were shown as especially the Queen's who uses them daily for her drive, and tries to fancy she leads a Paris life at Stockholm. She was a Mademoiselle Clary, daughter of a Marseilles merchant. What she may have been when young can hardly now be guessed. She is now a particularly good-natured, fat old woman.[2] Charles Jean himself was the son of a French *avocat*. He enlisted as a corporal, went to Egypt, and like many other of Napoleon's generals raised himself by bravery and talents to great eminence, but unlike them has continued to maintain it.[3] He is much liked and generally popular. So is Prince Oscar who has married a daughter of Eugène Beauharnais and has a very fine and interesting family.[4]

As far as I could learn and comprehend, the Swedish Parliament or Diet only meets every five years except [when] called together by the King. There are four estates—the nobles, the clergy, the bourgeois and the peasants. The latter are daily gaining power by purchasing land. The Norwegian Chamber is divided into two and is difficult to manage. They have thirty five thousand regular troops and a standing army and can bring together one hundred thousand more in a month and thirty thousand additional in six weeks. But though this appears a large number and a great force it would, I fear, avail them little if Russia had a fancy to place a paw of appropriation on Stockholm which, from the vicinity and situation, she might do at any time that she might feel inclined to brave the fire of the batteries.

On Sunday 4th we were invited to dine with Prince Oscar at the country palace, a curious old building at Drottningholm belonging formerly to the Vasa family and lent by the King who is not fond of it to his son.[5] It is about six English miles from Stockholm and a very pretty drive over three bridges of boats, through a picturesque country and lovely scenery. The castle is beautifully situated on the edge of an immense lake. At the back are large old French gardens with fine *allées*. It is a great resort for picnics and parties. Steamboats filled with people arrive hourly. There are little vessels of one and two horse power but the principal ones are of thirty and forty. On Sundays and fête days Drottningholm presents a most animated scene. The surrounding scenery is lovely, the foliage in some places feathering down to the water's edge. Our dinner was at four o'clock and the company in uniform. The Prince is extremely good looking and the Princess very pleasing and amiable. I could not help thinking how gentle and contented she must be to be cheerful and satisfied with a thirteen years' uniform *séjour* between Stockholm and this place. She was married and came here at sixteen and had never stirred or even seen her mother till this year when the latter came to pay her a visit.[6] The children seemed all fine and healthy, with very good manners, and she herself a kind looking person with beautiful and expressive eyes.

The Swedish ladies are not pretty and they have the additional disadvantage of being obliged to appear at Court in a peculiarly unbecoming costume. In town this is black with great sleeves, in the country grey, and for gala white. It is an ancient custom and a most troublesome one. The Queen and Princess Royal are the only women exempt on general occasions and even they are obliged to conform to the rule on presentations. The shops in Stockholm are quite barbarous and literally nothing is to be got but the skins of unborn *rennes* of which I purchased a quantity and sent them to Paris to be made up. The beauty, softness and luxury of such gloves are not describable and can only be appreciated by experience.

Monday, the 5th September, I went to see what is called the *Musée* which is under the Palace, and shown by a civil little man who seems very proud of his charge and wholly unconscious that it is one mass of rubbish. Not a single fine statue or good picture, and except some curious antiquities from Herculaneum and Pompeii there is literally nothing worth looking at. The Palace has an Italian façade and though the mass is of stucco there is a fine double flight of stone steps. It is very large, fine and forms a square.[7] The Queen's and the Princess Royal's apartments are *au premier*, Prince Oscar's below and the King's above. They are handsome as a suite but nothing extraordinary except in the view which is quite beautiful. The salt and fresh water meet under the great bridge beneath the castle windows and on one side may be seen the ships for foreign wines, while on the other are the means of communication with the interior of the country. The stone façade and ascent to the *château* is ex-extremely handsome.

We dined with the French Minister, Count Charles de Mornay, a most agreeable, good natured, clever person who was very kind and attentive to us. We there met General Suchtelen, the son of the Russian chargé d'affaires who had died lately after a twenty two years' residence here. He has been replaced by Count Potocki, a Pole, who was daily expected in the Emperor's yacht. The library of the late Minister consisting of about a hundred cases had been all bought by the Emperor and was to go to St. Petersburg by the return of the transport that brought the new Minister's luggage. Mr. Hughes, the American Minister, also dined at Count Mornay's.[8] We were in all the horrors of uncertainty as to how we should reach St. Petersburg from here, there being no possibility of engaging or obtaining a safe vessel. The weather was stormy and bad. The steamboat to Turku (Åbo), going only once a week, was small and dirty and dangerous, added to which the five days travelling through Finland with bad roads and an absence of all accommodation made this journey tremendous in perspective. However Count Potocki most opportunely arrived and placed at our disposition the beautiful Imperial yacht. He begged to take me on board and show me all over this *palais flottant* which goes straight to Kronshtadt, and really my gratitude was unbounded.

Tuesday 6th we dined at Court. Above forty people were there. I was presented first to the Queen and afterwards to the King whom I was very anxious to see. This interesting man fully repaid my curiosity. I found him most agreeable and kind. However, he conversed principally with Lord L. and left me to the Queen and Prince Oscar. We were invited on the following Thursday to dine with their Majesties at Rosendal, a beautiful little villa the King has built in the park, of which, being very fond, he was anxious to show it to us. Their dinner hour is six and always in full uniform.

Wednesday 7th. The day was not inviting and I devoted myself to finishing my letters for the English Minister's courier till five o'clock when we again all met at Count Mornay's very *recherché* round table where we had the same party as before with the addition of Count Woyna, the Austrian Minister. In the evening, with some persuasion, we succeeded in prevailing on Count Mornay to sing. He has a beautiful voice and a great deal of expression. He showed us some very curious sketches that had been taken during his mission to the Emperor of Morocco.

Thursday 8th. We were rather alarmed, like Aladdin when he looked and saw his palace gone, at seeing the *Ischora* no longer lying alongside the quay; but finding she had only gone up to the Gulf of Bothnia to tow up the frigate with Count Potocki's baggage we accepted other invitations and perforce protracted our stay. The King's house is beautifully situated in the park which is lovely with the wildest and most picturesque rocks and forest scenery. The whole of the furniture is Swedish and very magnificent, beautiful and in perfect taste. We were shown into the suite on the ground floor. Before the windows to the garden is seen a large porphyry vase of beautiful shape and of a rose colour and of wonderful size. The King on showing me this assured me that the execution of it and a *jardinière* that stood in the middle of the room was by the peasants. He then informed me he meant the *jardinière* for me. I was so amazed that I succeeded very ill, or rather, I fear, entirely failed in expressing how much I was gratified and pleased, and in the midst of this the Queen entered and we soon after went to dinner. There were about thirty in a gallery, fluted like a tent, with red pillars.

The dinners in Sweden are very long. Nothing is placed on the table and everything handed round. Before sitting down to the regular meal the men assemble at a small table to eat a little salt fish and bread and butter, and drink brandy by way of getting an appetite. After dinner we went upstairs and saw the suite of rooms there. The satin hangings and *teinture* like everything else were of Swedish manufacture and as beautiful as the Lyons *fabrique*, but at double the price. The painting and gilding of the walls, inlaid porphyry tables, indeed the whole decorations are in good taste. Seaham was this evening presented to the King who lectured him well on his bad carriage. The conversation of Charles Jean is particularly agreeable and *bienveillant*. He seems to forget the sovereign, to *penser comme individu* and I felt I could give him a very long, undivided attention. He was extremely candid and kind to his *ancien frère d'armes* as he called Lord L. whom he had known long and in momentous and interesting times. He explained his fondness for this residence by the interest naturally felt for what one had created and compared it to the feeling of a mother to her child. He talked of Napoleon who, he said, was *très matériel* and of his fear of and dislike to Madame de Staël who did him much injury.[9] He related an anecdote of her that is best given in his own language. "*Madame de Staël se trouvait toujours sur le chemin de Napoléon, qu'elle ennuyait avec ses questions. Elle ne pouvait pas être en société sans dominer un salon. A la fin elle lui demande, 'Sire, qu'elle est la femme la plus célèbre en France ?' Espérant sans doute un compliment à son esprit Napoléon lui répond, 'Madame, je pense que c'est elle qui a donnér les plus d'enfants à la France'."*

At Rosendal Prince Oscar took leave of me; the Princess was unable to leave Drottningholm, one or two of her children having the measles.

He is to come to England in a year or two which will do him good and give him more aplomb and *usage du monde*. The succession seems thoroughly established. The children speak Swedish as their natural language. Charles Jean has no knowledge of it and this has always been felt. I believe Prince Oscar cannot speak it but the Princess has learnt it. Before we took our leave the King informed himself, in the kindest manner, how our time was bespoken and what day we were disengaged and enquired if it suited us to dine with him. Nothing could be more considerate than the way he consulted our convenience and arrangements before he finally settled we should dine on Sunday at Nacka, the Queen's country residence.

Friday 9th. The Russian Minister, Count Potocki, was presented to the King and the aforementioned custom took place of the Master of the Ceremonies going in state with the eight white horses to fetch him, the etiquette being for the minister to receive him on the third step. I went to see the procession which was, however, extremely *mesquin*, and I thought the Russian chargé d'affaires' equipage the best worth looking at. We then drove up to a height to see the view which is really beautiful. The town, the park, the water, the shipping, all form a beautiful panorama. At that distance the poverty in detail is lost and the general effect only caught. We dined with the Austrian Minister, Count Woyna and met the Russian, Prussian, French and American chargés d'affaires and Count and Countess Loewenhjelm.[10] There was a great deal o difficulty and embarrassment about precedence which is here a matter of vital importance, and knowing how much this is thought of and strictly adhered to I regretted that their civility and hospitality should make them give us a rank we so little cared for and were not entitled to. It is curious to observe in a small Court and a circumscribed society how much importance is attached to the trifles of the day, and where there is nothing for anyone to do each one busies himself with the concerns of his neighbour and the slightest thing forms the theme of a week's gossip. We had a very fine dinner at Count Woyna's and admired his house which was *meublée et soignée* like a lady's and we went to the theatre to see the scene of Gustavus III's assassination.[11] The house is small for a foreign theatre, well lighted, and the performances Swedish which language, though I did not understand it, appeared to me very musical.

Saturday 10th. The rain came down like a second deluge and entirely prevented my stirring till we went to dine with the American Minister, Mr. Hughes. I sat next to Count Mornay who told me a most amusing story of old Madame de Bourke whom everybody knows. She lost her husband in the south of France. They were very much attached and really lived *comme Philémon et Baucis*. At his death, being inconsolable, she had him preserved in a barrel filled with brandy which she took in the carriage with her. On her journey she met with an old friend, a general, who offered to be her *compagnon de voyage*, suggesting that *Monsieur le Comte* might be put *avec les gens*. To this, after some consideration and consultation, *Madame la Comtesse* agreed, and she and *Monsieur le Général* travelled on comfortably and agreeably till they arrived at *l'octroi* where they passed without difficulty and proceeded to her hotel. The carriage with *les gens et le baril* containing *Monsieur le Comte* was stopped. "*Qu'est-ce que c'est que cela?*" "*Cela, mais c'est Monsieur le Comte.*" "*Comment, c'est Monsieur le Comte, c'est de la contrebande*", vociferated the man piercing the barrel and tasting the brandy. Madame de Bourke in the meantime, missing the second carriage, became uneasy, when a servant appeared *tout essoufflé pour annoncer qu'on avait arrêté Monsieur le Comte*. Measures were immediately taken and the barrel was forthwith released but not before the brandy was all drunk and the remains of poor *Monsieur le Comte* shrivelled up like an old apple.

Mr. Hughes was very agreeable and I saw nothing national about him except that when Lord L. proposed to him to see my jewels he declared he should be *glorified*. It is very ungrateful to remark upon a person who is kind and hospitable and I feel as if this observation was unjustifiable. Mr. Hughes has been here nineteen years and is very much liked.[12] He is well informed and good-natured.

Sunday 11th. There not being an English church in Stockholm, Mr. Barlston read the service at home. The day was very bad—a continued deluge of rain—and the Court changed their dinner from Nacka to the Palace in town, a wise measure considering the weather. We were not tempted to stir till six when we went there and found about forty people. This time Prince Oscar was absent and I had the good fortune to sit near the King whose conversation is peculiarly interesting. He certainly is an extraordinary person. He must have been very handsome and fascinating and is wonderfully strong and straight for his age which is seventy two. He sits up very late, seldom going to bed till two or three o'clock, breakfasts on chocolate, gives himself up entirely to business and sometimes is twelve and fifteen hours without eating. This he told me himself. Count Loewenhjelm declared to me, however, "*Le Roi mange comme un ogre, il est d'une force étonnante et il reste à la maison cinq et six semaines quelquefois sans bouger.*" I know for a fact that the King had not stirred out for five months when a great fire broke out during the winter and when intensely cold. It was the middle of the night. Nevertheless, he immediately got on horseback, rode to the spot to see and direct and was not the least the worse in consequence.

He talked to me a great deal of England, expressed his satisfaction at the manner the King had received Count Wetterstedt (the Prime Minister and since dead) who had sent him great accounts of the magnificence of Windsor, London, etc.[13] To my great astonishment he told me he had never seen the Duke of Wellington whom he thought the greatest general of the age. I observed that he was cold hearted. He replied, "*C'est plus facile de commander que de gouverner*". I said that admitting his genius, talent and judgement did not prove that the man had a heart to which with *chevaleresque galanterie* [he replied] "*Madame, s'il était plusieurs fois votre voisin à table vous verriez.*" We then talked on the march of events which he remarked went too fast to go safe. The reforms of the last ten or fifteen years were too rapid, "*qui va piano va sano, mais malgré tout*", he said, "he trusted that *la haute civilisation* of the immense population of England on one side and the brute force of that enormous empire of Russia on the other might *tenir l'équilibre*".

After dinner he established himself on a sofa in a distant corner with Lord L. leaving me to the Queen and her ladies—a pert little Madame d'Otronte just divorced from the husband of ten years, a Madame Davey, a good natured little woman, the wife of the Norwegian Minister, and a few others who all struck me as equally silly, plain and ill dressed. One can hardly wonder at the Queen's desire to visit her own country. She openly avows it. She was in error to remain twelve years and this has not been expiated by a thirteen years' *séjour* in Sweden. She came back for her son's marriage and declares she only accepted the crown of Sweden on condition of visiting her country *quand bon lui semblait*. She is a most kind hearted, considerate old lady. I expressed a wish to see her own rooms to which she instantly assented ordering them to be lighted up and assuring me they were not worth looking at. After a short time we went in and found her maids taking off the covers. She sent them off, saying, "*toute maîtresse de maison sait qu'il font* [sic] *des housses*" [sic]. Her rooms were filled with tapestry worked by her own ladies, pictures of her family and the children of Prince Oscar. Count Potocki had brought a present from the Emperor of Russia to the King of Sweden—a large vase of jasper *ondulée*. The Queen kindly ordered the room where this was placed to be lighted up for me to see it. I thought it beautiful—a square tazza shape, very large and highly polished. The King, however, condemned the form as being neither ancient nor modern.

He took a most cordial and impressive leave of us, assuring us repeatedly how much pleasure our visit had given him and how much he wished us all happiness. He then kissed me, giving his blessing, saying, "*la bénédiction des vieillards, comme celle des enfants, porte bonheur*". Soon after the Queen *congédié'd* us with great feeling and kindness. She embraced me and taking a bracelet with a watch from her arm begged I would use it to mark the hours on board the steamer. The *bienveillance* of this Royal Family and the kindness and hospitality of the *Corps Diplomatique* made a great impression on us and were the more marked and valued from our arriving as we did *en particulier* without any right or claim to such a reception.

Monday 12th. The last day of our very agreeable *séjour* at Stockholm was devoted to receiving visits and adieux from Count Mornay, Count Woyna, Count Brahe[14] (who brought the King's handwriting which I had asked for) and Count Potocki who called to settle definitively about our sailing next morning and, in spite of all my entreaties, declared he should see us off and that he always got up at seven. He requested our carriages etc. might be on board early the day before. I told him we had seen and admired the vase but he treated it as a mere nothing to what I should see at St. Petersburg and described a lapis lazuli one of prodigious size just finished for the Empress. Count Ardenfeldt then came in a small phaeton with four milk white tiny ponies, belonging to the young Prince, and drove me to see Nacka, the Queen's residence which the bad weather had prevented my seeing. The ponies are extremely small with long tails and manes and very beautiful. The park is à l'Anglaise with fine large trees and a piece of water. There is a pavilion built and formerly inhabited by Gustavus III who was nearly shot here, but the assassin seeing him asleep at a window had not courage to consummate his crime.

Tuesday 13th. We rose at six to take a long leave of Stockholm and embarked on board the *Ischora* which lay under the palace windows. I was handed in and duly installed by Count Potocki. The whole of the *Corps Diplomatique* accompanied us and all Stockholm assembled to see the Russian vessel depart.

The morning was dark and wild and the wind threatening. The vessel weighed anchor, salutes were fired from all the batteries and answered from the steamer. The scene was very striking and as we sailed down, with the firing on each side, I began to think Stockholm much more difficult of approach than I had imagined. No ships could resist the defence that might be made from these commanding heights. The whole day we passed through the most picturesque and beautiful scenery on each side and at no great distance. The vessel was a fast sailer and well manned with a crew of sixty, but we stopped every two or three hours to take in pilots, strange, wild looking beings that came off in skiffs from the islands. At eleven the breakfast was served in the state cabin for the officers—meat, pies, wine and brandy, and at five o'clock they dined. I had my cabin to myself and my maids. They were fitted up in satins and coloured woods and really beautiful. My own bed was put up in the largest and it was arranged as a boudoir. The night being dark they were unwilling to take us into open sea. We therefore anchored and the next morning the wind having gone down and there being little sea we crossed the Gulf of Bothnia, passed the island of Åland and anchored at the entrance of the Gulf of Finland.

Thursday 15th. We sailed up the Gulf. The weather was beautiful and the sea calm. We saw the towers of Tallin (Reval) which is exactly twenty four hours from St. Petersburg. The night was lovely and still and the sea like glass. The Northern Lights appeared and the Russian crew assembled on deck and some danced and sang for me in their own wild national manner. I was told they improvised as they sang, poor creatures. Their dirt and want of civilization shocked me and their food would hardly be touched by our pampered dogs—hard black bread soaked in salt and water and doled out to them in small wooden bowls. There was grace in their dancing notwithstanding its grotesque *sauvagerie,* and music in their singing though it was a wild howl. The Captain could not speak a word of anything but his mother tongue, one lieutenant spoke good French and the other good English. We had a doctor and a great librarian on board and General Suchtelen, the son of the late Russian Minister at Stockholm. He was a very agreeable companion. There was, likewise, an English engineer. The dews fell so heavily I was not allowed to remain on deck and at ten o'clock was preparing to descend to my cabin when alarm was given of a ship in distress, and the *Ischora* answered by signals and coloured lights which spoke a language unintelligible to all but the initiated. We stopped and distinctly heard the guns fired but after our blue lights these ceased. Nothing could be seen or heard and supposing it to be a false alarm we retired for the night and while sailing up the Gulf of Finland slept soundly notwithstanding all the noise, the pacing of the decks and in the morning, the toilet necessary for the vessel—the cleaning and scrubbing before she appeared in her own capital, though I must remark *par parenthèse* that she really was so clean and *soignée* all this trouble seemed superfluous. I tried to make the Captain accept a little souvenir, a *bonbonnière,* but nothing would induce him. As he only spoke Russian we could not converse but at last he declared he would only accept a small glove or some such trifle and I gave him a ring which he promised should never leave his finger.

Next morning, Friday 16th, we had the pleasure of seeing Kronshtadt which is a wonderfully fine creation rising out of the sea as it does. The magnificent and enormous granite harbour and fine batteries, the long range of immense line of battleships, strike one as the most formidable and splendid defence to a capital that art and nature could unite. The sea was literally covered with vessels. General Suchtelen observed how *blasé* we were since the day before when each sail on the wide waste of waters was an event and now we were surrounded, we could hardly count them. There were guard-ships, men of war, frigates, steamboats, packets, floating light-houses—in short vessels of all sizes and of all countries. Contrary to our hopes we passed Kronshtadt and entered the Neva. Our vessel drew nine feet of water and we were afraid of being obliged to take a smaller one and so near was it that the pilot who came on board at Kronshtadt said there was only eight and a half feet and the whole crew collected at the furthest end of the vessel to enable her to pass the sands and *bas fonds*. Many boats and steamers filled with workpeople are employed in cleaning out the Neva. The quantity of water depends very much on the wind.[15]

CHAPTER IV

St. Petersburg

ST. PETERSBURG lies low which spoils its approach by sea. The magnificence and the stupendous size of Kronshtadt surprises and excites in the mind great expectation, and the bright blue and green domes covered with gold, the gilt spires and the white houses keep curiosity alive till the traveller reaches the granite quays with their fine buildings on each side. One of the first great edifices is the *Corps des Mines* and on the opposite shore enormous sheds are seen for building vessels under cover.[1] Arriving under the protection of the Imperial flag, we were exempt from all visitation by the *douane*. Our carriages and effects passed the custom house at Kronshtadt and were immediately landed. The carriages were brought from the pier by the horses of two hackney coaches and we drove to our temporary lodging passing the splendid equestrian statue of Peter the Great.[2]

It is by far the finest monument I ever saw. The hind feet of the horse rest on the rock which is an enormous block of granite with the simple inscription upon it, "Catherine II to Peter I". It appeared to me smaller than I expected but this is to be attributed to the colossal scale of the surrounding buildings and emplacements. The effect of these immense palaces, enormous squares and wide streets is to make the people look like pygmies and the carriages shrunk to nutshells.

The Alexandrian column, lately erected to the memory of the Emperor Alexander, is very inferior in size, grandeur and conception to the monument of Peter. The site has been well chosen. It is of granite and [has] beautiful proportions though small.[3] The hotel was on the great *place* and opposite the Admiralty, an immense building with a beautiful gold spire.[4]

The next day, Saturday 17th, was employed in a fruitless search after lodgings, reading an accumulation of letters, receiving visits from Lord Durham and others.[5]

Sunday 18th, being fatigued we remained at home.

Monday 19th. We had a visit from Count Nesselrode whom I had known at Verona and found unchanged.[6] He invited us to dine with him the Thursday following, arranged for us to see the Hermitage and the Winter Palace next day, and informed us we should be presented to the Empress the Sunday afterwards at Tsarskoe Seloe where we should dine and stay all night on our way to Moscow. We had a visit from General Ficquelmont, the Austrian Ambassador, and drove out again in search of lodgings. The difficulty of procuring any in this magnificent city is perfectly incredible—all dirty, some unfurnished, others only to be let for a year or six months. In short we decided on remaining in our dirty, comfortless abode for a week and to postpone settling ourselves till our return from Moscow. The cheating is terrible and possessors of hotels and lodgings seem to consider all foreigners, especially English, their lawful prey.

Tuesday 20th. Count Nesselrode very kindly sent us Baron Brunnow and gave us a young Russian *employé* as cicerone and interpreter, and we all set out to see this wonderful Palace.[7] The Hermitage and Winter Palace are connected and form one immense solid mass of building.[8] The entrance to the first is a long dirty staircase. The first room is a great gallery, beautifully painted, communicating with the salons which are filled with magnificent pictures and *chefs d'oeuvre* of most of the great masters. I did not observe any Rembrandts or Corregios but I saw splendid Murillos, Carlo Dolces, Guido Renis, Albanos, Andrea del Sartos, Romanos, Canalettos, Rubenses and some magnificent Paul Potters, especially one of a rough dog starting as it were from the canvas. One room contained landscapes only, another was hung with the most beautiful Wouwermans, a third was filled with Tenierses. In short there is a surprising *richesse* of pictures collected by the different sovereigns and now enriched by the addition of the greatest part of the Malmaison collection[9] and two statues by Canova.[10] One salon is lined with *armoires* filled with gems and curiosities of singular beauty and immense value, snuff boxes of every age and country, Imperial toys, jewelled *babioles*, infant *toilettes* of the most precious materials, costly caskets, ancient clocks, watches studded in diamonds, books, etc. cased in gold and precious stones. To describe one quarter of these curiosities would be impossible. There was a curious ornament in the middle of the room said to be of English manufacture, a large tree of gold with a peacock and other birds that moved and sang. In another room is an extraordinary organ clock that played beautifully. It cost the maker years of labour and at last, as no one would buy it, a lottery was made and the wife of a poor *pasteur* won it. The Court gave her forty thousand roubles and a pension for it. From these windows is a fine view of the Neva, its granite quays and magnificent buildings.

The Hermitage was built by the Empress Elizabeth.[11] One salon opens into an *orangerie* which also opens on a gallery, curious only from being raised *au premier*. The riches, gems and treasures of this Palace are like the fancied contents of those described in the Arabian Nights and the magnificence of the vases, jars, tables, consoles, etc. of porphyry, jasper, malachite, is perfectly astounding. I observed some superb china vases of immense size and was told they were made here. The gilding equalled and the painting surpassed the modern Sèvres.

I subjoin the proportions of the great *salles* as given me by Prince Volkonsky.[12]

Mésures des grandes Salles du Palais

	Pieds Anglais	
	Longueur	Largeur
Grande Salle de Marbre	196	63
Salle Blanche	133	49
Salle St. Georges	133	49
Salle des Maréchaux	112	55

From the Hermitage we passed into the Winter Palace and here it is impossible for memory to retrace the succession of enormous *salles* all opening one into another. The first was coloured scagliola gilt. The second entirely white called the *Salle Blanche* and, I daresay, when lighted up has a dazzling effect, but by daylight I thought it looked heavy and would be improved by gilding. The lighting is managed by wreaths round the columns, with candles, besides lustres and candelabras. Four immense stoves are disguised under trophies and banners. This communicates with another scagliola *salle* used as a supper room. All these salons have galleries above supported by columns but they are seldom used except on the sixth of December, the Emperor's fête and on the first of

48

January, Old Style, when both the Hermitage and Winter Palace are entirely thrown open. There is an immense room of beautiful proportions and, though not like the others, a gallery shape, it struck me very much. It is called *la Salle du Concert* and is lighted by the largest and most magnificent lustres I ever beheld. Here the weekly balls are given during the winter. There is also a fine suite of rooms with a beautiful staircase fitted up for the Empress Mother who died there soon after they were finished and did not inhabit all of them. The Throne Room belonging to them is very handsome— red velvet worked with gold eagles and there are magnificent silver tables, lights and sconces. This suite is a palace of itself. The beauty of all the parquets, the bright Italian painted ceilings and the quantity of scagliola, particularly the white, gives an air of great cheerfulness. Here again the surprising succession of vases, tables, pedestals, etc. of jasper, porphyry and malachite call forth unbounded admiration. The Empress's salon for reception is beautiful —the same bright arabesque painting on white scagliola walls, columns and fireplace of the finest jasper, the furniture red velvet and gold, with malachite tables, candelabras and lapis lazuli vases. The chapel is like all the Greek churches with a fine screen and richly gilt and painted. It smelt strongly of incense. No one is allowed to sit down. The Emperor and Empress stand together in a corner and, on particular days, receive congratulations there. The gallery, called *la Salle des Maréchaux* with Dawe's pictures, was repairing and most of the paintings were taken down.[13] There are portraits of three hundred generals but these are only *en buste*. At the top of the room is a fine picture of the Emperor Alexander on horseback, the King of Prussia, the Grand Duke Constantine, Potemkin, Suvarov and a few others are *en pied*.[14] We were told that Dawe had made above a million of roubles here—even these bust portraits were one thousand each and most of them were painted twice. The extraordinary fact was added that he had left nearly all his money to the Lancasterian schools and hardly anything to his relations.

We next saw the crown jewels which are very fine. They are kept in one small room under the care of a *valet de chambre* of the late Empress Mother. The crown is of large diamonds and pearls and has an immense ruby of which a very long story is told by the exhibitor of its having been stolen and carried away concealed in butter. In the centre is the famous diamond which really looks like a piece of glass. The Empress's crown is very small. The remainder of the jewels are in glass cases round the room. A large diamond necklace with drops, some immense emeralds, a *parure* in pearls and a quantity of beautiful old jewelled fans struck me very much. We then quitted this wonderful Palace amazed at its colossal size and singular magnificence with but one regret, that its exterior was not of stone instead of crumbling, whitewashed brick, and a wish that some of its interior scagliola decorations had been solid marble.

I thought one room in the Palace very pretty, the walls white scagliola, *en faux marbre*, painted in panels of wreaths and bouquets of flowers. They have excellent contrivances for flowers during their long, dreary winter. Large stands for filling up corridors and fireplaces and recesses and a particularly pretty manner of portioning off corners or posts [parts] of rooms by railings or *treillages* on which creepers are trained having their roots in a tin box on the ground. Another great ornament to the Russian houses is the large panes or sheets of glass which give an unbroken view. A peculiarity in the Russian streets besides their immense width is the wooden or coarse mosaic pavement. The middle is stone and with a gutter and on each side is a parquet of wooden *pavé* of pieces of wood, neatly cut as out of a mould, dovetailed together and tightly wedged down over a *fond* of planks. I only saw this in the *Nevsky Prospect*, the Regent Street of St. Petersburg; how it answers in winter and long snow which must wet and rot the wood I know not. In summer it is very agreeable to roll on without jolt or noise.

Wednesday 21st. We started to see the *Académie des Beaux Arts* which is an immense building and a very fine liberal institution.[15] The Emperor gives the greatest encouragement to genius and talent and every aid is afforded to study and improvement and, under the enlightened system pursued, this immense and powerful Empire is making rapid strides in civilization and perhaps the last twenty years have accomplished as much as a century or two formerly. We saw two galleries filled with modern works preparing for the exhibition, and a fine library which is open to the students. We then passed through various rooms where they were copying. One part was a school for architecture where each, unseen by his neighbour, prepared his plan. At the end of all we saw a very large and clever picture of the last day of Pompeii executed by an artist whose name

I forget, for the Emperor. He was ten years about it and received for it forty thousand roubles.

From thence we drove to the great cabinetmakers where we were greatly struck with the beauty of the *meubles*, the inlaid *boiserie* and different coloured woods. In this respect they surpass the English in taste and the French in solidity. We then went to the glass manufactory which is a great way out of the town and where large looking glasses, sheets of plain window glass and beautiful coloured glass tables are made. It is a royal manufacture and a very fine one. The prices, which are moderate, are marked on everything. We drove down the Nevsky, passed a magnificent palace of the Grand Duke Michael,[16] a large private palace belonging to the Emperor called *le Palais d'Anischoff*,[17] and saw the great church of Alexander Nevsky[18] with its splendid shrine of silver weighing a ton and a half and brought from Novgorod by Peter the Great whose picture as well as that of the Empress Catherine is in the church. There is a range of buildings connected with the church to lodge the monks and a large house for the Archbishop.

Thursday 22nd. A very bad day and being tired I remained at home to write. Lord Durham called and at five o'clock we went to dine at Count Nesselrode's. Very pretty *campagne aux sales* [*sic*], which is about twenty minutes drive from St. Petersburg. We there met the *corps diplomatique*—the Austrian, Prussian, Swedish, Dutch and Danish Ministers. The dinner was perfect. At least everybody pronounced the cook without a rival and the wine nectar. I heard a great deal of a sort of snipe called *les doubles* which come for six weeks only and are greatly esteemed and really formed an endless subject for conversation. I was at last persuaded to taste them and found them greasy and strong. We then went to the French theatre which is a remarkably pretty one—very clean and bright looking, well lighted, and the Imperial boxes in red velvet and gold looked very handsome. I admired everywhere the white scagliola *fond* painted in wreaths of flowers. The acting was very good and the theatre quite a *salon de société*. However I was tired and did not stay long.

Friday 23rd. The morning was wild and stormy and the rain came down in torrents. Nevertheless, we drove to Lord Durham's villa from whence we were to go to see the palace and cottage at Peterhof. On arriving we found they were all invited to dine with the

Grand Duchess Hélène.[19] Having therefore prayed them to go without minding or considering us, we proceeded in Lord Durham's carriage to the palace which is a curious old place, gilt and ornamented in the Louis XIV style.[20] It is uninhabited and overlooks an old French garden with terraces, waterworks and gilt statues. The number of spires, domes and statues all quite gilt are very bright and striking. I should think the six months' snow much injures them. On this first and our twelfth [recte thirteenth] of July an immense fête is given here for the Empress's birthday. The gardens are magnificently illuminated, the waterworks (which are said to surpass those of Versailles) play and dinner and supper are served for five thousand persons. I regretted we were so much too late to see this fête of which I heard great accounts, as the weather had been warm and lovely though the days preceding and subsequent were rainy. We then drove to the small house or cabin of Peter the Great. There is nothing to see. The contrast of its simplicity with the gilded magnificence of the *Grand Château* and the remembrance of the man whose habitation it was makes it interesting.[21]

We took a long drive, passed a very pretty Swiss cottage built by the Emperor as a surprise for the Empress and, fortunately meeting with a *conseiller de la Régence* for whom we had a letter, were conducted by a beautiful drive coasting the Gulf of Finland to the cottage where the Emperor and Empress pass [a] great part of the summer. Here they live with their children in retirement. The cottage consists of three storeys. The Emperor and the children occupy the second which is plainly furnished and in beautiful yellow wood. The Empress's rooms are on the *rez de chaussée* and though neither large nor magnificent are quite charming. The taste and elegance of all the furniture, the beauty of the sheets of glass in her bay-windowed salon giving the lovely prospect unbroken struck us very much. The views from this little retreat are beautiful—the Gulf lying before the windows with St. Petersburg on one side and Kronshtadt on the other. We were greatly delighted with this place and regretted it was too late for us to remain longer. We returned to dine at Lord Durham's and drove back at night to St. Petersburg.

Saturday 24th. I remained at home to receive Madame Nesselrode who came to see my jewels and advised with me about setting them. I was very sorry not to find Princess Lieven here, though, poor woman, after such cruel calamities one cannot wonder she should dislike returning to the scene where they occurred. *Elle se jette dans la politique pour trouver distraction* and who can marvel ? Having lost all she cared for her object seems now to kill time and get through life, and if she must have a Ministry to make and unmake why should she not be allowed to reside at Paris, and when she can procure such playthings amuse herself with them ?[22]

Sunday 25th. We were invited to Tsarskoe Seloe to be presented to the Empress and we were advised to take it on our way to Moscow. The Emperor was absent; he had been overturned in travelling and still suffered from his accident. It is about two hours' drive from St. Petersburg. This was our first specimen of Russian posting and strange and wild it was, the four horses abreast to the chariot and a like number to the britska. A *courier de poste* had been given us by Count Nesselrode and he preceded us in a britska with our cook. We left Seaham, who was not very well, behind. The dirty, strange coachmen drive their little wild steeds at a wonderful pace and we soon arrived at the Palace and with some difficulty discovered the apartments destined for us. Not being able to understand the servants whose replies were in Russian, they kindly gave us a negro who spoke English and we proceeded to establish ourselves and prepare for dinner which was fixed at four o'clock, but as we were to be presented we received orders to be ready at half past three.

The Palace where the Imperial family reside is a little distance from the great one and was built for the Emperor Alexander's marriage by the Empress Catherine.[23] Carriages were sent to fetch us, Lord and Lady Durham, Count and Countess Nesselrode, etc. We found a very large party assembled and after a short time were conducted into an adjoining room and Lord L. was presented by Prince Volkonsky and I by Countess Nesselrode who was accompanied only by her son and daughter. The former is about eighteen, very tall and good looking. They say of him *"qu'il est beau et bon comme l'ange gardien du ciel"* and I have no difficulty in believing it. The Empress is a tall graceful figure, her face not very handsome, but her little head beautifully set and her expression pleasing and features regular, her hands and arms beautifully shaped and an air of imperial dignity and grace I never saw before.[24] Her dress was perfect—simple and of dazzling whiteness, with a necklace, fringe, drops, etc. that I can only compare to dark blue glass

53

eggs for never did I see their like. The eldest daughter was ill she said and unable to appear. The Grand Duchess Olga, her second daughter who is only fourteen but looks seventeen is very lovely— slight and fair as a lily, with beautiful blonde hair, singularly tall for her age and very conversable and agreeable. There is a peculiar charm about this family. They are gifted by nature more than the generality: tall, handsome, graceful, well made, clever, agreeable and different from most royal persons. They appear conscientiously good and, like the late Emperor Alexander, living to fulfil "their being's end and aim", to be useful, to do good and to distribute comfort and improvement on a great scale. The children seem carefully educated, and in the interior appears the domestic comfort, affection and simple privacy of a *ménage* in humble life, and this is singularly set off by the immense power, wealth and great magnificence that surrounds them.

We dined in an immense *salle*, the bay windowed middle of which was partitioned off on each side by open columns, orange trees and plants. [There was] a horse-shoe table and about sixty people. The Empress sat at the top, her son and daughter one on each side. I was next the Grand Duchess Olga whom I found very agreeable. The women were generally plain but remarkably well dressed, the men all in uniform. About twenty or thirty blacks waited. Their appearance in white turbans and scarlet and gold dresses, mingling with the other attendants, was very eastern. The establishment is on an enormous scale. For instance there were four hundred cooks there—forty travel with the Emperor and when the Imperial family move four hundred carriages are required. After dinner two little Grand Dukes came in dressed in the Russian costume—a sort of loose red and gold shirt buttoned up one side without a collar and with a sash.[25] They seemed very happy, quite at their ease rolling on the floor. Their attendants were all English. An old Scotch nurse made acquaintance with me and spoke of the whole family with enthusiastic affection. She had been with them nineteen years, said they were angels as good as they were handsome and the Empress a model to all as a mother and a wife. She concluded by declaring that they all doted on her and could not exist without her; that she kept their money, their jewels, etc. and had charge of everything. This old lady seemed quite a character. After this the Empress came and talked to me, and after enquiring about my

Lady Londonderry and her son

From a painting by Sir Thomas Lawrence. *By courtesy of the Marquess of Londonderry*

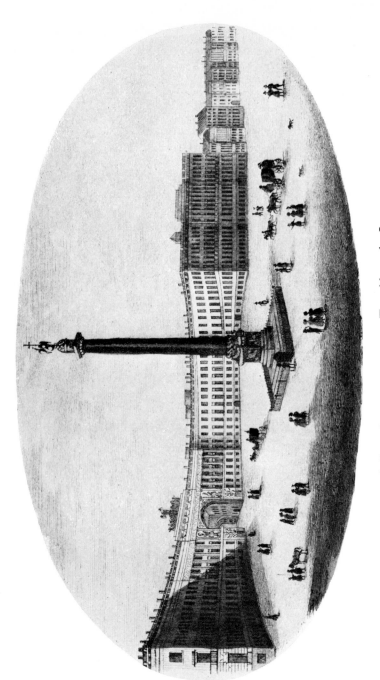

St Petersburg: monument to Tsar Alexander I

children, told me she had her eldest son and three daughters while Grand Duchess but it was not until she ascended the throne that her three other sons were born. She then dismissed us all about six o'clock requesting we would *reposer* and return for the ball at eight o'clock, saying in extenuation of the hour, *"C'est à la campagne et pour les enfants que nous vivons comme des paysans"*.

We returned to our rooms and after an hour's *causerie* prepared to make a second *toilette* and at the appointed hour returned to the Palace where the great *salle*, the scene of the dinner, had been cleared and prepared for dancing. I had a long conversation with Tchernischev about the Emperor Alexander's death. He died in his arms and might have been saved had he consented to be bled; but no entreaties or prayers could persuade him.[26] The fever rose and the last two days he was delirious. Tchernischev, whose fortune he had made, doted on him and told me his situation forced on him the cruel duty of being present when the body was opened and that he had fainted four or five times. He then related to me a circumstance that with a fatalist like the Emperor Alexander must have had great weight. He was busy in his *cabinet de travail* one beautiful day in August previous to his setting out to the last fatal journey when a dark cloud appeared and increased till darkness forced him to ask for candles. After a time the cloud passed, light returned, and immediately his *valet de chambre* came to take them away. In Russia burning candles *en plein jour* is considered as an omen of death. The Emperor, remembering this, asked his servant if he feared the bad *augure*. The man eagerly denied this and the event passed away, but the poor Emperor on his deathbed recalled it to all their memories. The veneration and almost idolatry that love and gratitude pay to his memory, however deserved and just it may be, is as creditable to the nation as it is honourable to himself.

At eight o'clock, on returning to the Palace, the first objects we saw in our outer room were the two little Grand Dukes going down *les montagnes russes* at a great pace. There was a much larger party in addition to those at dinner and the Empress soon after appeared more beautifully dressed than before. A simple white crape dress laced up each side with diamonds and turquoises, several rows of pearl on her neck and one row she told me belonged to the crown and really were like filberts. She observed the redness of my skin and enquired the cause and I was obliged to tell her the fleas had half

devoured me. "*Ah ma chère, quelle honte pour vous.*" She knew
Lord L. before her marriage when a girl at her father's the King
of Prussia's Court and declared she remembered his perfume and
knew it again after twenty years. She recalled scenes of conversations
to him. She danced with great grace and dignity. After the ball,
supper was served on little round tables that appeared as if by magic
and disappeared in the same way. Just before we sat down, the
Tsarevich came up to the Empress saying, "*Maman, voilà un
courier qui arrive de Papa*".[27] Upon which she sprang up from out of
the room followed by all her children. On returning she told us
the Emperor would arrive in a few days and that he hoped to see us
"*souvent et beaucoup*". After supper she took leave of us, wished us
bon voyage, prompt *retour*, etc. and we retired exceedingly fatigued.

Mésures des grandes Salles de Tsarskoe Seloe

	Pieds Anglais	
	Longueur	*Largeur*
Salle du Grand Palais	161	56
Salle du Petit Palais	147	49

Monday 26th. I was so unwell that I was unable to get up early
to see the dairy which is *à l'Anglaise*, the Arsenal and many other
interesting things which Lord L. went over.[28] But at two o'clock,
after a fine *déjeuner dinatoire*, we went over the Great Palace
formerly occupied by Catherine and Alexander. My bedroom had
a door opening into the chapel which, like all Greek ones, had a
screen and the whole was in black and gold and very handsome. A
uniform of the late Emperor's is preserved here and near it hangs the
key of Adrianople. From thence we proceeded through an endless
and magnificent enfilade of rooms in the Louis XIV style, richly
gilt, with beautiful parquets, one room of amber walls and pictures
of *pietra dura*,[29] another with a floor inlaid with mother of pearl,
an immense ballroom, but astonishment at the beauty and magnificence of all this was forgotten in the absorbing interest with which
one contemplated the simple apartments of the Emperor Alexander,
religiously preserved in the state he left them. His boots, his hat, his
pocket handkerchief, his worn pencil, the little tortoiseshell eye
glass, the emptied bottle of perfume, the books he was reading, the
miniature of his favourite sister the Duchess of Oldenburg,[30]

afterwards Queen of Württemberg where she died, the very plate with broken bits of toasted bread, all remained intact. It was sad and painful to go through these rooms and feel that he alone was missing who had been their inhabitant.

This magnificent Palace is full of interest and historical souvenirs and we examined with curiosity the rooms of the Empress Catherine and the Empress Elizabeth, wife of Alexander.[31] We saw the Empress on horseback from one of the windows and at about four o'clock set out on our journey to Moscow and arrived that evening at Pomeranye where we found an excellent supper prepared by our cook and very pretty, comfortable, clean rooms at the Imperial post house. Here we passed the night.

CHAPTER V

Discovering Moscow

FROM ST. PETERSBURG to Moscow is above four hundred miles. The road is very wide, perfectly flat and straight and beautifully macadamized. It is a magnificent work, was made by the Emperor Alexander, and is kept in excellent repair. It is by far the finest road I ever saw. The little bridges are all cast iron decorated with the Imperial eagles. The houses for the road surveyors are all alike and at regular distances. The versts are all marked in the most solid and clear manner.[1] Fine stations at post houses are built, some by the Empress Catherine, some by the late Emperor, and it is curious to find there lofty rooms twenty feet by thirty, with their fine parquets and Italian ceilings, their satin furniture and beautiful *boiserie* in the midst of so much reputed barbarism. I never saw a bed in a Russian inn, and I am sorry to add fleas, bugs, and vermin abound amidst these magnificent decorations. It is dirt and barbarism that shocks one for there is no squalid misery and want as in Ireland. The men are a fine, tall, wild looking race, well and warmly clothed. Their great boots, coloured morocco gloves, great folding pelisse of sheepskin and variegated sash, their long beards and tangled hair, all are covered with a thick crust of dirt. Animals clean, scratch, rub and lick themselves but these people seem to lie down and rise up living on in their dirt, letting it accumulate undisturbed by water. Few women are seen, and these are hideous in form and face. The villages are all wood, some cottages have rather pretty gable ends. In many of the great towns they are also wood except the government buildings which are whitewashed brick. At all these wretched villages a fine church rears its Moorish architecture, and the contrast between its beautiful green or blue and gold domes with the poverty around is very striking. The posting is admirably managed; the pace these little horses go is prodigious. There were one hundred and seventy horses ordered for the

Emperor but this did not impede our progress and we were assured very little notice was necessary to procure four thousand from the surrounding villages. The pains taken to advance civilization and promote improvement and comfort is incredible. Nothing is neglected yet the whole machinery is worked by one man.

We passed through several towns. The principal ones were Novgorod, Torzhok, Tver, and *la ville Klin*. At Torzhok we stopped to taste the famous cutlets of this place and thought them remarkably nasty. There was a small shop in the inn for shoes, boots, etc., made of morocco embroidered in gold and silver. Finding they spoke nothing but Russian I came out and meeting an officer, a traveller on the stairs, I prayed him to come and interpret for me which he did with great good nature. When my purchases were finished he said, *"A présent, Madame, soyez vous assez bonne pour m'expliquer comment se fait il que votre mari, Monsieur le Général, possède la croix de St. Georges"*. I told him that the Emperor Alexander had given it him when wounded at the battle of Culm.[2] He seemed greatly surprised, but I everywhere observed the respect this little white cross and small bit of black and yellow ribbon twisted to the button hole commanded, proving that the truth of the Emperor Alexander's words was felt when speaking of the Order in his letter bestowing it on Lord L., *'elle ne s'accorde qu'à la vertu militaire"*.

I had nearly forgotten to observe, we found the finest, whitest and best bread everywhere. The trains of loaded, one-horse carts extending miles delayed us but this is the sole communication with the interior. There are diligences for people and these are well arranged. The strange wild cries and howling song of the drivers are very peculiar. Their skill is extraordinary, notwithstanding the immense pace and numberless carts, etc. they thread through with wonderful dexterity and velocity. Droves of large white oxen are peculiar to this country and I must remark that the beef is excellent. I do not remember seeing any sheep in Russia and the mutton, wherever it may come from, is detestable.

On the fourth day from Pomeranye we reached Moscow, at twelve o'clock at night on the 30th of September. We were too tired and sleepy to be difficult about a lodging and took possession of some rooms that appeared clean and fresh in the house of an Englishwoman, Madame Howard.[3]

Saturday, October 1st. We eagerly drove out to gaze on this extraordinary city so totally different from anything we had ever dreamed of. St. Petersburg is a magnificent town and on a colossal scale but it can never be the capital of Russia. Moscow is Russia with an Asiatic colouring. The greatest difference of population is seen in the streets. The immensely wide ones of the former are thinly peopled, while the enormous size of all surrounding objects gives to these few the appearance of pygmies. But in Moscow the streets swarm and the crowds jostle. The different costumes, the long beard and anxious face of the old Jew, the stir, the movement and the busy hum of many tongues bespeak a city of trade and flourishing commerce. We first looked at the outside of the Kremlin which has risen like the phoenix from its ashes.[4] We saw the immense bell which has just been raised out of the ground and we walked round the ramparts of this glorious and unique palace gazing on the gardens below and the beautiful panorama around us[5]—the great extent and size of this city, the brilliancy of its domes and cupolas of every colour, shape and size, its minarets, gilt towers and fretted spires with their golden crosses and glittering threads floating in the air. From here we went to a very different but equally singular scene—the great bazaar of Moscow—and with our dandy contracted ideas of English bazaars we are not prepared for the extent, dirt and slovenliness of this immense place concealing in its recesses the riches of the East. There are fur shops, furniture warehouses, images, lamps burning, jewellers, lapidaries, money changers—every trade, and each shop has its little ladder stairs which, to those who have the courage to ascend and brave the dirt, the smells and the fleas, conduct to its treasures. The cheating, however, of the merchants is outrageous. In one place we saw a quantity of turquoises and the man asked fifteen thousand roubles for a paper full that might be worth fifteen hundred!

We had visits paid us by *Monsieur le Directeur des Postes*,[6] Count Tolstoy, Military Governor of the place in the absence of Prince Dimitri Golitsin, Monsieur Neboulsin the Civil Governor, etc. We dined alone and Lord L. went to the theatre but I was too much tired.

Sunday October 2nd. Not being well I remained at home and received visits. *Monsieur le Directeur* came, young Count Nesselrode brought his uncle Count Gouriev, the Russian Minister at Rome, a very agreeable man. General Kisselov also called and strongly dissuaded us from executing a plan which held out great temptation, namely, that being thus far on our road, one thousand miles to Odessa and two days' sail on the Black Sea might carry us to Constantinople. I own I was very anxious to see Mahmud and penetrate to the heart of the seraglio but on enquiry all agreed that the road from Moscow to Odessa at this season was almost impracticable, and the Black Sea far from safe during the equinox. Besides, the certainty of bad weather on our return and the detention of quarantine would delay us so long as to risk the possibility of our [not] being able to return to St. Petersburg during the winter. We reluctantly abandoned our scheme for the present, but General Kisselov strongly urged our executing it next year when the Emperor was to review sixty thousand cavalry on the immense steppes or plains in the south.

We set off early next day to see the Kremlin, the beautiful exterior having made us very curious to behold the interior.[8] The *rez de chaussée* is very interesting. The first *salle* is filled with armour, mounted knights, etc. and pictures. Among them is a fine full length [portrait] of the Emperor Alexander by Lawrence, with the huge keys of different fortresses tied with the yellow and black ribbon of St. George.[9] These hang under the picture, and, at the foot, the Emperor Nicholas has placed in a box the constitution of Poland. The banners and colours of the same country surround it, and opposite is a picture of Peter the Great with a homely peasant's chair-bed placed under it. This was the litter Charles XII was placed on when wounded at Poltava.[10] On either side of this great *salle* are long galleries supported by scagliola columns. The one on the right is filled with a great collection of fine old plate, all shapes, sizes and ages. In one *armoire* is preserved Peter the Great's memorandum book, plate, etc. Next to this gallery is a room with a most interesting and splendid collection of thrones and crowns. The latter are all more or less enriched with jewels— the Siberian, Astrakhan, Kazan, Georgian, Polish, etc. All are placed on pedestals with cushions; each has its little dark sable band. They are beautifully worked and very magnificent. Two gold armchairs encrusted with turquoises struck me very much. But to bring the throne of Poland from Warsaw I thought rather hard.

Mercy should temper justice and, however rebellious the Poles may have been, they are conquered and it is cruel to trample on the fallen and strip their ancient capital of its throne, its pictures and all its objects of interest. The Emperor Alexander was never crowned King of Poland. One curious throne is seen here with two seats for Ivan and Peter the Great, with a conceded [concealed] place behind from which their sister might prompt them in whispers what they were to say. The clothes worn by the Sovereigns at their coronations are deposited here and their boots, from the huge ones of Peter the Great to the last fashion of the Emperor Nicholas.

Retracing our steps we went into the gallery on the left where Catherine II collected the pictures of all the Sovereigns of her own time—George III of England, Gustavus III of Sweden, Louis XIV of France, Frederick the Great of Prussia, etc. There is also a large armoury and an immense collection of all kinds of curious things in old enamel and precious stones beautifully worked. In another room are four housings for horses, of great magnificence, embroidered in pearl and jewels, one with lapis lazuli and diamonds, the other with emeralds, a large collection of saddles and different ornaments for horses, also enamelled and jewelled with great taste and beauty. We then went to another part of the building to see the curious old equipages of some hundred years ago—large coaches of great width and length, magnificently gilt, lined with curious velvets and having glasses of one immense sheet. We saw a curious old Gothic hall below where the Emperor dines alone, under his throne, after his coronation, with all the nobles at tables round him, and on this occasion the fine old plate shown above is brought down and displayed.

The apartments of this Palace are simple and not remarkable. Napoleon occupied a suite on the ground floor and from one of the windows first perceived the conflagration of the city. The suite inhabited by the late family are [sic] simple also, and, as usual, the poor Emperor Alexander's room is left intact and even the little camp bedstead with its leather mattress which he always travelled with. When he left Moscow previous to going to Taganrog he uttered the singular foreboding respecting this little pallet, "*Laissez là tel qu'il est, car je ne reviendrai plus*". The Empress's suite and the public rooms follow. The Empress Mother's salon is likewise preserved as she left it—her letter commenced, dated the day of Nicholas's coronation, the envelopes, papers, the dead flowers she had gathered—these souvenirs so carefully and religiously preserved give great interest to the locale. I was also shown a most curious room like a vault, very ancient, arched, and painted like an old missal. This was called *la Chambre d'Or* and formerly was used as a *salle d'audience* for the Tsars to receive ambassadors, foreign princes, etc. in state.

There are three churches in the Kremlin.[11] In the Cathedral the Sovereigns are crowned, in a second they are married and in a third buried. Since the time of Peter the Great, however, they have been interred at St. Petersburg. The Cathedral is very fine and like a magnificent old illuminated book—the richest colours in gold. The walls are washed and painted gold. They were stripped by the French who, amongst other outrages, made a stable of this church. The shrine of the Virgin is gold enriched with large emeralds and diamonds and very magnificent. The doors of the screen were opened for us to look in but no woman is permitted with step profane to approach. I regretted not seeing the letter of the Emperor Alexander announcing to the Archbishop the taking of Paris and desiring thanks to be returned to the Almighty for this great event.[12] It is in Russian and attached to the altar. Being fatigued I returned home and received the Governor, Count Tolstoy, who brought his daughter and was kind enough to invite us to dinner on the following Tuesday. In the evening we went to the opera and saw *Le Pré aux Clercs*.[13]

The theatre is said to be larger than the Scala at Milan or the Carlos at Naples.[14] The latter I never saw and the former being dark and dirty I can hardly form an opinion about it, but I should not have thought that at Moscow so large. It is, however, considerably more extensive than our opera house and lighted by a lustre with two hundred lamps.

Tuesday 4th. My first *sortie* was to some of the Bukhara merchants where I saw piles of magnificent shawls, one finer than another, of every shade and pattern. I was quite bewildered amidst these beautiful things most of which were just brought from the great fairs where they are sent from the East. I then went to a horse-dealer's, an old Jew with a flowing robe and long beard who served me perfumed tea while I sat and looked at his horses. There were *attelages* of white, brown, bay and black, and the trot and high action of these animals were perfectly wonderful. They are only to be procured from the barrack of Countess Orlov. They are beautiful and go like the wind. We dined with Count Tolstoy. The Governor's Palace is large and magnificent and we met about thirty people, among them Prince Serge Golitsin who kindly invited us to dinner on Thursday. I found everybody amiable, conversable, hospitable and most anxious to be obliging and useful.

Wednesday October 5th. My whole morning was spent among the Persians and shawl merchants who made a positive fair of the ante-room. After seeing hundreds of shawls I finally bought a magnificent one for which I was first asked twelve thousand roubles. We then went to see the archives of the Foreign Office which are curious and interesting, beginning in the thirteenth century with the treaties of Novgorod. We saw the correspondence with England beginning by a letter from Philip and Mary, several, beautifully illuminated, from Elizabeth and Charles I, [and] a copy of one the Russian Emperor refused to receive from Oliver Cromwell. All these letters give the title of Emperor. We were shown Chinese and Indian letters and one from the Grand Lama, a collection of original letters of Peter the Great, a Koran and many very curious and interesting things.

The Bukhara merchants flock every morning with heaps of shawls of every shade and pattern. They are a very odd looking people with their embroidered caps and long beards. Their cheating is quite proverbial and so well understood that it is excused by an argument that it is *"tout simple qu'ils tâchent de gagner"*, and moreover those who are taken in by them never meet with pity but are considered fools.

At twelve o'clock we went to one of the largest buildings in Moscow, *les enfants trouvés*.[15] This establishment is on a gigantic scale; above thirty thousand children are brought up by it in the town and its environs. When a child is brought no questions are asked but whether it has been baptized; the limits are prescribed for the number admitted which is from twenty to thirty a day. Those who bring with them a hundred and sixty roubles are entitled to have the children brought up in Moscow. The boys are dressed in dark green jackets with white trousers. They are taught Latin, German, French and some English and drawing. Some are brought up to trade, some for the university or for the army according to their respective talents. We passed through various rooms where the different ages and classes were studying to the chapel which is beautiful, white and gold. The boys stand below and the girls in the galleries above. We then saw the endless department of nurses and young children and it is quite impossible to give sufficient praise to the cleanliness, comfort and system of this magnificent establishment. The large airy dormitories, the clean beds, the neat little cradles—everything, to the smallest detail, is well attended to. This institution was founded by the Empress Catherine but has been brought to perfection by the Empress Mother and is now protected by the present one who is said to take a great interest in it. We then saw another department where young women receive a most careful education and, after every possible advantage of masters of all sorts, and having learnt music, drawing, French, English, German, Italian, etc. they are sent as governesses into the different provinces where they generally prove treasures. Some again are brought up to inferior situations as broiderers, lace makers, dressmakers, milliners, etc. and one class as *sages-femmes* and when thoroughly taught are sent into the interior of the country. There are about seven thousand belonging to this establishment which comprises an hospital for sick children and another for lying-in women. It costs more than a million of roubles annually and is really a splendid charity, I should think on a scale unrivalled in any country.

At four o'clock we went to dine at Prince Serge Golitsin's who has the most magnificent palace in Moscow.[16] The stairs, the suite of drawing rooms, dining room, ballroom were all beautifully lighted up and we had a splendid dinner. There were some fine pictures, an Albano, Carlo Dolce, Murillo, etc., some fine *pietra dura* tables, a malachite table that cost sixteen thousand roubles and was the fellow to one sent by the Emperor Alexander to Napoleon. The satin hangings were manufactured on his own estates and are as handsome and, he assured me, as cheap as those of Lyons. We next went to the theatre where a Russian piece with national airs and dances had been given for me.

Next day I set off early to walk about the bazaar with Count Nesselrode. We were first attracted by the magnificent binding of the Russian bibles, from three hundred to three thousand roubles each, in gold and enamel. The golden images of the saints, the

Toula [?Toledo] work, a sort of steel inlaid on gold of which all sorts of plate are made, glasses, cups, spoons, *sucrées*, etc. After a long search and endless enquiries we succeeded in finding a small shop where cloth of gold and silver and gold velvets were made. Such magnificent stuff I never saw, literally realizing the hackneyed simile of standing on end. We then drove out of the town to see some races. The famous trotting horses of this country are harnessed to little droshkies and their swift pace and high action is quite wonderful.[17] We dined at home and went to a soirée at Countess Gudevich's to hear some Bohemian musicians. Their singing is strange, wild and extremely noisy. It is perfectly national and more extraordinary than pleasing.

At nine o'clock every morning the Persian and Bukhara merchants arrived and established themselves as usual in the ante-room with their shawls, *cachemires*, silks and turquoises, keeping up a constant fair for two or three hours and all in perfect harmony together. We were to undertake a pilgrimage to the convent of Zagorsk (Troitse), a distance of sixty versts, and as the road was very bad indeed we were counselled to go early.[18] By some mistake about the horses which were taken to a wrong place we were delayed till a quarter past four when, after an early dinner, we started. This convent is most interesting to Russians being rich in historical recollections and, after the one at Kiev where the first Christian church was built in Europe, is the richest, finest and most ancient in Russia. Napoleon never reached it and though his soldiers pillaged within a hundred versts all round Moscow they never attacked this place. On a former occasion when the country was invaded it stood a siege of six weeks and though only defended by the monks could not be taken.[19] It has never been occupied by strangers. We found the road even worse than was described, like a deep ploughed field with enormous holes, and I really expected every moment would see us overturned and our carriage smashed to pieces. After seven hours' desperate shaking and three relays of six horses to a very light carriage we arrived at an immense, large, dirty inn that formed one side of a square. Here we found our kind friend and constant cicerone Monsieur Novosiltzov anxiously looking out for us and alarmed at our delay.[20] The stairs, passages and galleries of this dirty abode poured forth crowds of astonished Russians to stare at us and our packages. We proceeded to settle ourselves for the night

66

and having supped on cold meat we brought with us and and taken all possible precautions against the bugs and fleas for which this inn is infamous, we went to bed.

At four o'clock in the morning the convent bells began and unweariedly continued every half hour, and on looking out of my window at seven and gazing on the scene before me I bitterly regretted my inability to sketch it. The whole place, an immense square, was one great *marché* up to the walls of the convent—the enormous number of little carts loaded with the freshest vegetables, the stalls, the shops, the quantities of fruit, cakes, and wares of all sorts, the strange, wild appearance of these picturesque looking men with their long beards and peculiar costume. It is singular to find the women so plain generally and the men so fine a race of beings. The number of horses in this country is extraordinary. Here every peasant has four or five each worth from fifteen to twenty roubles. They are cheaper as winter approaches as they can be less used. This accounts for the hundreds of little carts one meets every moment.

At ten o'clock we drove to the convent and first entered the cathedral where service was performing. It is lined with gold and painting. The monks were singing. The screen was open, behind which are the tabernacle, the host and all the mysteries of the Greek religion. The priests were officiating in their magnificent robes of cloth of gold and silver blended with the richest and brightest coloured velvets, embroidery, etc. The thick wax tapers were burning. Incense was thrown into the farthest corners of the church. The host was carried round; the people stood together in a dense mass; rich and poor, prince and peasant mingle their devotions continually crossing themselves and at different periods of the service falling down to kiss the ground in the deepest humiliation. A sermon was preached by one of the young academicians in Russian.[21] The language sounded sweet and musical. After this the Superior gave the benediction and distributed the blessed bread. The screen closed, the priests took off their magnificent dresses and put on the black monkish cap and robe and the Superior offered to show us the treasures. This man, whose name is Father Antoine, is about forty, tall, pale and handsome with regular features, fine teeth and interesting expression of countenance. His raven, silky hair parted down the middle fell on either side below his shoulders. His glossy beard without a grey hair and his graceful, dignified bearing

67

were very peculiar and his history made him still more interesting. He was carefully educated and tenderly brought up at the Court of a Georgian Prince, his friend and benefactor, who had an only child, his daughter and heiress. These young people thrown together from infancy and enjoying each other's society became attached and their mutual affection increased till they determined to gain the Prince's consent to their union. On hearing Father Antoine's prayer the Prince, greatly shocked, unfolded to him the dreadful secret of his birth that he was his own illegitimate son and had fallen in love with his sister. Overpowered with horror and remorse at his involuntary crime the unfortunate young man threw himself into the arms of religion and sought refuge in the cloister, and oblivion of these unhallowed passions in a strict monastic life, secluded and shut out from the world and its temptations. This happened about fifteen years ago. During the last seven he has been Superior to this convent where his mild and amiable manners and his benevolent disposition have endeared him to all with whom he holds communion or with whom he is connected, while his austere and holy life has secured for him universal respect and veneration. The Princess, I was told, has never married, but though she did not take the veil and still resides at her father's Court, she is almost a *religieuse*. She is one of the greatest heiresses in Russia and to complete the interest and romance of this true history ought to be beautiful. I regretted to hear she was not, but fat and short.

We followed the Superior over the different churches etc. This convent was founded in the fourteenth century and has been gradually added to. The last building was in the seventeenth. The Sovereigns have made presents to it and its treasures are very considerable. We went first to the tomb of St. Serge, the patron saint of the convent. This is richly gilt and ornamented with jewels. From thence [we went] to the treasure—old gold plate, embossed all shapes and forms, crowns of pearls and jewels, magnificent bibles bound in gold and studded with large emeralds, sapphires, diamonds and rubies, jewelled crosses, and chains given by different Empresses, and several *armoires* filled with quantities of *habits des prêtres*, all covered with embroideries in pearls. The principal riches of this convent are in pearls. Tables, crowns, sleeves, caps, aprons, robes, etc. are entirely covered and on [of] all colours.

68

We next went into an old chapel built by Peter the Great and opening into the refectory where dinner was preparing for the monks who seem to fare remarkably well. We then proceeded to the house of the Metropolite, the great dignitary of the Church. There are four —one of St. Petersburg, one of Moscow, one of Kiev and another of Novgorod. The suite he inhabits is on the ground floor, very simple, old and Gothic. We then visited the academy belonging to the convent and saw the library—one room devoted to Russian books, one to French, another to English, etc. We saw an edition of the bible in sixty nine languages and a curious composition of Moses on Mount Sinai receiving the tables [tablets] of stone. This had been constructed by a former Metropolite of the name of Platon, a clever man of singular ideas and inventions.[22] To represent the smoke of the thunder and lightning he had pastilles and incense burnt in the interior of the rock which was perforated with large holes to let out the smoke. There is a collection of Russian minerals and old coins and one shown that Peter the Great always gave for a beard, being anxious to abolish them and encourage his subjects to shave. We next saw the Cathedral of the Virgin which is large and old, painted and gilt, and then back to the one where service had been performed. It was now empty and we inspected the shrine of St. Serge with its candles burning and its lamp of emeralds, rubies and diamonds. Two monks always remain by it. The Superior then ordered the great bell to be rung for us.[23] The effect was surprising —like a thunder of drums, and even after it had ceased to strike the echoes long fell on the startled ear and hung on the air. We then heard the sweetest carillon of bells. The morning was lovely and the sun shone bright on all the gilded domes made of the purest ducat gold, enduring all weather and looking brighter and more dazzling than anything just polished.

We then took leave of our handsome and interesting Superior regretting we could not converse with him and tell him how much we had been interested and gratified by our visit to his convent. He gave me two enamelled images, one with our Saviour's head and the other with St. Serge's vision of the Virgin, and, further, two large loaves of blessed bread whiter than the driven snow. We then drove out of the convent's high walls and to Moscow where we arrived at seven to dinner. The road was dreadful, the country flat and, excepting a few churches with their green and blue domes, we passed

nothing worth looking at. The day concluded with a glorious sun-
set like an Italian sky in painting or imagination, not a cloud or
"frown upon the atmosphere", and the sun dropped into a sea of
gold leaving the sky tinted with the brightest shades of silver and
blue. I never saw anything more beautiful.

Monday 10th. Lord L. went to see two magnificent establishments. *Le Corps des Cadets* struck him so much I regretted not
having accompanied him.[24] I stayed at home to attend the usual
ante-room fair of Persian and Bukhara merchants, jewellers'
turquoises and merchants with gold and silver stuffs for priests'
dresses and magnificent Court trains.

I had a visit from Countess Gudevich, a good natured old Polish
lady married *en deuxième noces* [to] a Russian noble. She assisted me
in choosing, purchasing and bargaining for these cloths of gold and
silver. I then dressed for a great four o'clock dinner at Monsieur
Neboulsin's, *Gouverneur Civil de la Ville*. The house was very
fine, the stairs carpeted, heated and perfumed. A large party was
assembled in a great salon fitted up in white satin and about fifty
sat down to dinner in a large hall or gallery of which the walls were
of what is termed here *faux marbre blanc* and beautifully lighted. I
could not resist enquiring if this sort of decoration, resembling
scagliola was expensive. I was told that the principal ingredient in
its composition is alabaster and the cost for this large room was not
above a thousand roubles. One peculiarity at this dinner was the
absence of salt cellars. There is a general and ancient superstition
of ill luck attending accidents with salt and in some old Russian
families it is shaped and piled on the table so that everyone may
carry off a little while no one can upset it. We then went to the opera
and saw *Robert le Diable*, an opera I particularly dislike.[25] It was
inferior in decorations, numbers and horrors to Paris or London.
Besides the *prima donna*, who is not a good one, was ill and ill
replaced. The theatre, however, was full and everybody seemed
pleased and satisfied with the performance.

Tuesday 11th. The shawl merchants came even earlier than usual,
the turquoise ones followed, the furrier with his bearskin, the
banker with money, all appeared in the usual succession till
twelve o'clock when our kind and patient friend Monsieur Novosiltzov came to take us [on] our rounds. First we went over
l'Hôpital de la Ville, a large edifice with a handsome Grecian façade

Moscow: Cathedral of St Basil

Moscow: a view of the Kremlin

St Petersburg: Cathedral of Our Lady of Kazan

St Petersburg: Palace of the Grand Duke Michael,
now the Russian National Museum

and portico built by Prince Dimitri Golitsin, the Governor of Moscow, with *les fonds de la ville* added to by the Emperor. It was finished three years ago and is a perfect establishment where four hundred and fifty patients are received. The most indigent are admitted without questions or difficulty and the system, kindness, comfort, regularity, order, cleanliness and airiness are beyond all praise. The view from here is magnificent commanding the Kremlin with its gold domes and the many coloured, bright, variegated spires of Moscow. It was sad to see suffering human nature in so many forms and shapes in turning from the gay panorama before this fine building to its interior, but while one pitied the melancholy and in some instances sinking and hopeless victims, it was impossible not to admire and respect the benevolence and skill that administered to their wants and soothed their misery. The doctor who conducted us through this magnificent institution led me to the bedside of an Englishwoman who was dying of consumption. He said she would be comforted by hearing the voice of a *compatriote*. She was a very respectable person, had been a governess and, falling into bad health, had requested to be received into this hospital where, poor thing, she seemed too feeble and ill to derive benefit from anything that could be done. A beautiful chapel in white and gold is attached to this hospital. We then went to the Golitsin Hospital—a very fine private charity.[26] It was built with a sum of money by a Prince Golitsin and is supported by the revenues of estates also left by the founder. A hundred and fifty patients are relieved, a hundred old women and a certain number of incurables are admitted and allowed to remain. This is on a more luxurious plan than the former which is large and destined for the poorest. Every bed had its bath, each patient every comfort. The room with depots of linen was well filled. The chapel had a fine monument to its founder. The kitchen was beautifully clean and upon a new and excellent plan, no fire being visible as was the case also in the bakehouse, both lately built by Prince Serge Golitsin, a successor of the one who founded the hospital. This edifice is large and has a Grecian façade but neither as pretty nor as modern as *l'Hôpital de* [la] *Ville*.

The hospital for the children of those who fell victims to the cholera is also a large establishment. Indeed it is impossible to express half one's admiration and respect for the fine, excellent and numerous benevolent institutions in this city, all on so great a scale and conducted on so perfect a system. We concluded our expeditions for the ⟨day⟩ by a visit to the Empress's private palace which, though neither large nor magnificent, is extremely pretty. It belonged to Countess Orlov and the Emperor occupied it during the coronation and as a surprisal to the proprietor placed a magnificent staircase in it. Some time after he bought the house with its furniture and presented it to the Empress. The rooms were panelled *au fond* of *faux marbre blanc* painted in wreaths of flowers a particularly pretty way I have before described and often admire. The view from the windows and the garden is very pretty and I was presented with an immense bouquet, very bright and sweet for the time of year.

Wednesday, October 12th. We were invited to see the villa of Prince Serge Golitsin whose magnificent palace in town I had before seen and at twelve o'clock we drove to Melnitsa. The road was very bad and the country flat; our carriage broke; however, with six horses we got on and arrived there. We found the Prince's sister a kind old maid who received us with her pug in her arms, and I rather envied him his Persian gold collar encrusted with turquoises and thought I could have better employed it as a bracelet. We found as in all Russian houses a number of persons inmates of the house though in what situation it is difficult to ⟨be⟩ precise. There were two English women, a Persian and a little orphan niece. There is a great deal of charity and a universal spirit of benevolence in this country from the Emperor downwards. I never saw education so carefully attended to nor so much general attention paid to the wants, comfort and relief of the poor, nor so much observance of duty and respect to decorum. The good effect of all this system is seen in the conduct of the young people. The girls are well informed, well principled, accomplished, ladylike, *distinguées*, gay and natural; discipline is early introduced among the boys and submission, respect and obedience impressed. The young men are all brought up to serve whether in the military or civil or diplomatic service, and this is universal however high the rank or large the fortune. The greater part are in the army. No officer is ever seen out of uniform. I asked Monsieur Novosiltzov, aide de camp of the Governor of Moscow, to walk with me in the bazaar of Moscow if he could put on plain cloth[e]s. "*Moi! Madame, je suis né en uniforme, je suis venu au monde comme cela*" was his reply, and I was told that one good result was that the fear of affixing a stain of disgrace on their uniform and being known and exposed was a great check on youthful follies and often prevented riotings, disturbances and improprieties. The police is [*sic*] extremely strict and the greatest attention is paid to morals and decorum in public. No women of doubtful character are allowed to be in the streets at night nor at the theatres. How different from England and Paris where these unfortunate beings are continually presenting themselves to observation. It is a marvellous thing to reflect that this vast empire and its sixty or seventy millions are governed by one mighty mind, the inspiring and directing spirit of the whole. Everybody satisfied, and more than that, worshipping and venerating the memory of the late Emperor and almost adoring the present monarch whose example has the greatest influence on the morals of the Court and of the people. In his own *ménage,* they see him the devoted husband, excellent father, *et heureux comme un bourgeois au sein de sa famille.* Nothing passes without his knowledge, order or signature, and from the furthest corner of this enormous empire couriers can communicate in eight days. Russia has been singularly blessed in possessing such Sovereigns but it is fearful to think how great is the responsibility of an individual for all depends on him—the advance in civilization and virtue or the falling back into barbarism and darkness.

It is in Russia alone that so great a man as Peter I is appreciated, and especially at Moscow, for different as it is now to what it was in its rude state, still one never ceases to marvel how he could leave such a capital to found another in St. Petersburg. Many, however, assert that he projected only a port for commerce and did not anticipate a residence for the Court to supersede the old capital of the Tsars. The last twenty years have added immensely to Moscow and, by all I could learn, the fire from which it has risen like the phoenix from its ashes has, by destroying all the miserable old wooden buildings which are replaced by regular ones, improved the town which is now about thirty five versts in circumference and reckons one thousand six hundred versts of *pavé.*

On arriving at Prince Golitsin's we went out to see the gardens and pleasure grounds which are very extensive and filled with ornamental buildings—a kiosk, a pinery, peach houses, etc. and a temple built in memory of the Empress Mother. After seeing these buildings we got into a beautiful barge and were rowed round the grounds. There is a large sheet of water and a great extent of shrubbery and walks all well kept by a German gardener who has a hundred peasants to work under his directions. In Russia the peasants belong to the soil and the Prince told us that five hundred are annexed to this estate. To them he gives the land and its produce and they furnish him with a hundred serfs who receive no wages but their food. At about four o'clock we were conducted into a beautiful *orangerie* with a forest of the finest and healthiest trees I ever saw and, under their shade and perfume, was served what was called a *déjeuner dinatoire* but was in reality a regular dinner— cups of soup, beefsteaks, fish, etc. the finest fruit and thick cream. Nothing could be more kind and cordial than the reception we met with. We returned in the evening tired but very pleased with all we had seen.

During the evening I heard a trait of the present Emperor which is so much to his credit it deserves to be recorded. During the reviews, he desired Prince Radziwill[27] who was near him to send an aide de camp to request the General commanding to perform a particular manoeuvre. By some misunderstanding the aide de camp gave a totally different order. The Emperor seeing the result differ- ent from his expectation flew into a passion, sent for the General and said many harsh things to him expressing his displeasure with great severity. The General bowed and murmured that he had fulfilled the orders received. The Emperor, however, was too angry to listen but the unfortunate aide de camp, the cause of all the confusion, came to Prince Radziwill and intreated him to explain to the Emperor that his was the fault, having misunderstood the message and given a wrong one. The Emperor on being informed of this commanded all his general officers etc. to assemble in his tent next morning when, addressing the one he had so severely reprimanded the day before, he said, "*Mon Général, je vous ai parlé durement hier, j'étais injuste, je vous démande pardon devant tous ces messieurs; êtes vous satisfait?*"; and, as the person who related the anecdote added, "*Il faut bien penser ce que c'est qu'un Empereur de Russie pour bien apprécier le trait*".

Thursday 13th. The fête of the Virgin—the bells began earlier than usual and continued all the morning. At eleven we went to the

74

Church of St. Basil, one of the oldest and most curious in Moscow, built by an Italian architect for *Ivan le Terrible*.[28] The chapel, though small, is immensely high and was full and hot to suffocation.

The Metropolite officiated and the service was very imposing, the singing beautiful, but the incense was so strong I was quite overpowered and obliged to come out. An immense crowd was collected in the *place* before the Church to see the procession of priests bearing banners, images, etc. pass from there to the Cathedral in the Kremlin going through *la Porte Sauveur* where everyone takes off his hat to drive or walk through.[29] As I sat in the carriage I watched the poor people: not a driver of the humblest droshky omitted to deposit his hat on his lap with an air of reverential devotion while he drove through, and not the poorest peasant omitted to turn, bow and cross himself. The procession consisted in a number of images carried by monks followed by the priests in their fine gold and silver dresses of every colour. We then saw the riding house, a magnificent building, well lighted and heated with stoves and about eight hundred feet long, a flat ceiling inside.

From thence we drove to see *la Salle de la Noblesse* where balls are given in the winter.[30] I could not get the dimensions of the ballroom which struck me as the largest I ever saw. It is immensely high and broad as well as long, with a gallery supported by pillars of imitation white marble and lighted by double rows of lustres between each column and thousands of candles. There is besides a fine suite of rooms for refreshment, cards, etc. We then went to the Institution of St. Catherine where three hundred of the daughters of the *noblesse* are brought up.[31] The greatest pains is [*sic*] taken with their education. They are taught English, German, French, music, drawing, etc. Their dress is green with a white apron and sleeves and for fêtes a white frock with a scarlet sash. The building is very large, the whole thing admirably managed with the greatest system, order and regularity. We went through all the dormitories and the classes, the beautiful white and gold chapel, a large hall with scagliola columns where the young people play, the refectory where they dine and the hospital where any invalids are kept separate. I was very much struck with the good manners, perfect carriage and ladylike appearance of these girls. They sung [*sic*] in chorus a prayer for the Emperor. From thence we proceeded to another institution very near and on the same plan, but with fewer masters and less luxury though equal comfort for the children of the bourgeoisie—the *Institution St. Alexandre*.[32] Gardens are attached to these establishments which, like the others, are on a magnificent scale and perfect plan. The late Empress Mother, Marie, the wife of Paul and the mother of the Emperor[s] Alexander and Nicholas, was a Princess of Württemberg, and though she never reigned, or at least for too short a time to exercise power, yet she appears to have laid the foundation for the great and numberless institutions now existing for education and charity.[33] Her memory is worshipped as the beneficent genius of Russia. The impulse and example she has given to charitable establishments and moral improvement in this country seems to have been followed by her successor the Empress Elizabeth, wife of Alexander.[34] She was a Princess of Baden and a most amiable person and at the time of her marriage very beautiful. An equal interest is taken in them also by the present Empress Alexandra who devotes much care and attention to these institutions for the ends of charity and education in St. Petersburg and Moscow. We then saw a most curious building for supplying the town with water. There is an immense basin from which all the engines are filled simultaneously in an incredibly short space of time. The height of the building is five hundred steps which was more than I could accomplish and I did not climb to the top but I was told the view from it was very fine.

Friday 14th. I went out early *pour parcourir les bazars* and after searching and climbing into all sorts of extraordinary places I succeeded in buying some beautiful gold and silver stuffs or cloth of gold like that of the priests' garments. I returned home to receive farewell visits and in the evening paid a visit to Countess Gudevich. From thence I went to the theatre. A Russian ballet was given at the French theatre which is a singular and very ugly *salle* of a deep, narrow, oval shape, badly lighted.[35] We were received in the Director's box which is over the stage. The German tragedy is a most detestable, *exaltée* and unnatural one. It was not finished and we saw its conclusion. After this was the ballet with all the Russian and Bohemian costumes, dances and music. The dresses were beautiful, many gorgeous, the most curious stuffs and the whole thoroughly national.

Saturday 15th. Lord L. went to see the Russian Prison and the Cholera Hospital which is a fine institution for the education of the orphans of those who die of that disorder. I remained at home to receive Prince Serge Golitsin who was to call on me to take leave. We had a long conversation and he told me some interesting anecdotes. He was a great friend of the Empress Mother and lived a great deal with the Imperial family. He said that during their youth the Empress Mother one day reproached the Grand Duke Nicholas with not having the smile and the charm of his brother, the Emperor Alexander. *"Mais Maman, c'est votre faute"*, was the child's answer. *"Comment, c'est ma faute?"* *"Mais oui, c'est vous qui m'avez fait comme cela."* Prince Serge had given me a bust and now gave me a little picture of the Emperor Alexander, strikingly like him. He bid [*sic*] me adieu promising to visit St. Petersburg in the winter.

I then went out to take a last drive, a parting walk through the market and bazaars, and bid a long farewell to this bright and lovely city. No one can conceive or imagine these curious scenes, peculiar to the place, without having been there. No description or words are adequate or capable of placing them, with all their locale, details, interest and entourage, under the eyes or before the mind of another—the endless and varied riches of the East in all shapes and forms, *cachemires* from Persia, piles and bales of every hue and pattern, chests and chests of tea from China, furs from Siberia, Kamchatka, etc. golden images for the adoration of superstition, the money changers, the beggars, the dense mass of beings young and old, rich and poor, the product of every clime and every soil, the inhabitants of every country from the refined visitor brought by curiosity to the old merchant tempted by gain or the savage idolater bowed before the glittering images and their burning lamps. The dirt, the filth, the extent, the concealed and displayed wealth in these extraordinary places where the piteous moan of the beggar, the sharp cry of the fruitseller, the growl of the driver, the scream of the shop boy and the smooth invitation of the wily, long-bearded old merchant all bewilder, your ears and your eyes being engaged by the glittering stalls in dark, dirty recesses filled with magnificent, massy *évangiles* in splendid bindings, jewelled cups, glittering crosses, etc. and all your mental powers being absorbed in contemplation of the strange and novel scene before you there is a great danger of your being knocked down by the trays of fruit, bales of goods, the mooning idler or the bargaining Jew etc. who impede and arrest every footstep. Nothing is so easy as to lose oneself in these endless *allées* all crossing and intersecting and one like another, but this is indescribable and must be seen to be at all imagined or understood and I bade the scene adieu with a feeling of regret. I went to the English Church at Moscow. It is a small neat building, thinly attended. I was startled at hearing for the first time the prayer for his Imperial Majesty added to our service. I then went to Monsieur Novosiltzov to take leave of him and his children, and returned home where the shawl merchants awaited me, and after much bargaining and quarrelling I became the possessor of another very fine shawl. It was really with a *serrement de coeur* I set out at seven o'clock in the morning to take leave of Moscow. This bright, lovely, half Asiatic, half European city had so captivated my admiration by its fine buildings, its coloured cupolas, gold domes, shining crosses, floating threads, glittering minarets and fretted spires. We had spent a fortnight there and met with the greatest hospitality and kindness. We were fortunate in having heavenly weather and were altogether delighted with our *séjour*.

CHAPTER VI

Conversations with the Tsar

WE INTENDED to reach St. Petersburg the fourth day, *mais l'homme propose et Dieu dispose,* and the first stage out of Moscow witnessed the fracture of our carriage with the baggage. Nothing is more vexatiously tiresome than these accidents which turn you in to the power of a tribe of cheating blacksmiths who demand a large sum at each stage and are in league by doing and undoing each other's work to make you their prey during your journey at the end of which, when the fifties and hundreds of roubles are added up together you find it would have been wiser economy to buy a new and effective carriage than spend five or six hundred roubles before you started in repairs. At this first stage we found a Russian officer coming from Odessa and bringing up a *remonte* of black horses for his regiment. He said the Crown allowed him four hundred roubles a horse and they were all chosen out of the best barracks. Here we were obliged to leave the chariot and, putting our luggage on the britska, proceeded as we best could to Mednoye where we found our cook and courier, but unluckily a whole family of Golitsins had already arrived and secured most of the rooms. The next morning at six we started again. The chariot had not come up in the night as we hoped and expected but we heard of it near and decided not to lose our time in waiting for it. We stopped at Torzhok for more of the gold embroidery on leather and having bought boots, gloves, slippers, etc. we proceeded without further delay to Zimogorye, a miserable place, where we found our supper prepared, and we determined to wait for the chariot which came up in the night and Wednesday 19th we started together but had not gone far before both carriages broke down. After repairs and great delay we proceeded again, but these misfortunes were so often repeated we were unable to get on or accomplish our day, the cook and courier being fifty versts off. We endeavoured to stop at Novgorod but found it utterly impossible—at Jargivo, however, the inn was kept by Germans and we rested. The night was spent in repairing the carriages and we were obliged to abandon our intention of reaching St. Petersburg in four days.

Thursday 20th. We arrived at Pomeranye, the best inn on the road, and early next day at St. Petersburg.

Friday 21st. We found a large collection of letters, the gathered snowball of a month during our absence. We had none forwarded not wishing they should be read which all that pass through a Russian post office are. We found our room at the *Hôtel de Londres* spacious enough but the noise of a club above, a *restaurateur* below, dancing children and smoking generals on either side were nuisances not to be endured with patience. We were, however, forced to bear these ills for no other lodgings could be heard of. Next day was spent in answering letters and writing for the English courier. Lord Durham, Baron Brunnow, etc. came to see us. Lord L. received an invitation to attend a grand review of the Cavalry Guard in the *Champ de Mars* at twelve o'clock.[1] As I before observed the Emperor was absent from St. Petersburg when we arrived. His accident delayed his return and, having passed him on our road to Moscow, flying but invisible (for he was in a shut carriage travelling like the wind), we had not had an opportunity of being presented to him. Baron Brunnow came at eleven to fetch us and Lord L. was presented with a horse of the Emperor's for the occasion, and I was deposited at the house of Monsieur Novosiltzov, the President of the Council, whose windows commanded an excellent view of the whole thing. He was not at home but his niece Madame Agarev received me and I found a great many acquaintances, among them Count and Countess Stroganov whom I had met at the Hague and who had kindly promised their friendship and protection here. The Emperor reviewed the troops himself. There were not less than ten thousand. First came a small troop of Circassians, wild looking people with mail caps, scarlet shirts, armour and long spears, looking like warriors of old. Then followed two magnificent regiments of the *Chevaliers Gardes* and the *Gardes à Cheval*, the Hussars commanded by the *Héritier*, Lancers, Cossacks, Grenadiers, etc. I was greatly struck with the numbers *en masse,* so different from our reviews of one thousand five hundred or two thousand men. Every horse of a regiment is the same shade of colour, size and

80

shape and this perfect matching has an admirable effect. Most of them showed blood and race. The review lasted some time and when over the Emperor and the *Héritier* got off their horses and [into] their little *galèches*² to return to Tsarskoe Seloe, as we were told, where the Court was resident.

We returned to our inn and had not been there five minutes before a bustle in the house was heard and the Emperor was announced. Lord L. was taking off his uniform and unable to appear. He had seen the Emperor at the review who had waived all ceremony and presentation, meeting him as an old acquaintance and unchanged, he said, beyond being *un peu grisonné*. The Emperor came in his little open *calèche* quite alone and unattended by any servant except the long-bearded driver. I had never seen him and being wholly unprepared for this sudden visit was at first confused and embarrassed. However, his cordial and friendly manner soon put me at my ease. He excused his abrupt and unceremonious visit by his great desire to make my acquaintance. I enquired after his health and his accident (his arm was still in a sling) and I said I feared he had not been taught prudence for he had returned as fast as ever *et sans coucher*. *"Voilà, Madame, comme tout le monde tombe sur moi pour mon voyage de retour mais j'éprouvais le besoin d'être avec ma famille et d'être soigné par ma femme."* He was surprised to hear I had seen the review and said *"Si j'avais sait cela j'aurais fait d'autres arrangements; ce sont des braves gens, Madame, et sincèrement attachés"*. I told him in answer to his enquiries about Moscow how charmed I had been with it, how much struck with its peculiar beauty and of my astonishment at the gigantic scale of the hospitals and the institutions and my admiration for the perfection of all their details; that it appeared wonderful to me how this immense empire and all its millions and machinery were directed and guided and governed by one man. *"Cela vous effraie, Madame?"* *"Non Sire, mais il me semble que si vous réfléchissiez à cela, vous aviez plus de soin de votre santé car votre vie est bien précieuse pour votre pays."* He then made a reply that reminded me of a speech of his brother's thirteen years ago at Vienna. He, the Emperor Alexander, in answer to some caution given him, said, *"Madame, pendant que ma vie est utile elle sera conservée, quand elle cessera de l'être tous les gendarmes du monde ne le préserveraient pas"*. The Emperor Nicholas, in the same spirit, said *"que la Providence veillait sur lui*", and that were he cut off suddenly his family were all educated on one system and actuated by one feeling, and that his son would be fitted to replace him.

I told him how much I had been struck by all that was done for the alleviation of poverty, the comfort of the sick and the education of the young. He said much of it owed its existence to his mother of whom he spoke with the greatest respect and affection, "*et ma femme les surveille et les augmente*", he added. Remarking on the veneration and good feeling of the people to their Sovereign, [he replied] "*oui, Madame, ils servent que c'est comme à leur père qui leur est sincèrement attaché*". He then took up the pictures of my children and admired them, talked of his own girls being delicate and that he feared they had been brought forward too young and ought not to have entered the world till seventeen or eighteen when their health and strength were established. He then invited us to Tsarskoe Seloe, saying, "*J'espère que vous nous accorderez un jour entier, il y a un jour de deuil cette semaine; après cela nous espérons vous voir*". He said I was *indignement logée* but that I must not be in a hurry to go and having taken the trouble to make so long and *pénible* a journey I must stay through a Russian winter. "*Moi, je vous préviens, Madame, que je ferais tout au monde pour cela.*" He talked of the Emperor Alexander as his *bienfaiteur* to whom he owed everything. "*Je sais, Madame, que vous avez été honorée d'avoir de l'amitié pour lui et je sais qu'il vous portait une affection toute particulière.*" He then took leave of me, kissed my hand *à plusieurs reprises*, saying "*à présent, Madame, j'espère que la connaissance est faite et la cordialité établie—plus de cérémonie*". He shut the door, rolled himself up in his cloak and jumped into his little *calèche* which waited for him. A crowd had collected and there was more of humble veneration in their mien and their uncovered heads than of curiosity. It was a quiet, anxious gaze of affection and not an impertinent stare or a noisy ebullition of feeling.

The Emperor Nicholas is not like his brother Alexander. He has neither the softness, the gentleness, nor the winning smile; he is taller and larger, a perfect colossus combining grace and beauty. His face is very handsome; if it has a fault I should say it was too long. His countenance is severe, his eye like an eagle's and his smile like the sun breaking through a thundercloud; and on the whole, I think everyone must admit he is a singular and magnificent looking being, and if seen among hundreds and thousands would, from his personal appearance alone, certainly be selected as the one best fitted for the situation he was born to fill. After his visit we went to a family dinner at Lord Durham's.

Tuesday 25th. Count and Countess Stroganov came to see me and most kindly asked us to share their box at the French play, the Count adding, *"seulement, permettez que ma femme y vienne quelquefois"*. Lord Durham then came in and I introduced him to them and after some talk about Constantinople they took their leave. At three o'clock I went to Countess Nesselrode to meet the great jeweller and see designs for mounting and resetting my jewels. After this we had some conversation and I asked her to take me to pay some visits which she agreed to do on Thursday. In the evening we went to the French play and were very glad to find our box next to Madame Stroganov's. The *Michel* theatre is quite one for society. It is small, well heated, open boxes and of which there are only a certain number eagerly taken by the first people. The Court go constantly and people are sure of meeting and seeing everybody there.[3]

Wednesday 26th. I went to Madame Stroganov to see her furs which are magnificent, so dark and fine the sable. Count Stroganov kindly undertook to procure whatever I might want from Tobolsk for half its price in St. Petersburg provided I waited till a certain fair in February or March. *"Je fais rassembler une certaine nombre de ces petites bêtes on coupe tout cela et on les conde chez moi; j'ai deux valets de chambre qui surveillent, car je suis un peu Arabe et je ne souffrais pas qu'on triche, et même après qu'on a tout assemblé je trouve plusieurs urchines de queues sur lesquelles on n'avait pas comptait."* A conversation on furs then commenced and a chapter was opened wholly unknown to me, and I found I was in a state of gross ignorance on the subject. I was told the black fox was more esteemed than sable. I had not seen one beyond seven thousand roubles and I thought the long fur too hot to use in England but I found the finest fox linings cost near fifty and sixty thousand roubles and that their beauty consisted in the black of the raven and the lightness of eiderdown. To collect enough to form one cloak lining two thousand foxes and five or six years were requisite as but one small bit near the tail is fine enough to be used. Count Stroganov advised my going to see the furs at the *garde meuble*, and then concluded with,

83

"Je voudrais que l'Empereur écoutait à la porte, savez vous ce qu'il ferait? Il chercherait ce qui se trouve de plus beau dans le cabinet Impérial pour le déposer à vos pieds". I thought the house pretty; a long suite of rooms ending with the Count's bedroom and boudoir and all the *ameublement* and *boiserie* in good taste.

Thursday 27th. I went at two o'clock to Madame Nesselrode to pay visits. We set out in her carriage, a fine rough chariot-and-four, and paid a visit to Madame Ficquelmont, the Austrian Ambassadress, a very agreeable, handsome person. She received us in a long room filled with towering greenhouse plants and *treillages* like a conservatory, while the bearskins with the head stuffed and reposing on its paw gave an Eastern look to the floor and luxury for the feet. The room was filled with pretty things. Madame F. is a Russian by birth though an Austrian by marriage. She met General F. at Naples where he was Ambassador and married her. They have been six years at St. Petersburg and are very much liked. We met as old acquaintance[s] although for the first time, having heard so much of each other from a mutual friend Madame Apponyi, the Austrian Ambassadress at Paris.[4] From here we went to Madame Narishkin's, the wife of one of the great *chargés de la Cour* and lodged in a corner of the Palace.[5] She is not young, has travelled a great deal and is an agreeable person, rather *maladive* and inclined to stay at home and happy to receive visits. She conversed a great deal on all subjects, said she had *beaucoup roulée*, as she called it, in foreign lands. She urged our stay at St. Petersburg and the impossibility of travelling during the winter. We then paid several other *visites de cérémonie* but did not get out of the carriage, and Madame Nesselrode took me home after giving me a severe scolding for coming out too thinly clad as the weather was piercingly cold, a cutting wind and snow.

Friday 28th. Great alarm spread all over the city from a fear of inundation. There was a tremendous one in 1824, the year before the Emperor Alexander's death, and I understood that the distress and destruction it had caused had greatly affected him.[6] There had been one the year of his birth and it is calculated one occurred every forty five years. It was described to me as the most fearfully sudden and awful visitation without any previous threatening. The westerly wind set in strong, the Neva rose, the salt water poured in, and in an incredibly short space of time the streets filled and boats were going to save the unfortunate people from the first, second, third *étages* and finally from the roofs. The destruction of property and the loss of life was fearful and a few hours more would have destroyed the town. As it was, so much mischief was done that it became a consideration whether Moscow should not again become the seat of empire. The great drawback of St. Petersburg is its situation. It is built below the level of the sea, and by an unfavourable combination of wind, water and weather, might be annihilated. This is a formidable contemplation and sufficient to keep people in a fright during a long, rainy autumn. Excitement was kept up all this day and during the night by the cannons firing at Kronshtadt proclaiming the rising of the water, answering shots from St. Petersburg and coloured lights and signals in the dome of the Admiralty. There was continued bustle and commotion during the night. The Neva rose and overflowed the English Quay above four feet, and all Lord Durham's horses were removed in the middle of the night. The next day, however, the wind changed and the thaw was succeeded by a clear frost. All anxiety ceased and people recovered their spirits. The damp of St. Petersburg is, I am told, felt in summer even in the hottest weather. There is a famous story of a Fin[n] peasant seeing Peter the Great seeking a site for the town, saying, "Oh, I can show you a much better place than this". They followed and were led to a sort of morass half under water and on being asked why he had conducted them there he replied he thought they were looking for the dampest and most unwholesome place in Russia or they never would have thought of building a town there at all.

Saturday 29th. Lord Londonderry received intimation of a second review and we were desired to go as before, he to the *Champ de Mars* where he found a charger of the Emperor's waiting for him, and I to the house of Monsieur Novosiltzov. By some mistake of clocks we were rather late and unfortunately the Emperor was already on the ground. He is, however, always entirely absorbed by his occupation and seems to have neither eyes nor ears for anything else. The *coup d'oeil* was fine—the immense mass of twenty four thousand men very striking, but an infantry review is far less interesting than that of the cavalry. The horses and varied uniforms add greatly to the scene; there is a sameness in so many regiments of foot-soldiers, almost all alike, except one distinguished by the privilege of wearing brass helmets. This favour was granted for their conduct in 1812 and most of the helmets are pierced with balls. There is a singular custom in the Russian service that astonishes a stranger. When a regiment passes the Emperor, if he is pleased with their appearance he says, "How are you, my children?", and hundreds of voices reply, "We thank you, my Father", or, "You have done well, my children", the same wild scream answers, "We will do better next time my Father". I have heard much discussion whether this habit being allowed in the army was likely to be productive of good or ill; for myself I can form no judgement and I leave the matter to speak for itself. On this occasion, however, the Emperor was greatly dissatisfied and after dismissing the four regiments he was pleased with and also the ambassadors and strangers by taking leave of them, he pronounced the rest *"pitoyable"*, and remained on the ground reviewing them till they went through the manoeuvres better. His displeasure created a great sensation and a sort of mysterious fear seemed to fall on everyone. It was, however, undeniable that he had cause for anger for nothing could be worse or more irregular than the way the men passed, some running and none keeping their ranks.

At four o'clock we set out for Tsarskoe Seloe and took leave of our dirty, cold hotel which certainly was, in many respects, as objectionable as an English alehouse. Two hours brought us to the Palace where we found the same suite of rooms prepared for us as before and we commenced our *toilettes* for the concert at eight o'clock, where, as usual, we were summoned. The party was small and without form or ceremony. The eldest Grand Duchess, Marie, whom I had not seen, appeared and seemed very delicate. The concert commenced with *les chantres de la Cour* who sang beautifully. The Empress, whom I had not seen since my return from Moscow, talked to me a great deal about my journey and asked me many questions about all I had seen, and then led me to the sofa and made me sit by her while her young children grouped at her feet seemed entirely absorbed by the music. After these choruses we had a piece on the violin by an aide de camp of the Emperor's. This was declared very fine but I dislike the instrument and could not help admitting this when asked my opinion. The confession was treated as a barbarous taste and the instrument pronounced *plus touchant et plus fin que tout autre*.

A maid of honour then sang. She had a fine voice which the Empress told me was the reason of her having taken her. They estimate and appreciate music here and regret and bewail the climate and the distance that prevents the great singers coming. They declare they are all spoilt and overpaid in England. Catalani was here and Caradori and Sontag and they were very well received and fêted, but neither Malibran or Grisi have they ever heard.[7] They say the great mistake in these people receiving such immense sums in England is increased by the fact that from its vicinity to Paris they ought to receive less than in any other country. During this concert the Emperor, having previously made his *tournée*, formed his *partie* and played at whist with three of his generals. He admired my *toilette* very much, adding, *"Mais on s'y attendait, Madame, votre réputation vous avait précédée"*. I took this opportunity to thank him for the yacht and express what an advantage and comfort it had been to us. I was introduced to Prince Menshikov, the head of the navy, a very agreeable, gentlemanlike, goodlooking man.[8] At eleven o'clock supper tables of all sizes and shapes were brought in without tablecloths; in an instant *le couvert est mis* and supper handed round. The Empress called me to sit near her at a table with about eight or ten covers. Lord L. sat on the other side and the Emperor, having finished his *jeu* and drunk his tea, came and sat by me. He suffered a good deal from his accident, complained of his arm which was still in a sling, and said the pain always occurred when a change of weather approached. He conversed a great deal of England, his residence there, his recollections of the country, and talked over the most remarkable beauties he had known and admired, Lady Peel,[9] Lady Mount Charles[10] etc.

On Sunday morning, while I was puzzling what I ought or was expected to do, I received a message from the Emperor to inform me *la Messe* was at eleven and that I should find a door in my room that opened into the chapel. This I understood as a command and therefore got up and commenced dressing, an occupation that certainly took up a good deal of time with everyone during a visit at this Imperial Court. Lord L. accompanied me in uniform. The chapel I have before described having seen it on my former visit to Tsarskoe Seloe. On this occasion it was full. The ladies stood on one side and the gentlemen on the other.

The Imperial family entered and placed themselves near the

screen. In the Greek church even the Sovereign does not sit. The singing was very fine, the dresses of the priest extremely rich and the whole ceremony imposing. The ladies appeared entirely absorbed in devotion, crossing themselves, kissing the ground, shedding tears and prostrating themselves with the deepest humiliation etc. This lasted about an hour and when it was over the Empress spoke to me and I retired to my room to receive visits while the Emperor took Lord L. in his own little *calèche* to the parade. The day was deplorable—rain and snow, and it was impossible for me to stir out had I been so inclined. At four o'clock we were dressed for dinner, and as usual the Imperial carriages were sent for us. We found a large party assembled and the Empress, who the night before was dressed in muslin and bands of gold like a Greek statute without a jewel on her classically shaped head or her graceful figure now appeared clothed with Eastern splendour—a Turkish dress of gold stripes with green and red velvet, a necklace fringe, strings and drops of enormous emeralds and diamonds. The dinner was very magnificent—above a hundred people. The Grand Duchess Hélène, wife to the Grand Duke Michael, a very pretty person, Prince Dimitri Golitsin, the Governor of Moscow, the French Ambassador, Monsieur de Barante,[11] his wife and daughter, Prince Menshikov, the head of the navy, Count Tchernischev, the head of the army, and the latter introduced his wife to me, a pleasing person who had just returned from a visit to England for her health. The dinner passed as usual, the ladies going to dinner first, the Emperor and the other gentlemen following. I sat next the Grand Duchess Olga who talked a great deal to me and spoke most perfect English. At half past six o'clock we were dismissed and desired to return to the *spectacle* at seven.

The time was short; nevertheless all contrived to change their *toilette* and the Empress reappeared in a still more lovely one than the last—the richest blonde over the palest pink, trimmed with large opals and diamonds and strings of pearl down to her feet.

The French actors performed two little *vaudevilles* in a *salle* fitted up as a theatre and afterwards we returned to the *grand appartement* and the dancing began. Soon after eleven supper was brought in and the same magic wand cleared the whole away and the dancing was resumed.

It was gay and agreeable with an absence of all form and etiquette, the Empress sometimes dancing in the same quadrille with her children and talking to different people. The Emperor this evening devoted himself to a beautiful Madame Kindener, natural daughter of the Princess Thurn [Tour] and Taxis,[12] who is aunt to the Empress. This Princess is sister of the Duchess of Cumberland and the beautiful Queen of Prussia, the Empress's Mother, and has led a most extraordinary life.[13] She is the mother of Princess Esterhazy[14] and resides principally at Frankfurt. She has had several illegitimate children, hates them all, and has not provided for any. One is now a singer on the Berlin stage, and this Madame Kindener was brought up by the wife of the Princess's lover. She is tall, very fair and lovely; her likeness to the beautiful Queen Louise struck the King of Prussia forcibly when he first saw her. I thought the Emperor in speaking of her to me took pains to explain that they saw a great deal of her *"parce que c'est la cousine de ma femme"*. I was told she had killed a bear, that he had been lamed or tamed for the purpose, but she actually had shot him with her own fair hand.

After supper the Emperor came and sat by me and we had a long talk. He again reverted to his English recollections and among them to the beauty of Mrs. Howard, now Mrs. Cavendish,[15] saying he little thought then her brother would be ambassador here and added that having been disappointed of our filling the situation he was very much satisfied with Lord Durham whom he believed was loyal. I said I believed he was *envers lui* but that for my own part I could never esteem a man who was a tyrant in his home, a radical at Glasgow and a conservative in Russia. The Emperor said he had nothing to do with Lord Durham's family not being a member of it, but that as to his political errors, he was arriving at an age to see their fallacy. I said I never attributed them to *étourderie*. *"Mais à quoi donc, Madame?"* "Why to vanity" I replied, and that the same feeling which made him *pérorer* as he did to a Glasgow mob to obtain popular applause and now made him a convert to the reverse here where he found liberal opinions execrated would, when united with self interest, decide his future line and career in England.

The Emperor then talked of the horrors of an inundation in St. Petersburg and the terrible anxiety kept up by the awful possibility of its recurrence; of the Emperor Alexander, his goodness and perfection. He remarked on the shortness of the women generally, as they danced by; he enquired about the Princess Victoria and said he had heard much praise of the Queen.[16] He spoke with great regard of George IV, who, he said, had shown him much kindness; enquired about the Fitzclarences;[17] and in answer to my remark that the Duchess of Kent was a clever woman, *"Je ne la connais pas, Madame, mais elle vient d'une famille que je n'aime pas, une famille qui aime de l'argent, c'est vil, c'est bas"*.[18] There is a truth and straightforward manly principle in the Emperor Nicholas which, though it makes him at times brusque and is totally different from the soft, winning manner of his late brother, is too fine a trait not to be valued and appreciated in any individual. It is doubly rare in a monarch, and being the leading feature in his character calls for unbounded admiration. Our conversation was interrupted by the mazurka and after that I retired to bed.

Monday 31st. The weather was still horrible but I went with Madame Rauch, a Prussian lady, to see the arsenal which was built by the Emperor Alexander.[19] It is very fine and there is, *au premier*, a collection of armour greatly added to by magnificent presents from the Sultan after the Treaty of Adrianople[20]—the housings and furniture of a horse, embroidered in large brilliants, the sword, pistols etc. of enamel and diamonds. Madame Rauch herself had on a magnificent shawl just given to her by the Emperor worth, she said, ten thousand roubles. He had, I was informed at Moscow, bought above forty of the finest at the great fair at Nishni Novgorod in August. We then dressed and went to dinner at a palace called Pavlovsky belonging to the Grand Duchess Hélène about three or four versts from Tsarskoe Seloe.[21] It belonged to the Empress Mother who left it to the Grand Duke Michael and, as he is unwilling to alter or disturb her apartments, the *corps de logis* of this immense palace is uninhabited and they live in a corner of it.

The Grand Duke was absent. The Grand Duchess sent for us before dinner for a private audience and was very agreeable and amiable. The dinner was small and *sans cérémonie*, a round table and about twelve persons. Her children, three little girls, came in after dinner. She is clever, much given to literary pursuits and not in good health, very pretty and *d'une humeur un peu inégale* as I heard whispered.

Rooms were prepared for us to stay at night but we declined, and having retired, a French maid of the Grand Duchess's offered her services and I took off all my *toilette* and, having wrapped myself up in *bonnet et douillette de voyage*, we returned to St. Petersburg and took possession of our new house which belonged to the *Grand Chambellan*, Count Golovkin. Next day our *beau idéal* and visions of comfort were destroyed by discovering the nastiness and filth of our abode, the rooms filled with dirt and vermin and the satin sofas absolutely stuffed with bugs. It is not possible for any English person to imagine the horrors of this lodging without seeing them. As one of the servants expressively said, "if only the edge of the dirt had been taken off, but the creatures positively form ropes of themselves"; earwigs crawled over my toilet, bugs literally dropped from the ceiling and I can declare what I hardly expect anyone to credit without seeing, that I have seen them in the water poured out of the bottle and out of the pitchers. I never touched a thing till it had been examined and never put on a single article of dress till it had been thoroughly shaken and looked through. Fleas we ceased to mind, there were such swarms, and they were forgotten among the horrors of larger vermin.

Madame Stroganov came to see me, also Madame Narishkin. The former sent me a beautiful little miniature model of the Alexandrine column.

Wednesday 2nd. We went to a great dinner at Lord Durham's who had taken a house on the English Quay. Among the party were Countess Voronzov-Dashkov,[22] a daughter of Madame Narishkin's, General Benkendorf, brother to Princess Lieven, General Kisselov, Count Tchernischev, Prince Menshikov, etc.

Thursday, November 3rd. Lord L. was taken ill and Dr. Doratt, the physician of the British Embassy, was called in. In the evening Baron Heeckeren, the Dutch Minister, called and sat with me. He has been a great many years at St. Petersburg and is an agreeable, clever man.

Friday 4th. Lord L. was still very ill. Madame Nesselrode bringing [*sic*] Madame Ribeaupierre with whom I had a discussion regretting the stoppage of the steam boats to England by the closing of the navigation, while she rejoiced in the necessity for the messengers going by Berlin where her husband is the Russian Minister. Madame Nesselrode closed the argument, wisely remarking, "*Chacun prêche pour sa paroisse, vous pour les paquebots qui vont droit en Angleterre, Madame pour les couriers par Berlin où son mari est*". In the evening Sir James Wylie came to see me.[23]

Saturday 5th. Lord L. was a little better and went out for a drive and I called on the Stroganovs where I was received with a kindness and cordiality at all times that made me invariably feel welcome. The Count talking of the severity of the climate told me what appears astonishing, that the gardeners (who are principally German) so well understand the management of the hothouses that any dish of fruit may be ordered for a particular day; for example, a plate of cherries commanded for any date in January would punctually be ready, "but", added the Count, "*il faut les payer chaque cérise quatre ou cinq roubles, et comme il faut, quatre ou cinq cents pourrait s'élèver à une assiette de deux milles roubles*".

Sunday 6th. We were all invalids and unable to go to church, but had prayers at home and in the afternoon Count Nesselrode and his son called to see us.

Monday 7th. We went to a great dinner at Lord Durham's. We met the French Ambassador, Monsieur de Barante, a very clever, agreeable man and his wife and daughter. I was so ill I fainted away, lay on the floor for some time, and when I came to myself I was taken home and attacked with violent spasms. Dr. Doratt attended me and for the whole week I was confined to my bed, very ill and suffering every sort of annoyance that a small bed and inconvenient lodging filled with vermin must entail. In spite of every care and attention, incessant scrubbing and washing, nothing could eradicate the smell of smoke and other poisonous odours. Cockroaches came up in the wood for the stoves, bugs fell heavily from the ceiling and crawled out of the cracks of the walls and floors, earwigs walked over the glass of barley water by my bedside. In the enjoyment of health one less regards hardship and inconvenience and one bears patiently and sometimes laughingly the ills which are repaid by the novelty, curiosity and interest of a new scene; but when sickness debilitates mind and body the loss of comfort is felt tenfold and every trifle becomes irritating. I certainly suffered *mort et martyre*.

The returning Monday [the] 14th found me still ill and so I remained till Saturday 19th. During all this time my existence was a blank as far as sightseeing or interest. My kind friend Madame Stroganov visited me daily and sent me a bug hunter who came loaded with bug washes and bug decoctions, but though he opened chairs, sofas, mattresses, etc. and killed thousands and thousands by the touch of his magic brush and mysterious preparation, still the professor was conquered and as many remained. We received a most kind invitation from the Imperial family to Tsarskoe Seloe but my health made this impossible and Lord L. very kindly was unwilling to leave me. The Emperor and Empress sent every day to enquire after me and, according to the Court etiquette, Lord L. always answered the messenger in person. Our friends were busily exerting themselves to provide for us a better lodging but none could be found. Nothing is so difficult as to *caser* oneself in St. Petersburg. One was too large, one too small, one not furnished, another damp, none to be let under a year. We really were in despair and actually began to talk of attempting our journey to Berlin. This however no one would hear of. We were to remain for the fêtes [of the] sixth of December and first of January, Old Style. Besides, we were assured the roads were impassable and that the moment when the summer ones are broken up and the frost and snow not established (which was precisely the case just now) is the very worst for moving. Add to this the difficulty of crossing the river when the bridges are carried away and the ice though not strong enough to be driven over is sufficiently so as to endanger the boats. Thus *bon gré malgré* we were forced to say.

Saturday 19th. I was a little better but unable to go out and Lord L. went alone to dine with the French Ambassador.

Sunday 20th. The fête of the St. Michael Regiment. Lord L. was desired to attend the parade and was invited to the great dinner at the *Palais d'Hiver*. The Imperial family were not however residing there though they had left Tsarskoe Seloe and settled in town. They prefer passing six weeks in the *Palais d'Anischeff*, a private one at the end of the Nevsky Prospect. They are both very fond of this residence where they passed so much happy time before they ascended the throne. Here they live as Monsieur and Madame Nicholas and more *comme riches particulières* than *en Souverain* giving balls, dinners, etc. without the form and ceremony of a Court.

The great fêtes, however, are always at the Winter Palace and Lord L. returned dazzled with the splendour of the scene. Sir James Wylie passed the evening with me. He had been the Emperor Alexander's confidential friend and physician and I had a long and interesting conversation with him about his Imperial Master's last illness. The details will one day be published but the doctor was desired not to do so during the lifetime of the Empress Mother, the Empress Elizabeth, wife of Alexander, and the Emperor Nicholas. The two first are dead. There is not a vestige of truth in the suspicion entertained in England that he was poisoned or assassinated, nor is there the least doubt that he himself wished to die and for many years had taken leave of all worldly feelings. The knowledge of the conspiracy against him had caused him the deepest anguish and the ingratitude of those on whom he had heaped favours disgusted and sickened him.[24] He had the names of the traitors and the whole of the details in his writing box. He could not be prevailed upon to take or do anything for his health, went through great extremes of heat and cold and long fasting often shutting himself up in convents to pray, and when he grew worse nothing would persuade him to be bled or follow any advice or take any remedy. He died at the wretched, ill fated place, Taganrog, on the shores of the Sea of Azov *"au milieu des médecins sans les secours de la médecine, il voulait mourir et il est mort"*; and such was the poverty and misery of the spot where the last remains of the mighty Emperor of millions lay that sufficient black cloth could not be procured to hang the little room in which he expired. When he was in the greatest danger, Sir James, who had been four years with the Emperor Paul, approached his bedside and said, *"Je suis votre fidèle serviteur depuis vingt cinq ans, vous avez refusez mes remèdes, vous ne voulez pas écouter votre médecin corporel; je ne puis vous cacher qu'il faut voir votre médecin spirituel"*. The poor Emperor took his hand and thanked him and the priest came, received his confessions and went through all the last ceremonies. With a sort of expiring hope's last effort they persuaded the priest to tell him it was his duty as a Christian to listen to his medical advisers and this, added to the prayer of the Empress on her knees, made him consent to have forty leeches applied behind the ears. But hardly had they placed four or five on each side when, finding she had left the room, he pulled them off and refused to put on any more so impatient and anxious was he to be released from an ungrateful wicked world for which he was too good.

"And what is Empire, what is man,
A noisome vault, a narrow span
Confines that mighty King,
Whose will was erst supreme command

94

From far Kamskatka's lonely strand
To warlike Poland's plains of sand
And Euxines bowers of spring.

Nations peal his funeral knell
The wild Kossac with barbarous yell
And ash besprinkled head
Hetman, Palatine and Peer,
Warrior and sage throng round his bier
And sorrowing Europe drops a tear
O'er the illustrious dead."

Hon. H.[enry] L.[iddell][25]

CHAPTER VII

St. Petersburg Society and the Imperial Court

MONDAY 21ST. I went out ◇ and we heard of a small house likely to suit us. Aided by the advice and counsel of Count Stroganov I bought myself a magnificent sable, very dark, almost black and with the occasional white hairs that attest its merit. I bought another, less fine, for Lord L. as the weather was beginning to get piercingly cold. I had got myself a fox lining at Moscow but being ignorant about furs (as everybody is who has not been in far northern climes) I had not bought a nice or a light one. We dined at Lord Durham's and met a large party of English.

Thursday 24th was entirely occupied by moving into our new house which, though small, was very nice and warm and clean, newly furnished and quite a paradise after the dirty hole we had existed in for three weeks. We were obliged to take it for three months. However we resigned ourselves to this not seeing much chance of leaving sooner. No one can imagine a Russian move without seeing it. There was not half the difficulty I expected in moving all the effects. We had hired a great deal of furniture and had an immense quantity of things. The drawers and wardrobes were snapped up as they stood, quite full, deposited in sledges, whisked off with inconceivable velocity and placed in the new house. When I beheld the commencement of this transit I gave up things as lost but, to my amazement, nothing was missing and in a couple of hours we were *installé de nouveau*.

The intelligence and quickness of the Russians is incredible. The lower orders are so clever it is easy to make them understand any thing by signs. We dined with Lord Durham, a family party.

Monday we dined with the Stroganovs. We also improved in health in our new house though the weather was dreadful. The first break-up makes the streets like a ploughed field and the previous sudden change from droshkies to sledges was now reversed. The snow and ice melted and the streets were one sea of mud and slop. Wednesday 30th. We dined at Lord Durham's and met a large party of English bankers and merchants. I was much surprised to meet Mr. Nicholl, one of the proprietors of the English *magasin* and who literally stands behind the counter.

I have omitted to give some account of a ball we went to at the *Palais d'Anischoff*. The balls are strictly private and without form and the *corps diplomatique* are never asked. The entertainment began at half past eight o'clock. The rooms are beautifully lighted, the supper was served on round tables in a large gallery. There was no ceremony, the Emperor and Empress both occasionally dancing and generally conversing. I was very weak not having entirely recovered from my illness, and being extremely tired I asked permission to withdraw early.

Friday, December 2nd. Madame Stroganov took me to her box at the Alexandrine Theatre[1] to see the *Revolt of the Haram* [*sic*].[2] It was the fête of the accession. The national anthem was played. The Court mourning for Charles X was cast aside and everyone appeared in the gayest colours.[3] The theatre is large, very handsome and well lighted. The ballet was old and the dresses not fresh but the acting was good and we were informed that the Emperor and the Grand Duke had drilled the young ladies who went through their exercises with great skill.

Saturday, December 3rd. Lord L. dined at Court for the fête of the Simonisky regiment and Seaham and I dined at Lord Durham's. Next day Lord and Lady Durham and Prince Lieven dined with us. We found our house warm and clean and our little *ménage* comfortable. I thought the provisions all bad; nothing tasted natural or wholesome. The meat appeared worried [*sic*] and beef alone was seen. The game from being frozen and thawed never was good, the vegetables were equally bad, the wine tasted like brandy. The sturgeon *sterlette*,[4] caviar etc. were good, I suppose, but I never could touch them and I don't remember ever thinking anything good or ever feeling hungry while I was at St. Petersburg.

Monday 5th. I did not go out but had constant visits; indeed by this time I had made a great many acquaintances and was seldom alone when at home. Count and Countess Stroganov and their son and his wife dined with us.

Wednesday 6th [*recte* 7th].We dined at the Austrian Ambassador's, a magnificent fête for forty people. The lighting in this country is very brilliant—there were above a hundred candles on the dining table and the whole hotel was equally *éclairé*. Count Ficquelmont was many years Ambassador at Naples where he married and from whence he removed here. The Emperor asked him during his first winter, when the cold was excessive, how he bore the change, "*Mais, Sire, comme l'acier qui devient dur après le feu*".

Thursday 7th [*recte* 8th] was devoted to paying and receiving visits.

Friday 8th [*recte* 9th]. We went to a great dinner at Lord Durham's, meeting the Stroganovs, Prince Lieven, Count Palfy, etc. and immediately afterwards we adjourned to the great theatre to see its first opening.[5] This was really a beautiful sight: the *salle* is immense, a horse-shoe shape, entirely white and gold, and magnificently lighted.

I have already remarked on the perfection of the system of hot air in Russia. Excepting during the momentary transition from the door to the carriage when the piercing cold sometimes takes away one's breath and seems to cut one down by its severity, the temperature is beautifully regulated however large the building. Stairs, passages, halls, theatres, riding houses are all thus admirably managed.

The opening of this theatre was a great event and a beautiful *coup d'oeil*. The men, as usual, in uniform—the Court present and the mourning laid aside. The ladies were in the brightest colours, and *en grande toilette*. The opera was entirely Russian and more national and extraordinary than pleasing. From the theatre I went with Madame Stroganov to a ball at Madame Soukhozanet's, a pretty house and beautifully lighted. Most people here who do not dance play cards; politics are rarely discussed and there is little general conversation. To give some idea of the distances in St. Petersburg, this *réunion* was about four miles from my abode and yet both were in good situations, the one at the end of the Nevsky Prospect and mine close to the English Quay which is the great walk, and during all the winter is kept carefully swept and sanded as at two o'clock every day the Imperial family are almost certain to drive there to walk.[6] They go out in all weathers and I have sometimes been amazed to hear of the Empress walking in a snow storm when I would not have left my own fireside. The immense distances in this capital make it absolutely necessary to have four horses even to drive about shopping or visiting. The Russian coachmen are very picturesque looking people. They have a long beard, bare neck, round black hat, and their folding flowing robe of blue cloth is confined by a girdle or sash of bright colours. A person thus attired drives the first pair of horses to which are traces of endless length and on the second pair is a little boy riding the off horse. At balls or any other large assemblage of carriages there is great inconvenience in these long *attelages* which of course nearly treble an English "string".

Sunday 10th [*recte* 11th]. We attended divine service in a handsome chapel well warmed and lighted. It was performed by Mr. Law, the resident clergyman, a relation of Lord Ellenborough's.[7] On returning home I had visits from General Kisselov, Madame Boberinsky, etc.

Next morning we set off at twelve o'clock to see a very fine and interesting establishment called *le Corps des Mines*.[8] It is a large and handsome building with a long façade to the Neva. We were conducted through many galleries and shown scientific models of all sorts and some, said to be very exact, of the gold mines in Siberia. The different arrangements and processes for washing the sand and extracting the precious metal are curious and interesting. It is found sometimes in large lumps. Siberia is rich in minerals and precious stones of all sorts. The amethysts are much finer than those found in Brazil; opals and emeralds have also been discovered but of inferior description. The iron mines are very productive. Some belong to individuals but the greater part to the Crown. The collection of minerals at this institution is very fine and there are contributions from every country. I saw one large case filled with various sorts of Derbyshire spar, a quantity of fossils and the bones of an animal supposed to be the mammoth; also an enormous block of malachite and some very curious specimens. We were then conducted through the dormitories of above three hundred of the pupils. They were as neat, clean and orderly as all the other establishments in Russia. We went through the kitchen, the baths, the hospital (where there were only ten invalids) and finally we saw the inmates at dinner. We were then conducted *dans les souterrains* which were lighted up and are constructed precisely as the galleries are cut in the mines with the veins of ore, the windings, etc.

The day was very bad which prevented our enjoying our expedition as much as we should otherwise have done. Lord L. dined with the Prussian Minister and we paid visits in the evening and went to a *soirée* at the Saxon Minister's.

Tuesday 12th [*recte* 13th]. We were to have gone to the mint but the bridge had been taken away and the river not being sufficiently hard to bear driving over, we gave it up. The courier arrived from England with the letters which we answered by a Russian one just going and we dined with Monsieur and Madame Seniavine who have a very pretty, small house, *meublée et montée à l'Anglaise*. At ten o'clock I accompanied Countess Stroganov to *la Princesse de Waldemar*, an old lady of ninety nine *qui tient salon* and to whom everybody goes *pour lui faire sa cour*; even the Emperor and Empress visit her on her fête. She is a wonderful person, seemed quite herself, and though rather deaf, was seated in an armchair supported by cushions, deeply interested in her game at Boston.[9] She was playing with cards of an immense size to aid her failing vision. She has kept a journal since she was fifteen and her recollection and details are said to be most interesting. The number of reigns she has seen, the number of celebrated individuals she has known whose names belong to the past make her interesting and historical, *et tout cela date de si loin* that it really revives and realizes all one's ideas of "the Undying One". Her son, Prince Dimitri Golitsin, I have already spoken of as the Governor of Moscow and much respected and beloved. Her daughter Madame Apraxin is between sixty and seventy and was very handsome as one may judge by the remains of her beauty and her picture painted by Madame Le Brun.[10] She, as well as the old Princess, had been a great deal in England; they both conversed in English. Madame Apraxin was much admired by George IV who gave her his picture. The old lady made me sit by her, conversed a good deal, and when we left the circle begged us to return. I heard she had been painted by Hogarth.

It is surprising to find how many people here speak English. It appears to form a part of every woman's education. They are excellent linguists which was accounted for to me by the difficulty of their own language: "*cela leur délié la langue*". I almost fancied myself in England seeing Madame Stroganov receive all the annuals, new publications, etc. The papers are not allowed by government but some people contrive to get them by couriers.

Saturday 16th [*recte* 17th]. We went to dine with Count and Countess Voronzov-Dashkov. He is Chamberlain[11] and she is the daughter of Monsieur Narishkin, *Grand Maréchal de la Cour*.[12] They give constantly magnificent dinners and great balls and have a very fine house; the only drawback is *les grands appartements* being *au second*. There is a fine collection of pictures—a Giulio Romano, Guercinos, etc. and a gallery filled with statues by Thorwaldsen.

About fifty sat down to a most magnificent and *recherché* dinner. I was next to the master of the house but on the other side was Count Orlov *le grand* who so gallantly and loyally stood by the Emperor Nicholas during the revolt previous to the accession.[13] He talked a great deal about Russia generally and her two last Sovereigns contrasting the late and the present one. He told me *un très joli mot* of the King of Prussia. Count Orlov attended him on his visit to Moscow. The King arriving late at night was lodged at a country house of Monsieur Narishkin's, and coming early into the town next morning was first conducted to the Kremlin. Among the gazers there collected he saw many Prussians, and addressing them and taking off his hat he said, "*Messieurs, saluez la ville qui a sauvé l'Europe*".

From the dinner we went to pay some visits and to a great *soirée* at Countess Nesselrode's.

Sunday [*recte* Saturday] 17th. *Il gelait à foudre la pierre* with a tremendous fall of snow and everyone hoped the damp, unwholesome weather was at end and concluded the winter was really setting in but, as usual, in a few hours a change of many degrees took place and there was a complete thaw. The most trying part of the climate of St. Petersburg is this sudden variation of temperature added to the extreme damp and unwholesome situation of the town. All the Russians agree in this winter being much worse than usual.

Sunday, December 17th [*recte* 18th]. This day in the Old Style is the sixth, and as the St. Nicholas is the Emperor's fête and a great day. I got up by candlelight to breakfast and dress for Court. We went at ten o'clock, the Emperor having given a special permission in these words: "*Jamais on n'a admis d'étrangers, pour vous exception*." I enquired if I ought to go in a Russian or Paris costume. I was informed any dress I pleased, but it was signified to me that it would be complimentary and good taste to adopt the Russian one. I therefore not only did so in shape and appearance but I determined to employ only stuffs and furs of the country. We drove to the door and staircase of the Empress Mother from which we were shown to *la Salle Blanche* where we found an immense number of people collected, the gallery round being filled with spectators. There are above two hundred maids of honour all wearing the cipher and crown in diamonds on their shoulder and distinguished by their red and gold trains. The *dames d'honneur et les dames à portrait* are dressed in green and gold, the maids of honour of the Grand Duchesses in light blue. These colours are prohibited for others. After passing through a *salle* full of magnificent troops the procession arrived, a great *cortège* of *fourriers de la Cour*, pages, *gentils-hommes de la Chambre*, chamberlains, etc. and at last, the Emperor in the uniform of Hetman[14] of the Cossacks leading in the Empress in the full Russian costume with a red velvet and gold train and her cap and gown a blaze of jewels, followed by the Grand Duchess Hélène and the two eldest Grand Duchesses with their youngest sister and a daughter of the Grand Duchess Hélène's. These were all dressed in the palest blue velvet and snowdown. They proceeded through *la Salle des Maréchaux*, a long gallery filled with Dawe's paintings, to the chapel which is white and magnificently gilt, very lofty and with the transparent Greek screen. The Emperor and Empress stood in front; behind them the Grand Duchesses, and then ranged the whole Court, the ladies all on one side, the men opposite. The heat was excessive. The Grand Duchess Olga fainted and a maid of honour suffered in a far less refined manner, Madame Nesselrode remarking in her usual imperturbable manner, *"Pauvre petite chatte, elle dégosille"*. I had expected from my own weak state of health to be incapable of standing for an hour and had retired to an anteroom *pour prendre l'air* when I found myself called upon to act as nurse to all the sufferers who were brought out. The singing in the chapel was very fine, the priests' dresses were magnificent and the whole scene very impressive. After the service the Empress received *les félicitations* of the clergy who kissed her hand, and the procession returned to *la Salle Blanche*. The Court then went into *le Salon de Pierre*, a fine room with a throne and that Sovereign's picture. Here they received the congratulations of

Zagorsk (Sergiyevo): the Troiste-Sergieveskaya Monastery
General view and the Cathedral of The Trinity

Zagorsk (Sergiyevo): the Troiste-Sergieveskaya Monastery
The Cathedral Church

the *corps diplomatique* and afterwards the Empress retired to her own room at the farther end of the Palace.

At last it appeared to me we walked miles to arrive at the salon. We passed through apartments filled with magnificent *objets*, porphyry, porcelain, crystal, orange trees, plate, etc. and at last, after the Empress had reposed and refreshed herself, the doors of her salon were thrown open and the immense assemblage were admitted one by one.

To describe the Empress's room and succeed in placing it in imagination before the eyes of one who has never seen it I believe would be impossible—the gorgeous magnificence and the perfect taste that are combined, the windows of a single pane, the walls of dazzling white scagliola painted with the brightest flowers, the splendid jasper columns, the gilded doors, the lapis lazuli vases, the malachite tables, etc. In the middle of this stood the Empress, her dignified, graceful figure resting on a malachite *jardinière* filled with flowers, her whole person one blaze of jewels but all arranged with such taste and perfection that their brilliancy struck you more than their weight. The Grand Duchesses were grouped behind her and the ladies entered one by one, first the two hundred maids of honour, then the *dames d'honneur, à portrait*, etc. I had been delivered into the charge of Countess Stroganov who was to enter first of the Russian ladies and she had been desired to conduct me in. I wished to kiss the Empress's hand as all the ladies did but she absolutely prevented this and embraced me, thanking me most graciously for putting on the Russian costume. I then passed on, Madame S. following. The Empress sent her after me to see that I did not lose myself and I was placed at a glass door where I had a full view of everyone that came in. The order was admirable—no pushing or squeezing or jostling; everyone knew his or her place and fell into it. After the ladies had all passed came *le Conseil* one by one, *le Sénat, les aides de camp de l'Empereur* at the head of whom they placed Lord Londonderry who had laid aside every order but the little ribbon and cross of St. George, an attention that was much appreciated by these refined, sensitive people whom we, in all the pride of our vanity and ignorance, call barbarians and uncivilized beings. Next came the Generals and, at the end of this string, the *Héritier* who, on that day, his father's fête, had been raised to that rank and kissed his mother's hand on the promotion.

I sat very comfortably looking through the glass door, delighted and interested with the scene. I was hungry and faint but, being absorbed in all I saw and heard, I did not find this out myself till I was fed by my kind and attentive friends. The same order prevailed outside; an enormous fire blazed in the middle of the *place* surrounded by snow. The carriages and four were all drawn up like a regiment of soldiers, and in one moment, without noise or confusion, were ready. The system and method, *jusqu'au moindre petit détail*, was not the least striking feature of this magnificent fête. The pomp and splendour was surpassing but nothing was more beautiful than the devotion and affection shown to the Sovereign whom this great people, collectively and individually, look up to as a father. He had conferred many favours and made many great promotions on that day. Some new maids of honour had been appointed by the Empress; the Emperor had done many things for the army and everybody seemed pleased. The evening ball was put off on account of the mourning for Princess Radziwill, the Empress's aunt who had lately died at Berlin and the account was just arrived. I thought the delay very fortunate, for after the morning's exertion no one had strength for a ball. Next day I was suffering so much from overfatigue as to be unable to go to a ball at the Saxon Minister's.

Tuesday 19th [*recte* 20th]. The Nesselrodes, Creptovichs, etc. were to have dined with us but early in the morning the first sent an excuse, being *commandés au Palais*. We put off our party and received an invitation to dine at Court at four o'clock that day. This is rather an inconvenience and one I found generally felt. These Imperial invitations are sent so late sometimes the person is not to be found, or has hardly time to alter his previous arrangements.

We went, as commanded, utterly ignorant whether the dinner was for ten or for forty. However as a Court mourning was ordered I thought I could not err in wearing black velvet. We were shown into the lovely salon where two days before the Empress had received us, and we found General Kisselov, Prince Lieven, Count Nesselrode, Prince Serge Golitsin and two others I did not know. We were soon called by the Emperor into an adjoining small room where the Empress, the Grand Duchess Marie and the *Héritier* were. Dinner was announced and the Empress and her daughter went in arm in arm. I followed. There was no other lady or maid of honour. The Emperor and the gentlemen then came and we sat down at a round table in a small adjoining salon—twelve persons. The Emperor, the Empress, the *Héritier* and the Grand Duchess sat together, Lord L. next the fourth and I found myself near the Emperor who immediately enquired if I was dissatisfied at his having *servi les intérêts de ces messieurs, mes amis, en les invitant.* The Empress was dressed in black velvet, with magnificent pearls; the Grand Duchess was likewise in black and dressed with great simplicity. There was an absence of all ceremony and form; the two children were playing about and coming to their mother for cakes. I mentioned having seen the Empress's private palace at Moscow in answer to some question put to me. *"Oui, nommément le mien"*, she observed, upon which the Emperor turned round and said, *"Comment, Madame Nicholas, pas le vôtre, qu'est-ce que cela tu veux dire?"* He afterwards related *un joli mot de Napoléon,* who was asked, *"Pourquoi il ne renouvellait pas Versailles?" "Voulez vous que j'aille loger chez Louis XIV"* was the reply. The Emperor's conversation is extremely open and unguarded. *Il ne se gêne pas* in his expressions against the French and Louis Philippe and openly avows his wishes for Don Carlos's success.[15] Talking of *la chasse aux ours* he declared his dislike to the whole thing and that as far as he was concerned *messieurs les ours pouvaient sucer leur pattes dans leur tanières* unmolested. He enquired a great deal about my health repeating his hopes that my faintings and ailings would end *dans un petit Russe.* In vain I assured him that there was no probability of such a thing, *il s'obstinait toujours à le croire.*

Wednesday 21st. The Stroganovs dined with us and after dinner the Saxon Minister and his wife called. They pressed us very much to see Dresden on our return and we talked over the possibility of our going there. I had always heard that the Court was *très aimable,* the society very agreeable, and great encouragement given to the arts; and that the finest collection of pictures, a splendid treasure chamber, lovely environs, and a beautiful porcelain manufactory were to be seen in that capital. Monsieur de Lutzerode made one very true remark that notwithstanding the proud aristocratic feeling in Russia, in no country are illegitimate children so well received. He instanced the old Madame Boberinsky whom Catherine had married to her son and whom all the Imperial family call their aunt.

I recollected on hearing this that the Empress had at the ball at the Anichkov Palace introduced this old lady to me saying, *"C'est notre tante à nous tous*". He then alluded to Madame Kindener, the natural daughter of the Princess Thurn and Taxis who is received and treated as the Empress's cousin. As he said, "*L'existence vient de Dieu*", and we have no right to visit the faults of the parents on the children. For my part I believe this arises from the peculiar delicacy and good feeling of this nation who make it a point of duty to *redoubler de politesse et d'attention* to any person whose position is doubtful or painful from circumstances over which they have no control.

Thursday 22nd. I paid visits to Madame Tchernischev, Madame Stroganov, etc. and in the evening I went to a great ball at Countess Voronzov-Dashkov's. It was in the gallery and apartments before described. The rooms were beautifully lighted and the heat proportionate. The host and hostess *très aimable* and, yet though I could find no fault, I never felt more bored or more rejoiced to depart.

Sunday 25th being only the 13th here, it seems but half Christmas Day. It creates a singular feeling, this difference of calculation. In a general way it is little thought of but on a great epoch like the present has a strange effect on the mind. The grand ball was again postponed at Court, to my great regret, especially as no time was fixed for it.

Monday 26th. We had a party at dinner, Count Nesselrode, Prince Serge Golitsin, etc., and in the evening the English courier arrived bringing a large packet of letters.

Tuesday 27th. Lord L. went with Sir James Wylie to see the hospitals but I had arranged to go to the *Cabinet Impérial* to see the jewels. It is a large establishment where everything concerning the Emperor's private *cassette* is managed: the gold, silver and iron mines, the precious stones of Siberia, the malachites, jaspers, etc. found in Russia belonging to the Crown. The stairs were covered with poor people who, as I was told, were waiting to receive their pensions. The anterooms were filled with persons writing on business and I passed through several rooms filled with clerks and secretaries till I reached the last one where Prince Volkonsky and Prince Gagarin,[16] the two *chefs* of this department, showed me a variety of fine stones. I also saw some fine furs, a black fox of great value, sables, etc. and some white sable which I thought very ugly.

From thence I went to the Palace to enquire after the Empress who had been ill. The etiquette is to go upstairs and enquire of the negroes who are in attendance and present pens and paper to write down one's name. While waiting General Benkendorf came through the room and gave me a favourable account. I then called on Madame Nesselrode and Lady Durham and returned home.

Wednesday 28th. We dined with Prince Volkonsky who has apartments at the Palace. There was a winding staircase of endless height and the cold was piercing.

In the room where we dined there was an immense tableau of Gobelins tapestry given by Louis XVIII and most beautifully executed. In the next room a very fine vase of malachite and a very pretty dessert service with views from the keepsakes. The Prince's daughter, Madame Dournkov, I found a particularly nice, *distinguée* person. We then passed the evening at Madame Stroganov's and talked over the possibility of giving a dance in our tiny abode, but after making out the list and gravely discussing it we burst out laughing at the absurdity of fancying it would hold fifty people and the idea was given up.

Thursday 29th. Late in the day we received a summons to dine with the Grand Duchess Hélène at five o'clock. The palace is of great size and very magnificent—a beautiful long Italian façade, the staircase immense and an endless suite of very fine rooms.

We dined, ten people at a little round table, in an immense *salle*. After dinner we went into the Princess's private apartments and I never saw anything prettier, the *ameublement*, the taste, the arrangement—perfect.

Her own *cabinet* is a very large room with divisions and compartments making different little *établissements*. In one corner greenhouse plants were grouped as in a conservatory; another was railed off with rosewood and coloured glass for writing; sofas and seats of all shapes, books in every language, prints and the annuals lie about. A corner was reserved for pictures and miniatures. Her boudoir was arranged in English chintz, her music room and library all connecting and apparently in constant use.

We were then shown the magnificent *salles* of this immense palace but I was so cold and ill I was very glad to get home. Next day I was confined to my bed. The cold had been daily increasing and now had arrived at nearly thirty degrees below zero. This is not to be imagined but is fearful when felt. Light furs feel like cold linen.

The eyelashes are painful, the breath freezes, the windows become opaque, and a sickening feel pervades the whole frame as of a knife cutting to one's very marrow. I had a little room with a fireplace and here I have sat on the fender and lain on the rug without feeling warm, and have gone from that to the next to *coller* myself against the stove and then back again in despair to look at the fire. At night I covered myself with eider-down which is lighter and I believe warmer than any fur. How the coachmen and horses stand this cold I know not. The[y] wait hours, their beards as white as snow with the frost. Neither can I conceive how the women bear it. It is very true, one instant suffices to jump into the carriage ⟨⟩. In full *toilette* these Russian ladies rush from a heat of twenty five degrees to a cold of twenty five below zero making a transition of fifty degrees in a moment.

Saturday 31st. The officers of the *Ischora* dined with us— Prince Menshikov, Monsieur de Lieberman, etc. Unfortunately I was ill and fainted away.

Sunday, January 1st. It seems so extraordinary to have commenced the new year when all around are still in the old one.

Monday, January 2nd. I went to a great diplomatic dinner at Count Nesselrode's. There were fifty people—the French and Austrian Ambassadors and their wives, the Saxon, Bavarian, Swedish, Prussian, Dutch Ministers, etc. The house is a very fine one; it belongs to the Emperor and the *Bureau des Affaires Etrangères*. The reception rooms are *au second* and the staircase very high. For this occasion it was all carpeted and lined with servants in scarlet liveries. We dined in a *salle* of *faux marbre* and the dinner was very magnificent but I was principally struck with the *plateau* which was of eight or ten pieces of malachite, large separate raised slabs supporting immense gilt figures holding malachite *jattes* filled with pyramids of flowers. The effect of this was beautiful and the whole thing quite unique. It was made at Paris for Count Demidov who had the malachite sent and it cost seventy thousand roubles but was bought by Count Nesselrode for forty thousand.

Tuesday, January 3rd. We went to the fortress, a large and very strong building at a great distance.[17] The high tapering gilt spires had attracted my admiration long before I knew what it was. After winding round and crossing two strong places we arrived at the mint which is very curious not only because the money is all coined there but the gold and silver are separated, purified and alloyed, being brought there as they are found in the mines.[18] We were first shown the gold mixed with the silver; then the process for separating it; then all the different processes of melting, coining, stamping, etc. and, after being presented with some medals, we went to the cathedral where the Sovereigns of Russia since Peter I are buried.[19] The cathedral is very large and magnificent, richly gilt. The coffins are not in vaults but in the church surrounded by railings on each side of the screen. Peter, Catherine, Paul, the late Empress and Constantine all rest here. On the Emperor Alexander's coffin lay the medal of 1814 with its little well worn ribbon and the cross of St. George. There was something touching in these two simple memorials, rewards of military virtue; and they spoke volumes to the heart, more than all "the boast of heraldry or pomp of power" "or storied urn" etc. It showed a refinement of feeling to preserve to him in death the simplicity and absence of ostentation that distinguished him in life.

Wednesday, January 4th. Countess Nesselrode asked me to go with her to a great *exposition* of porcelain in a large *salle* at the Winter Palace where it is exhibited twice a year, Easter and Christmas. Lord L. and Seaham were obliged to return and change their *toilette* as it is absolutely *de rigueur* to have on a frock coat to enter the Palace and they were in long morning ones. This caused a short delay. The glass exhibited did not strike me as superior to our own manufacture. There were some large vases but they were not white. The porcelain was beautiful and I thought both in painting and gilding surpassed ours.

In the middle was a large vase or *coupe* destined for the King of Prussia, a peculiar and beautiful shape with a portrait *en pied* in miniature of the Emperor Alexander. In the centre and on the flat edge or sides of the vase which moved round the standing portrait was the review at Vertus.[20]

Large vases were placed down the gallery on white pedestals. In an adjoining room were tables covered with toys, little vases, cups, perfumes, bottles etc. for the children and for lotteries, and while we were examining all this, to the surprise of everyone, the Empress walked in followed by her three daughters. The things were not half arranged and she was not expected till the next day.

Thursday, January 5th but Christmas Day [*recte* Eve] according

109

to the Old Style. At about twelve o'clock Monsieur Seniavine of the *Cabinet Impérial* arrived. I was hardly out of bed, but hearing he had a letter from Prince Volkonsky and magnificent *cadeaux* from the Emperor for me I hurried on a *peignoir* to receive him. I found a beautiful malachite table and a fine vase of the same. Quite thunderstruck at this unexpected kindness I was some time endeavouring to express my gratitude. I at last tried to do so in an English letter to the Emperor, and Lord Londonderry went to deliver it to Prince Volkonsky, when Monsieur Seniavine returned with two magnificent porcelain vases sent by the Emperor to Lord L. as specimens of the *fabrique*. He told me his Majesty had given away the whole that I had seen the day before and the *salle* was now empty. The King of Prussia,[21] the King of Saxony,[22] the Duchess of Saxe Weimar,[23] the Prince of Oldenburg,[24] Prince Charles of Prussia,[25] were thus distinguished. To crown the whole, in the evening the Emperor sent Lord L. the medal for the taking of Paris in 1814 with a most flattering letter from Prince Volkonsky inviting him to be present at the great military and religious ceremony next day at which no strangers are admitted. The celebration of the taking of Paris and the deliverance of this country falling on their Christmas Day occasions much solemnity and pomp and I regretted not being able to witness it. It must have been a magnificent sight, that immense Palace filled with troops, the religious ceremonies, the music, etc.

A kind offer was made me to see it from the galleries but I was not well and I went to the English church where the service for Christmas Day [*recte* Eve] was performed.

Friday, January 6th New Style, Christmas Day Old Style. At half past ten o'clock Lord L. went to the Palace to attend this great ceremony and did not return till two.

Saturday 7th, New Style, December 26th, Old. On this day the long looked for ball which had been postponed from December 6th Old Style took place. Only a part of the Palace was thrown open and that was lighted by ten thousand candles.

The *Salle Blanche* is a gallery one hundred and thirty three feet by forty nine with columns supporting a gallery which was filled with spectators. The room is of dazzling whiteness and without a line of gilding and with four immense stoves which had externally the appearance of banners and standards. The pillars were wreathed with candles, the whole a perfect blaze of light, and three thousand here produced literally the effect of daylight in which they themselves seemed to burn dim and blue.

When the company was assembled the doors opened and the Imperial family walked in and rarely does one find united so much grace and beauty. The Empress was dressed in white with *colonnes* of large single diamonds round her gown from her waist to her feet. She had a *couronne du moyen age* at the back of her head and a small low one on her forehead, the shape of the whole perfectly classic, not a jewel or colour but these enormous diamonds which she called *mes cailloux*, and which, except on her, must have been taken for the pickings of a great glass lustre. Altogether I never saw such a combination of simplicity and splendour.

Prince Charles of Prussia, the Empress's brother, had arrived and in compliment to the Emperor wore the light blue ribbon, the great cordon of *St. André*, the first order in Russia,[26] the Emperor and the *Héritier* having on the orange ribbon, the Black Eagle of Prussia.[27] Great attention is paid to these details and much importance attached to them. The Grand Duchesses Marie and Olga looked lovely, their beautiful skins, fair hair, graceful figures, simple *toilettes* and amiable high bred manner delighted everyone.

The polonaises began and continued some time. They are very agreeable for those who do not dance. When the Emperor took me I endeavoured to thank him for his *cadeaux* and his kindness in thinking of me at all. *"Mais, Madame, c'était une injure d'en doûter."* He said my letter was *charmante*, and the Empress who said the same, added, *"C'était trop bon pour lui"*. The ball began at nine. After the polonaises were quadrilles and at twelve o'clock we passed through a *Salle des Maréchaux* and a long gallery with between three and four hundred pictures of Dawe's to the supper room, an enormous *salle* with scagliola columns and blue glass lustres and lighted by four thousand candles. This was really fairyland—the endless vista, the quantities of massy plate, the abundance of lovely flowers, and, to crown all, the whole having the appearance of an *orangerie*, the supper tables being so constituted as to let the stems of the immense orange trees through so that we literally sat under their shade and perfume. The scene was perfect enchantment and eight hundred and fifty sat down to supper without the slightest confusion or squeeze. The Empress, according to the strict old etiquette of Russian hospitality, went round all the tables and spoke to every person until she fainted away. She soon recovered and after we returned to *la Salle Blanche* she retired with the rest of the Imperial family and thus ended this magnificent fête.

Sunday 8th. I was unable to leave my bed after the fatigue, cold and exertion of the previous evening. Lord. L. dined with Monsieur de Leuchenfelles, the Württemberg Minister.[28]

Monday 9th. We dined at Monsieur Laval's, an old Frenchman who has been fifty or sixty years in Russia and had married a great heiress. He has a magnificent house on the English Quay, with a very fine collection of pictures. The dinner was *très recherché* but the dining room was exceedingly cold and I was told this was a precaution that gourmands take that they may the better enjoy their dinner and be able to eat a greater quantity.

Thursday 12th. We had a large party at dinner—the Seniavines, Nesselrodes, Prince Volkonsky and his daughter, General Benkendorf, Prince Butera. Count Stroganov called in the morning.

We talked over the last attempt on Louis Philippe's life of which the intelligence had just arrived.[29] "*Qu'est-ce que vous dîtes de cela?*", said Lord L. "*Je dis*", replied the Count, "*que je vois le doigt de la Providence en tout cela. Il prolonge la vie de cet homme parce que l'Europe en a besoin, mais en la prolongeant il prolonge le martyre du remords*".

Friday 13th. This being the Russian New Year's Day, the great ball at Court was to have taken place but unfortunately the Empress was taken ill and it was put off. It was a great disappointment to me not to see this unique fête as it had been described to me so as to excite my utmost curiosity.

The whole of the Hermitage and Winter Palace are thrown open and lighted up and crowds of the commonest and dirtiest people admitted. Above forty thousand tickets are issued and coachmen, servants, moujiks, etc. are all allowed to enter, walk about and take refreshment.

The crowd, the heat, the smell, the squeeze are not to be imagined and nothing can penetrate the solid mass except when the Emperor appears, and holding up a finger requests his children to let him pass and the crowd falls back. It is spoken of as the most beautiful and touching sight to see the Sovereign in the midst of his subjects, the love and veneration shown, and the propriety of conduct of all these people high and low, rich and poor—not a case of drunkenness or dishonesty. Though all the treasures of the Palace are left open, not a bit of plate is ever missed.

There was a ball at Madame Rasumovsky's whose house, though small, is *très élégante et très soignée*. She is a most good-natured, kind-hearted person, and truly anxious that everyone should be happy and amused. She took Prince Charles of Prussia all over her rooms, and we admired her bedroom, dressing room, bath, etc. extremely.

Saturday 14th. We dined with the Seniavines at five o'clock, and at eleven went to a great ball at Madame Miatlev's. The dining so early is to me very disagreeable as it makes the day so short, and to those who have not strength to brave the cold and visit about afterwards the evening is so long before one can appear at the balls or *réunions*.

Madame Miatlev's house was large and cold but magnificently lighted. I was weary and ill and came home very early, but Lord L. remained till four o'clock and saw the supper.

Monday 16th. Lord L. dined with the Ficquelmonts and was rather shocked to see her and her mother Madame Keitsev smoke.

Tuesday 17th. My birthday, and here a great fast day. Lord L. gave me a malachite box and Count Stroganov filled my room with hyacinths and he and the Countess dined with us. I received a letter from Prince Volkonsky informing me the Empress desired to see me the next morning.

Wednesday 18th, Old Style 6th, and the day appointed for the Emperor and all the clergy to go in great state and bless the Neva. I went according to appointment and at the top of the great stairs Lord L. was conducted in one direction to join the Emperor's staff while I was shown into the Empress's lovely salon where the daylight displayed with redoubled beauty the lapis lazuli, the malachites, jasper and combined wonders of this lovely room which has so often called forth my admiration. Next to it are the private apartments of the Empress beginning with a little room fitted up in pink and white satin. She appeared, as she said, *"sortant du lit" en negligée* with a little violet velvet cloak trimmed with ermine. Madame Rouet, a Russian lady, Princess Trubezkoi[30] and one or two maids of honour were there. The Empress then took me on, *"Venez voir mes appartements"*.

The next was prettily furnished—some fine paintings, curious vases made of [sic] the porcelain *fabrique* in imitation of the Herculaneum. There was a large high gilt cage with a beautiful bird in it, a mackaw that looked like enamel of every colour. From this room we entered a large corner one with four windows, but how [to] describe this sanctuary where taste and a chimney corner were combined with magnificence and the riches of the east, while fine *objets d*[*'art*] were piled on all sides. It had the air of being constantly inhabited and even the little Blenheim spaniel that lay stretched before the fire looked comfortable. One corner was divided by a partitioning screen covered with miniatures while another was portioned off by a thick *treillage* and a third window by light bars and an archway of ivy. In one corner was raised a beautiful statue of Carrara marble, its pedestal concealed by piled up plants, a double writing table with a large malachite jewelled clock, and literally covered with the *bijouterie* of Vienna, London, Paris and Geneva—cups, urns, clocks and vases of the finest lapis lazuli and quantities of malachite. The only thing I did not see was old Sèvres china.

While I was examining all these things the Empress accomplished a *toilette* and appeared in Brussels lace with a little cloak of geranium coloured velvet trimmed with the darkest Imperial sable.

I then went into her bedroom where, in large glass cases, were displayed all her magnificent jewels, and in a separate *armoire* those of the Crown. The latter consisted of pearls like eggs and diamonds like crystals.

The Empress has had a fine *parure* given her at every fête and on the birth of every child; and emeralds, rubies, turquoises, opals, sapphires, pearls and diamonds vied in size and magnificence. It was literally the realization of the fruit described in Aladdin's garden.

The Grand Duchesses, who are charming girls, so gay and natural yet beautiful and high bred, carried me off to see the bath which is a mixture of Turkish, Indian and Chinese taste—a temple with a marble bath into which the water dashes from a large conch or shell. This little room is lovely with a ceiling like a page of an illuminated book. I was invited to pass through the *cabinet de toilette* into a private retreat of the Empress's. There was a cast of her mother, the beautiful Queen of Prussia, taken after her death, a miniature of the Empress Mother, a jewelled casket with all the present Empress's *souvenirs réligieux,* and a *cassette* with all her journals. This interesting little room was shown me by the Grand Duchesses. We then returned to the corner room to see the procession.

CHAPTER VIII

Russian Customs

NOTWITHSTANDING the piercing cold, the cutting wind and the thick falling snow, the Quay and the Neva were covered with spectators. The greatest order and quiet were observed, a deep devotional manner and reverential respect. Every person was bareheaded, even the Emperor who, as usual, towered above all and looked a superior being. He was dressed in the uniform of Hetman of the Cossacks. First of the procession came the priests bearing the cross and the whole of the clergy in gorgeous dresses of cloth of gold, the *chantres de la Cour* in scarlet, the Court officers, the Emperor and his aides de camp among whom walked Lord L. I really trembled for him bare-headed and thinly shod and not warmly clothed. The Emperor had sent Prince Charles of Prussia and the *Héritier* away and had advised Lord L. not to come declaring that his own head was shielded by a false top which he raised to prove what he said.

A platform—a covered temple—having been erected at the edge of the river at a little distance the whole cortège proceeded along the Quay. The priests formed themselves into an avenue through which the Emperor passed.

After the ceremony of blessing the water which is supposed to purify the river and send all evil spirits to the bottom of it, the procession returned in the same order as it went.[1] The poor people ran to the spot to fill their bottles with *l'eau bénite*. The superstition is so great that it is only lately their plunging newborn infants into the river at this time has been abolished by law, many having died of cold and exposure, and many by drowning, the hands that held them having become insensible.

Prince Charles of Prussia and the *Héritier* came up to the Empress's room and soon after the Emperor and his suite. Chocolate and a *déjeuner à la fourchette* were served during which the Empress conversed with me. Two goblets of the blessed water were brought and everyone tasted *pour porter bonheur* for the coming year. The Empress told me of her baptism on arriving and her having been unable to preserve her own name Charlotte as not being a Russian one, and that embracing the Greek religion had been an effort at first, *"mais pour tout au monde je ne voudrais être d'une autre religion que mes enfants"*, she added very feelingly.[2] She said it had all passed like a dream in ten days—her arrival the twentieth, her baptism and being made Grand Duchess, *les fiançailles*, and the first of the next month her marriage.

We were then joined by the Emperor and his suite. He enquired after my health. He disappeared and soon after returned in another uniform and took the Prince of Prussia with him to see the *Corps des Cadets*.[3] The Empress sent me after them saying, *"Cela fera plaisir à l'Empereur"*. We passed *la salle du concert*—an immense room with five large lustres and scagliola white walls; next, the Empress's salon, *la Salle St. Georges* and *la salle du souper* where the cadets, having dined, were getting up. In an instant each had his cap and his gun and they assembled in the *Salle Blanche* to be reviewed by the Emperor. This lasted some time and to a stranger has a curious effect. It is so impossible in our small rooms to see such an exhibition indoors. Among the cadets I saw one tiny boy, smaller than his musket, but going through all the exercises the others did and this I found to be the Grand Duke Constantine, the Emperor's second son of nine years old. So early does a military education commence in this Imperial family that even the two younger Grand Dukes Michael and Nicholas of four and five years old were called up by the Emperor and made to join in the drill. They were exercised in the *Salle Blanche* for some time and this, being the ballroom, the scene astonished an English eye.

Thursday 19th. We went to a ball at Madame Rasumovsky's and quite unexpectedly the Emperor walked in. He walked a polonaise but did not stay long.

Friday 20th. I was out all the morning *pour des courses* shopping and visiting and in the evening we went to a ball at Madame Soukhozanet's.

Saturday 21st. A party in the evening at Madame Ficquelmont's.

Sunday 22nd. After church Madame Rasumovsky proposed a *partie de traineau* and as she had a large one *à quatre places et à quatre chevaux* we set off for a *campagne* of Countess Laval's about four versts from St. Petersburg to see the amusement of ice mountains.

The sledges are very agreeable, much easier than a carriage and quicker, even the large ones; but I decidedly prefer the small ones which go like the wind with a high trotting horse and a *petit furieux* pulling and capering on one side. It is, however, very necessary in keeping one's mouth shut otherwise, as Count Stroganov explained, "*On a trente cinq petits canifs dans le gosier à la fois qui se querellent incertains s'ils rentiront ou s'ils sortiront*". We drove across the Neva which is as hard and as great a thoroughfare as the magnificent *Quai de la Cour* of which I had a fine view, with its row of palaces, the Admiralty, the Hermitage, the *Palais d'Hiver*, the *Palais de Marbre* (the finest building as to materials in St. Petersburg, where, alas, all the other fine edifices are but whitewashed brick. This palace belonged to the late Grand Duke Constantine and has been given to the young one[4]), the house of the Austrian Ambassador, the palace of the Prince of Oldenburg, etc.

These formed a splendid range on the granite quay on the one side, and on the opposite side was seen the fortress with its glittering spire of ducat gold, and at its foot, the tiny cabin of Peter the Great.[5] This scene was exchanged for a flat, ugly drive through rows of small wooden cottages that looked ill calculated to protect the inhabitants from the severity of their winter. However I was assured that each of these miserable abodes had its stoves, its double window, and was warm and comfortable. At last we arrived at our destination and found a large party assembled. All the young dandies were there in a kind of *Esquimaux* costume, Eastern caps, embroidered gauntlets, short jackets and furs *tous brignant l'honneur de conduire les dames*. A temple was erected with steps to ascend and, at a certain distance the same opposite, and from each of these was a descent of smooth ice nearly perpendicular of from sixty to eighty feet.

Immediately after we arrived, before I well knew what I was doing, I was half pushed, half lifted into a large sledge that stood in the middle of the temple. In this were three persons on each side who supported themselves by pushing against each other's backs.

I was told to shut my mouth, sit quiet, hold my tongue and not be frightened, assured there was no danger, and down they pitched us.

Russian girls on a see-saw
Russian dancing

A troika
A Russian street market

It is impossible to conceive how dreadful is the shock. Had an eagle pounced upon me and carried me beyond the clouds I could not have been more *saisie*. I neither breathed, saw, nor heard. There was a mist before my eyes and a singing in my ears, and in fact the only thing to assimilate this amusement to is running upstairs to be thrown out of [a] window. *Il fallait revenir*, therefore I climbed up the opposite steps to the second temple and returned in like manner, half dead, but satisfied with having accomplished this wonderful exploit. I remember Prince Talleyrand handing me down to dinner in a house he had in Portland Place which he disliked especially and took every opportunity of abusing, and when we arrived at the top of the stairs he said, "*Regardez, Madame, le précipice qui est devant vous*". What would he have said to the ice mountains?

However, to resume, I was seating myself very quietly but perfectly contented when I was informed that going down "*en diligence n'était rien du tout*", and, "*venez avec moi*", resounded on all sides. "*Comment*", I enquired, "*mais ici, vous serez à merveille, il n'y a pas de danger, j'aurai bien soin de vous*". I declined and begged to see others first. Immediately all the young men produced a sledge like a narrow plank with a cushion, the whole not higher than a low footstool and not larger than a small portmanteau, and thereupon they deposited themselves and between their knees a lady, having carefully wound her garments quite tight round her and divested herself of all floating drapery, placed herself. If the feet or any bit of clothes touch the ice the danger of upsetting is great and legs, arms and collar bones have been broken. After seeing repeated descents, in a weak moment I was half coaxed and half scolded into yielding. The instant I agreed to go everyone stepped forward to pack me up and they did not allow me to retain even my pocket handkerchief. I was consigned to a young Prince Trubezkoi in the *Chevaliers Gardes*, universally declared to be the best *conducteur*. "*Mais je ne fais que cela depuis que j'ai cinq ans. N'ayez pas peur, Madame, et si vous vous sentez mal jetez vous dans mes bras.*" These were his last words of comfort before "*êtes vous prête*", and down they pitched us. His last invitation was quite unnecessary for the first shock sent me back into his arms where I lay till we arrived at the bottom of the *montagne de glace*, half dead. In the diligence the person sits sideways and the danger is greater though the shock is less. But in the other way, being sent straight down it is impossible to conquer the impression that you must necessarily fall forward whereas, in reality, the force of the air so rapidly met drives you back. I was obliged to return and I cannot describe the sensation. All power of respiration seemed stopped and I felt as if I must be suffocated or burst a blood vessel. I lay some time on a couch made up of cloaks and furs to recover myself and returned home but did not for days lose the oppression on my chest though my face was not cut as I expected. Everyone seemed to enjoy it and no one to suffer but I. However, when a pleasure becomes a pain it is useless to continue doing what is disagreeable merely because it is the fashion. *Je me suis donc bien de ne plus y retourner.*

Monday 23rd. I went with Count Stroganov *en petit traineau* to see the Cathedral of *Notre Dame de Casan*.[6] It is a fine edifice though there are many faults in the architecture, the cupola being too small, the aisles too narrow. The inside is magnificent, a perfect mass of immense red granite columns. It was begun by the Emperor Paul and finished by the Emperor Alexander. The church is filled with banners, standards and colours taken at different times by the Russians. Here is the tomb of Marshal Kutusov[7] and one square column is covered with the keys of the different French towns taken, Rheims, Nancy, etc. and brass plates with the names and dates. The *baton de Maréchal* of Davout[8] and the keys of Paris hang here, and I was not surprised at being told that the French Ambassador did not like to enter this church when the great ceremonies take place at Easter. There are three screens of which the middle one is the most magnificent; the doors, the forms of the images, the balustrades of the ceiling are solid silver and estimated at eight thousand pounds. This has been lately done and is a striking trait of the good taste and religious feeling of Cossacks whom we choose to consider barbarous and uncivilized. When Napoleon pillaged Moscow the French stripped their churches of their gold and silver and melted it down. During their retreat the Cossacks retook this plunder, but scorning, poor as they were, to enrich themselves with the spoils of their country and their church, they made an offering of the whole to this cathedral. The story redounds to their honour and is quite true and *très touchant*. There is an image of the Virgin here, with a crown of diamonds, and richly decorated with jewels. Four beautiful columns of polished Siberian jasper support this screen. Candles were burning at the different shrines and many poor petitioners prostrate before them.

Tuesday 24th. We dined at Count Nesselrode's and in the evening paid a visit to old Madame Miatlev whose large house seemed in want of a thorough cleaning. I never saw so dirty a place and seeing preparations for tea, which was made and given out by a hideous dirty female dwarf, we shortened our visit and escaped. I foresaw this decoction thus administered would suffice *pour faire rendre l'âme* as effectually as a steamboat in a stormy sea.

We then proceeded to visit Princess Kotchoubey, a very agreeable, clever woman living in retreat since the death of her husband. One judges often from trifles and I had hardly crossed the threshhold before the difference between this house and the last struck me. The cleanliness and *comme il faut* appearance of the very servants formed a contrast which was heightened when we reached the boudoir of the Princess with its profusion of hyacinths and other flowers, its beautiful *boiserie* and tasteful furniture, and its various *compartiments* and *établissements*. From hence we went to Madame Soltikov's where a ball is given every Tuesday in a small odd house, singularly arranged, and where in a low room underground I was shown a wonderful collection of snuff boxes, watches, rings and *bijouterie*.

Wednesday 25th. We went by especial permission of the Empress with Madame Stroganov to see the establishment for *les demoiselles nobles* at the *Couvent de Smolna*.[9] Madame Adlerberg, a most respectable, distinguished old lady, formerly governess to the present Emperor and whose daughter now holds the same situation to the young Grand Duchess Olga, is placed at the head of this magnificent institution. There are seven hundred and fifty young people of the *bourgeoisie* and the *noblesse*. It was instituted by the Empress Catherine and brought to perfection by the Empress Mother, and now is, like all similar institutions, protected and *surveillée* by the Empress. The building is of the usual colossal size; the same almost military precision, order and exactitude are observed in the bedrooms, linen rooms, kitchen, etc. and pervade every detail. There are three separate classes, brown, blue and white. They seemed extremely happy and all looked very healthy. They learn English, French, German and Russian. The system appears excellent. We heard them examined in history ancient and modern, geography and arithmetic, and were very much struck by the talent of one girl who, without a moment's hesitation, traced on a large slate a map of the British Isles as correctly as possible. We then heard a wonderful performance on the piano by a girl called Eugénie Muller. Their drawings and work were then shown, and we accompanied the Superior over the whole building to the refectory where we heard the girls sing the grace beautifully before they sat down to dinner. Chocolate and a luncheon were handed round, and we sat down with the *Supérieure* and some of the professors, the children being at dinner at long tables. A little Kalmuck[10] Princess was called up to us. She was only about ten or twelve years old with nearly closed black eyes and a complete Tartar expression. She was the oddest looking little person I ever saw, as ugly as a Kalmuck face could be and yet interesting from her sleepy black eyes and sentimental look. She sang some romances in her own language in a pleasing manner and with a very sweet voice. I was greatly struck by the appearance of the young people and the way this system of education is conducted. Their health, their hearts, their heads, all appeared to be carefully watched and their comfort studied in everything—simplicity without luxury, excellent principles, solid instruction, good manners and ladylike appearance. Great neatness and order reign throughout. Indeed, with the exception of that most important bar—difference in religion—I think every English mother would be satisfied to place her daughter there.

Thursday 26th. We dined with Sir James Wylie and in the evening went to a magnificent ball given by the French Ambassador whose house is very fine and beautifully lighted. It belongs to the Russian Government who provide an *hôtel* for the French Ambassador in return for a similar attention at Paris where the Russian representative is lodged by the French Court. There was one magnificent *salle* for dancing and an immense one for supper. The picture of poor Charles X was said to be concealed in some unmentionable corner and was replaced by that of Louis Philippe. The supper room displayed the souvenirs of four reigns. The candelabra were of Napoleon's and Louis XVIII. Charles X and Louis Philippe had each his separate contribution.

Friday 27th. A great ball at Princess Belogilsky's, a magnificent house with a very fine staircase. Here I met General Benkendorf and for the first time he mentioned the Emperor's wish that before we went to Berlin we should see Warsaw.

Saturday 28th. We dined at Prince Butera's, the Neapolitan Minister. The house is lovely and furnished with perfect taste. It was last inhabited by Princess Lieven but belongs to the Princess Butera who was a great heiress and whose life is a *fond* for a novel. This is her third husband. She was brought up at the *Couvent de Smolna* and married a Count Shuvalov about twenty years older than herself. She had two sons and was in despair when she lost her husband, so much so that her health suffered and the physicians ordered [a] change of scene. She went to Paris where she made acquaintance with a handsome, agreeable Frenchman whom she married to the disgust of everybody. He was very young and very poor. However, on his coming to St. Petersburg, in time opinions changed. He won all hearts and gained the goodwill of everyone. He put her immense fortune in order and went a journey to her mines and lands in Siberia. Here he caught cold which went on to consumption and ended fatally. The Princess nearly sank under the blow. Her health, her spirits, even her mind seemed affected. It was feared she had caught this treacherous disease while nursing her husband and it was declared that nothing but a milder clime could save her. To Italy she went and returned with this Prince Butera— a Hanoverian by birth, but who had gained this title and a large fortune by his first wife. She is plain but amiable, retiring and good-natured, and of her I heard the Emperor had said, *"C'est la femme la plus vertueuse de la Russie, ne pouvant pas se passer de mari, elle n'a jamais pris d'amant"*. The staircase of this house was a *treillage* of ivy with mirrors. On the landing and first [floor] is a long gallery with a double fireplace in the centre of the room. I never saw this anywhere but it is peculiarly comfortable and agreeable. The whole suite of rooms is beautiful and everything in the best taste. The lighting, the plate, the magnificence of the *plateau*, the brilliant Bohemian glass, the scarlet liveries, the air of comfort, and the extreme *recherché* and perfection of everything surpassed all I have seen here. After dinner we saw the beautiful suite of the Prince below. In the evening there was a *grand bal de la noblesse* but I was too tired to go.

Sunday 29th. I was desired to attend the Empress and was informed that she wished to see my jewels. I took them in the carriage and they were brought upstairs for me to show them. She admired them excessively and wished for drawings of some, particularly of a cross given me by George IV. The Grand Duchess Olga did this beautifully. The Empress then made me write my name and affix my seal in her book of souvenirs. I sat with her some time and the Emperor, Prince Charles and the *Héritier* came in. We dined at Lord Durham's and in the evening went to the old Princess Waldemar's whose fête was the 17th O[ld] S[tyle] when she completed her hundredth year, I believe, but I heard some dispute whether it was that or the ninety ninth. Everybody makes a point of going to the old lady on that day. The Empress was ill but the Emperor went and sent her two fine porcelain vases.

Next day 30th. I sent my silver work-basket as well fitted up as I could to the Empress with a letter and many apologies praying *un petit coin* for it in some of her many rooms where she might now and then cast her eyes on it *en passant* and remember me. She wrote me a very pretty answer in English.

Tuesday 31st. We dined at Madame Miatlev's and saw some magnificent old plate *du siècle de Louis Quinze* which some ancestor who had been Ambassador at Paris had had made. It was very fine. I came home weary and cold. Prince Lieven called and to my horror I fell asleep during his political prose with Lord L.

Wednesday, February 1st. A very pretty ball at Madame Seniavine's—a small house beautifully lighted and filled with flowers.

Thursday 2nd. I took a walk in the *Ghastenai Dvor*. This is an immense bazaar full of shops of all sorts, but nothing sold that is not of Russian manufacture and no other language spoken. The merchants have a little frame with coloured balls for counting so I made my purchases by signs. They showed the piece. I then took the frame and diminished sometimes half, sometimes more. The merchant shook his head, I shook mine and walked off but he invariably recalled me on the threshold sometimes two or three times before we could agree, but once firm and fairly provoked I always succeeded. In the evening there was a great ball at Madame Ficquelmont's and a magnificent sitting down supper.

At twelve o'clock one day Madame Stroganov took me to hear *les chantres de la Cour* practise. This is in a concert room filled with spectators or rather listeners. There are between sixty and eighty voices, from the deep bass to the sharpest treble. They practise every Saturday for the Sunday mass in case the Emperor should desire a new piece.

I was told he had done this only once in six months and that was on the occasion of our attending the Greek worship in the chapel at Tsarskoe Seloe. The singing is unaccompanied by any instrument. *"C'est l'homme qui adresse son Créateur"*, they say, and the effect is thrilling. Rossini said it was sufficient reward for a journey to St. Petersburg to hear *les chantres de la Cour*. They sang the hymn of the angels and cherubims and Prince Butera exclaimed, *"en fermant les yeux on se croit en ciel"*. They then sang the sinner's prayer for mercy—*le Pater* etc. and Count Stroganov who, like all the rest, was *tout ému*, said, *"Ma foi, s'il y a cette musique en haut, je ne demande pas mieux que de creuser ma fosse et y aller tout de suite"*. The Emperor's military passion is displayed even here for all these young men were dressed like the cadets in green jackets. The regular *chantres de la Cour* are dressed *à la messe* in red and gold and the two choirs united are about eighty voices.

From thence we went to the *Palais Tauride* which is at a great distance from the centre of the town.[11] It is an enormous building and remarkable for an immense *salle* built by Potemkin that he might give fine fêtes to the Empress Catherine. This great room supported by columns has a large garden literally in it. The gigantic size, the height, the garden, the *orangerie*, all combined have an unique effect and for a fête must be perfect. The great *salle* and winter garden are connected, and in the latter are walks and shrubberies. The space is enormous. The rest of the palace is mediocre and requires repair and furniture. It is not used except when offered to lodge a stranger Prince who may visit St. Petersburg and not be at the Palace. Prince Oscar of Sweden[12] and the Prince of Persia[13] were here and one great fête has been given here since the Emperor Nicholas began his reign, and one was given by the Emperor Alexander to the beautiful Queen of Prussia.[14]

At a ball at Countess Voronzov-Dashkov's, Prince Volkonsky informed me that the Empress wished to see me at one o'clock next day and I accordingly went. I found her quite alone with her daughter in her private rooms looking *souffrante* but beautifully dressed in Brussels lace over light blue. The silver basket stood before her filled with her balls of worsted for knitting. *"Tenez"*, she said, *"j'ai mis cette robe pour accompagner votre panier"*. I sat with her a long time and she conversed on various subjects, regretted the necessity for our going, urged our stay and deplored that her health had made it dull for me observing, *"Nous ne nous sommes jamais vue dans le monde"*. She talked of the Queen of England[15] whom she praised and regretted not knowing and begged me to express to her Majesty how much she envied the Grand Duchess Hélène who had the advantage of making her acquaintance. She observed on the anxious and responsible situation the young Princess Victoria would fill; she talked over the various pretendants to her hand. *"A présent, ma chère, je vais vous demander d'accepter un petit souvenir de ma part, c'est mon portrait"*, she said, giving me a magnificent bracelet with a beautiful miniature of herself in the Russian costume set in large diamonds. At this singular mark of favour and kindness so rarely bestowed on any and thus conferred on a stranger without right or claim to expect such a thing I was *toute émue*; I would to take her hand which she would not suffer but embraced me and spoke most affectionately about seeing me again and make [*sic*] acquaintance with my children. She sent her daughter out to walk and I remained with her some time quite alone till at last, finding her talk increased by talking she bid me adieu. I asked her if I should see her again. *"Mais sûrement, c'est que nous désirons que vous dînez ici mais je suis trop malade pour me mettre à table, mais il faut que je vois votre mari et vous encore une fois."*

I took my leave and went to Madame Dournkov's (*née* Princess Volkonsky) who showed me all her jewels and there I found an old German nurse who had known me at Vienna. On returning home I received an immense number of visits and at five o'clock we went to dine at Lord Durham's. At eight o'clock the Stroganovs took us to a great Russian wedding in the Greek chapel of the Tchernischev's palace. It seemed a magnificent house but uninhabited. We passed through a long suite of rooms till we arrived at the chapel. It was lighted up and the priests and the *chantres* were there. After waiting a long time, the two *garçons de noce* arrived bearing images. These young men were in uniform, one in the Hussars, the other in the *Chevaliers Gardes*. Then came the bridegroom Monsieur Schevitz, nephew to General Benkendorf, *en uniforme de Housard*. He prostrated himself and appeared absorbed in devotion and then waited with his family, Prince Lieven, Madame Schevitz, Count and Countess Benkendorf, a young Princess Belogilsky, etc. the arrival of the bride. They all ranged on one side. After long expectation she was led in dressed, as all brides are, in blonde and orange blossoms. She had neither ornaments nor veil over her face; a long scarf fell from the back of her head to her feet. In all Russian weddings the bride and bridegroom have each what is called *un père assis et une mère assise*, the idea being that the real parents are too much affected by the event to be of use, and therefore the nearest friends are chosen to represent them.

The singing began—a long, lighted candle was placed in the hands of the *promis* and another in the hands of the *promise* who stood together in the middle of the chapel and the service commenced. Three priests in magnificent dresses officiated. The question was asked as in our service but repeated three times; their hands were joined, rings exchanged. Two jewelled crowns were then brought from the sanctuary by one of the priests. These nuptial crowns were shown to the young couple who kissed them reverentially. They were then held over their heads by the bridegroom's men and a piece of pink satin laid down on which the priest led them while the service went on. The belief is that whoever places his or her foot first on the satin will rule the *ménage* through life, "*et ma femme*", whispered Count Stroganov, "*a tout enjambé, que dans son empressement elle a passé autre pendant que j'ai mis le pied dessus*". Another superstition is observed about the two candles the couple hold burning during the service. These are carefully put with the gold images, and when the lady is to be confined the candles are fetched, lighted and placed before the images, and before they burn out the child is born. After standing some time the priest again joining their hands, covered them with one of the silver bands of his robes and led them three times round the reading desk followed by the *garçons de noce* holding the crowns over each head and carefully and skilfully avoiding touching or spoiling *la coiffure de la mariée*. Then come the sermon, the hymns, the devotion, the prostrations of the bride before the screen and then she was embraced and congratulated by everyone. The parents appeared terribly overcome; the father leant against a pillar entirely absorbed and overpowered and the sister was in hysterics. They were then accompanied to their own home where their friends assembled to drink their health in champagne and we returned home tired and worn to death but very glad to have been allowed to witness this interesting ceremony.

Monday 6th. Lord L. had a long audience of the Emperor and I received visits all day and in the evening drove to Count Stroganov's whose fête it was. (January 25th O[ld] S[tyle] *St. Grégoire*.) We then paid a visit to Madame Nesselrode and returned to dress for Madame Miatlev's ball. I was, however, too tired to go and Lord L. went alone.

CHAPTER IX

A Dreadful Journey to Warsaw

As THE TIME for our departure approached I had a great deal to do
to prepare for our long and tremendous journey. I had visits all
day. At last I was obliged to send away even the French Ambassador
to dress for dinner at Court, the Emperor having wished this though
Lord L. tried to decline fearing it might fatigue the Empress.
Just as we were descending the stairs we were met by General
Benkendorf who came with many excuses to put us off as the
Empress was unable to sit at table but had insisted he should come
himself and explain this and begged we would be present at a
petit spectacle at seven o'clock. We dined at Lord Durham's where
we had been previously engaged and afterwards went to the Palace
where in the *salle du concert* a little theatre was prepared. The
Empress seemed *très souffrante*; she was wrapped up *en toilette de
matin*. The Grand Duchesses, the *Héritier*, the Grand Duchess
Hélène and all the Court were present, but no one else. I sat next the
Emperor. The first was a German piece of which I did not understand a syllable; after this a clever little French *vaudeville* was given.
The Empress came up and took a most affectionate leave of me,
embraced me and expressed her hope of seeing me again. The
young Grand Duchesses did the same, and the Emperor begged to
call on me next day *pour faire les adieux*. I then went to a ball at
Madame Rasumovsky's to take leave of all my kind friends and
acquaintance[s].

Wednesday 8th. Early in the morning commenced visits of
adieux and while Mr. Milbanke[1] and Monsieur Novosiltzov were
with me the bell rang three times and the Emperor appeared. They
vanished, he seated himself and began a long conversation upon his
great position and domestic happiness. He spoke of the Empress
with the deepest devotion declaring he was as fondly and devotedly
attached to her as the day he married and that now I knew her he was

129

sure I appreciated her and would understand this. He spoke with great anxiety about her health. I said I trusted she was recovering. *"Dieu veuille, Madame"*, he replied. I remarked that the heat and excitement of that *salle de spectacle* could not be good for an invalid and that *un grand calme* must be necessary. *"Pour un que l'ennui ne s'en mêle pas"*, he said, *"mais elle ne voit que moi et ses enfants, son frère va dans le grand monde et son esprit s'attriste."*

He talked of his children whom I praised as they deserved. *"Oui, ce sont des bons enfants"*, he replied, and he went on to say they were arriving at an anxious age when their future happiness would be decided by their present choice. *"Mon fils doit bientôt choisir une compagne pour la vie, mes filles élevées dans un heureux intérieur, adorant leur pays et actuellement hereuses, doivent changer leur sort et chercher le bonheur en pays étranger."* He went on to say he looked to this with deep anxiety as in their situations the chances of happiness were very doubtful and when he looked at the fates of his own sisters and brothers not one had been happy. *"C'est à dire, comme moi, j'entends le bonheur dans le ménage. Ma soeur aînée a faite un mariage qui n'était pas pour son bonheur et elle est morte en couche. Ma soeur, la Duchesse de Saxe Weimar, charmante personne, ne doit qu'à son caractère heureux, de faire bon ménage avec un bel homme. Le Prince d'Orange est excellent, ma soeur est très aimable, mais ce n'est pas un heureux ménage.*[2] *Mon frère Michel est brave, excellent, la Grande Duchesse, que nous aimons comme une soeur, est charmante, mais voilà des caractères qui ne se conviennent pas.*[3] *Il faut se convenir pour être parfaitement et réciproquement heureux dans le ménage; au reste, comme moi, je l'entends"*, he always added. He then kindly regretted our departure and pressed our return hoping that if an opportunity occurred for Lord L. to come as Ambassador I should not object and that the Empress and his daughter would do everything they could to make it agreeable to me and mine. I thanked him for giving us his *feldjaeger* to manage our journey. *"Malheureusement, Madame, notre pays n'est pas assez avancé pour pouvoir voyager sans toutes les précautions, mais j'espère avoir consulté votre commodité en priant votre mari d'aller à Varsovie. Je désire qu'il voit ce pays si malheureux. Vous verrez le Maréchal Paskevich, homme froid, distrait, rêveur, mais un grand homme.*[4] *Vous verrez la maréchale qui à son âge a la prétention d'être ce qu'elle n'a jamais été même jeune."* I said I knew General Agerovsky there. *"Oui, mais vous le trouverez très changé.*" I observed that Prince Volkonsky was hardly changed. "*Parce qu'il est pétrifié et d'un âge qui ne change plus.*" I remarked that Tchernischev was the most changed of my old friends and that I attributed this being so evident to his *faisant le jeune homme.* "*Non, Madame, qu'il s'est fait mal en travaillant pour mon service.*"

After more conversation he took his leave and visits from Prince Volkonsky, Count Nesselrode, Count Ficquelmont, etc. succeeded till at five o'clock we went to dine at Count Stroganov's where all my most intimate friends were assembled *pour dire adieu.* It was a large party—the Nesselrodes, Prince Volkonsky, Prince Lieven, the Trubezkois, Madame Rasumovsky, Serge Golitsin, etc. Count Stroganov himself had most kindly directed the arrangements of all our carriages which were put on sledges for the journey. After dinner it was with real sorrow I took leave of Madame Stroganov. She was much affected and this is the great drawback to forming sincere friendships and close acquaintance with an amiable, agreeable person in a foreign land, that after weeks and months of daily communion and affection you are torn asunder without a prospect of meeting again. She and I had become so intimate, and I had met with such unbounded friendship and kind hearted hospitality and welcome from this delightful family that I had become a sort of *enfant de la maison* and,

> "Almost [*recte* And half] I felt as they were come
> To tear me from a second home".[5]

At eight o'clock we were fixed *pour prendre congé* of the Grand Duchess Hélène who changed her mind and determined to have a nine o'clock *soirée.* She said she had sent us some message which, however, we did not receive having dined out. Accordingly we arrived at the hour commanded and, being shown upstairs, found all in perfect darkness, she herself *en papillotes* not having begun to dress. She explained the mistake, begged us to wait, lay books and prints before us while she made her *toilette* and the servants proceeded to light up the house. She soon returned and sat down, talked of our departure, our journey, etc. of Lord Durham who, she said, everybody fancied had a passion for her. "*L'Empereur même m'en a parlé*", she added. The Grand Duchess Marie arrived soon after and made tea for all the party. Her governess, Madame

Baranov, talking of her to me, and both of us observing what a beautiful feminine miniature of the Emperor's her face was, told me it was a Russian superstition that when the eldest girl strongly resembled her father she was born to a happy lot. More company arrived and as the party seemed likely to last very late, I explained my difficulties to the young Prince of Oldenburg[6] who told the Grand Duchess that having understood she would give me a private audience at eight o'clock, I had promised to make other visits. She then very kindly dismissed us embracing me and wishing us a pleasant journey or rather a safe one through all our threatened dangers and difficulties. This Princess is certainly pretty, clever, and when she chooses agreeable and fascinating. She is not, however, as much beloved as the Empress of whom I heard touching praise in these few words, *"depuis vingt ans qu'elle est dans notre pays que d'heureux elle a fait, et elle n'a jamais fait de la peine à personne"*. Her passion for dress and *toilette* is chiefly to please the Emperor who is said to be most particular in examining the dress of his wife and daughters, and wishes them to be brilliant and perfect, and she perhaps exhibits it the more to show she has no desire to meddle and intrigue in business. She is the best wife and the best mother in the world, a gracious, dignified Sovereign, and an amiable being, and if anyone on this earth enjoys unallayed happiness and rests without being sensible that one leaf of her bed of roses is folded I should say it is she, and more wonderful still, that she deserves it. Prince Serge Golitsin said to her, *"Madame, que Dieu vous conserve votre bonheur actuel"*. The tears stood in her eyes as she replied, *"Dieu veuille, car c'est effrayant d'y penser"*. The same individual went on New Year's Day to *faire son compliment* to the Emperor. This was during the Empress's illness. He found him busy but dejected. He listened and putting out his hand to the Prince said, *"Mon cher, priez que ma femme se remette, depuis vingt ans que nous sommes unis je n'ai jamais même pensé à la possibilité de lui être infidèle, je l'adore comme le jour que je l'ai épousé; et si Dieu me prive d'elle ou de mes enfants je ne serais plus bon à rien pour vous autres"*.

The Grand Duchess Hélène is a great politician, said to be very jealous of the Empress, capricious and *volontaire*. When she came to England some years ago Madame Nesselrode was sent with her as a *gouvernante* or duenna, but they so entirely disagreed that Madame N. left her suddenly and returned to Russia. This displeased the Imperial family and was an *éclat* that no provocation hardly could excuse, besides the impropriety of the Grand Duchess being left unprotected and unadvised in a foreign country.

From the Michael Palace we went to take leave of the Ficquelmonts, and lastly of Lord Durham from whence we returned home tired and worn. I found Count Orlov had called twice to bring me the Emperor's autograph and General Kisselov had also called and brought me a little bust of the Emperor Alexander. I was very sorry to have missed them; indeed all the kindness shown us, the entreaties to us to prolong our stay and the regrets at our departure made me quite grieved to go. A singular sight in St. Petersburg is a train of little carts each loaded with one enormous, thick, square block of ice, all as if turned out of one mould of the clearest, transparent sea green, and when the sun plays on them as brilliant as aquamarines. Sometimes these huge blocks are set up like a sort of Stonehenge or miniature Giant's Causeway on the Neva. I asked Madame Stroganov one day what they were for, "*Mais je les appelle les violettes de Petersburg*", was her reply because it is a sort of hope of spring when people begin to fill their icehouses. Another peculiar scene I have often wished to sketch is a Russian hall and stairs during the ball above, the steps regularly lined and the space below filled with servants—immense creatures in large cocked hats and enveloped in the skins of wolves, bears, foxes, hyenas, racoons, etc. and looking like wild beasts or savages each carefully nursing his mistress'[s] rare and costly fur and holding it with a sort of reverential respect almost during his sleep.

On Thursday 9th we left St. Petersburg. Its climate is certainly as pernicious as the deadly upas tree;[7] the severe cold, the damp exhalations attendant on its marshy position, and the sudden changes of temperature make it most trying to the strongest constitutions, but it is a wonderfully magnificent city and a most agreeable *séjour*. The colossal scale of everything—its palaces, institutions, buildings, fêtes, etc. strike the mind with wonder, while the kindness, cordiality and friendly hospitality of the people warm the heart. They are the most intelligent, agreeable, *distingués*, clever persons imaginable.

The Emperor most kindly gave us his own *feldjaeger* to arrange our journey, and having expressed a wish that we should see Warsaw, "*ce malheureux pays*", where he was said to devour *des petits*

133

Polonais en côtelettes, and our carriages being arranged and packed and all our *couchées* for ten or twelve days settled we set out, and really the train looked more like a savage horde than an English family. First went the cook in a little britska laden with packages of all colours, shapes and sizes, the favourite dog wrapped carefully in the fur of a Siberian relative and a dwarf interpreter, a tiny black imp who had been rejected by his parents as incorrigible and was pardoned because he could speak French and Russian. Then flew on a kibitka[8] or open cart filled with straw in which sat the *jaeger* wrapped in shawls and furs over his uniform. He contrived to see us off at every stage and then darted forward to prepare for us at the next. His authority seemed undisputed and unbounded, and I believe if he had ordered one thousand horses and as many serfs to appear they would have been forthcoming. He was a Russian and could only speak a very few words of German. Next followed an enormous *berline* in which were Lord L. and myself. This was loaded inside and out. The servants looked like *Esquimaux* or savages in their various wild furs, jackboots and strange caps. After this came a chariot with Seaham and lastly came what was called the *traînage* which consisted of a kind of enormous low table on sledges on which were deposited first the wheels of all the carriages, secondly the trunks and carpet bags of every individual—the beds, mattresses, plate chests, wine, meat and other provisions, baskets, boxes, hair trunks innumerable, and bundles tied up in handker-chiefs of every colour of the rainbow—the whole covered with oil-skin and corded, and this uncouth, extraordinary edifice used to proceed at a pace that threatened destruction to all the things piled upon it which had to be unpacked every night and repacked every morning.

The snow was deep and uneven and the roads in a dreadful state. We expected to be upset every moment though in many places we were obliged to go at a foot pace. We were unable to go far the first day is there was much delay at starting. At Chirkovitsi (Ichinzkovitch)—about eighty versts—we remained the night and on Friday 10th set out early. At Opolye, the first relay, we met the English courier and went on through Kingisepp (Yamburg) to Narva, a fortified town very picturesquely situated.

This part of Russian Finland belonged to the Swedes and was conquered by Peter the Great.[9] We slept this night at ⟨⟩ and on Saturday 11th arrived at Tartu (Derpt) a large town with a university. The inn was kept by a dirty German who particularly praised the cleanliness of it, blessing his stars he was neither a dirty Russian nor an extortioner. This was the worst and dearest inn on the journey to Riga. There was a fair going on. We could only get three rooms and I slept in a little summer pavilion filled with plants and animals and with window shutters that let the light in through hearts and clubs cut in them. Here the roads improved and we glided or rather flew over the beaten track of hard snow without a jerk or jolt. Many people maintain that there is here a geographical line where the change from damp is felt and, after passing it, the climate improves. Bells were hung to the harness of the horses to frighten the bears and wolves whose footprints were visible on both sides of the road, but none appeared or emerged from the thickets. The country was flat and ugly and we went through dreary plains of snow till our eyes ached with the glare.

Sunday 12th. We slept at a very clean little inn at a small town called Valmiyera and from thence we made a very easy journey to Riga where we slept Monday 13th and remained Tuesday 14th during which day the carriages were taken off the sledges and put upon wheels. The Governor of Riga, Count Pahlen, called on us immediately to invite us to dinner. I, however, excused myself being tired and ill and not having a maid that could dress me. Mine, I omitted to mention, fell ill of a pleurisy at St. Petersburg. She was attended by Dr. Doratt and recovered when, one day, she proposed going to church, which I forbade as likely to give her fresh cold and lay her up again. Soon after she fell ill and the doctor declaring it was in consequence of having gone out, I asked her if it was possible she had been so imprudent. *"Mais oui, miladi, j'avais besoin de respirer l'air."* She had gone out without shawl or bonnet in the depth of a Russian winter literally *pour chercher la mort*. We delayed our journey but the physician said if she ever recovered she could not be moved till the spring and I was at last obliged to engage a person and set out without her. Poor girl, she died after months of suffering. The town of Riga is dismal and dirty, strongly fortified and with a great trade in flax. That in timber has been transferred to Klaypeda (Memel).

On Wednesday 15th we left Riga. There was a curious scene coming out of the town early, a market on the river we drove over.

We passed through Yelgava (Mittau) and arrived late at Shyaulyay (shavel). The inn, we heard, was not habitable, but we were received with great kindness and hospitality by Count and Countess Zubouv. We dined and slept there and went on the next morning. The change of costume and a certain stamp of nationality are very striking, even among the lowest orders is [in] passing, however rapidly, through Finland and Courland. The long hair and Swedish cap of the Fin[n] peasant and the resemblance to the Polish Jew in the Courlander cannot fail to excite remark. The picturesque Russian with his long reins, flowing robe, gay sash, long beard and bright gloves, gave place to the clumsy postillion with the German horn, leather and jackboots. The cottages are like Irish cabins and though the people are tolerably clothed there is an appearance of dirt and misery about them. The villages on the Moscow road, though composed of wooden houses, have a picturesque Swiss look, their balustrades and little balconies and flat gable ends are quite different from the cottages here.

On arriving at Shyaulyay we were soon set at our ease by our host and hostess who seemed to think it a perfectly natural thing to receive weary, famished travellers. We had an excellent dinner and the Countess insisted on giving me her room. The sitting room was filled with *bijouterie*, tapestry, pictures, birds and flowers, and a *treillage* concealed the beds.

[The] 16th. We found an excellent road to Ukmergė (Vielkomir), a clean little posthouse where we passed the night. The inn was small, the kitchen bad, and we were greeted on our arrival by the *feldjaeger* informing us *Herr Peron hat eine spectacle gemacht*—in short, there had been a regular quarrel about a room. This was settled, peace restored, and we had our supper and went to bed.

Friday 17th. We passed through Kaunas (Kovno), the Russian frontier, and entered Poland. We crossed the river on the ice. The town is a curious looking old place with very odd shaped buildings. Here Madame Tatischev, a beautiful Russian, wife to the ambassador at Vienna, died. She had long been in bad health but crossing the river, seeing the ice give way and one of the carriages go through, fright and horror so overpowered her she never could be moved from Kaunas. Here, to my regret, the high white verst posts ended. There is a great satisfaction in rapidly passing them and rejoicing in one's progress. We had now to count the dreary Polish miles which, like the tedious German ones, are seven versts. The horses are larger than the Russian ones and the number to our carriage was diminished to eight and afterwards to six. The roads were good and we went on prosperously to Marijampole, a dirty place where we were obliged to pass the night.

Saturday 18th. Having one hundred and seventy versts to go, we set out early. The day seemed marked by misfortune. We were terribly delayed by the badness of the roads, by jibbing horses, the pole of a carriage breaking, and various other disasters. At Augustov while changing horses, an old Scotch farmer came up to the carriage side. He had heard an English family were passing. He told us he came from Melrose, from Sir Walter Scott, "whom maybe you've heard of", he said. He had brought his wife out eighteen years ago to settle, hearing land was cheap in Poland, but he found it very disagreeable. He was a tenant of General Compatz whom he knew nothing of since the revolution and was determined to return to Scotland. He told us we should find dreadful roads and his prophecy was accomplished. We expected the carriage would be upset and smashed to pieces every moment. At last the *feldjaeger* procured a band of peasants who supported the heavy landau as it floundered and sank in the immense snowdrifts that lay across the road. But this, after going half a stage in the greatest peril and fear, was declared unsafe and open kibitkas or carts on sledges were procured from the cottages. In these were placed baggage and provisions for the night. The servants were divided, some remaining with the carriages to bring them on. The vehicle we had was filled with straw and four horses took it [at] a wonderful pace over hills of snow. Up and down we flew and reached Lomza at five o'clock in the morning more dead than alive. The cold was intense, the night air damp and piercing, and being so near the ground which we dashed over with inconceivable rapidity, snow, mud and lumps of ice covered us. I had immense bearskin jackboots, a footsack and a tin of boiling water. My fur cap covered eyes and nose and I was entirely wrapped in fur and eiderdown and covered with hay, furs and blankets. Yet I was cold, my face cut to pieces. I was bruised all over and when I was lifted out of the cart at Lomza after lying there nearly eight hours I could hardly stand. The jolting affected my head terribly. We found a *maison de la couronne*, the house of the *Commissaire du District*, prepared for our reception and we soon forgot our

137

troubles over a very consoling supper. It may be easily imagined that this was acceptable as we never stopped for dinner and on this occasion had breakfasted the preceding morning at five o'clock and had nothing during the twenty four hours but frozen pie, hard, dry bread, and hot brandy and water.

We lay down for a couple of hours and awaited the arrival of the carriages. As orders had been sent on and everything arranged it was important we should be exact in our arrivals. At every one of the little villages where we took fresh relays we found the Mayor, the *Bourgmestre*, the *Maître de Poste*, the Commissioner, the civil and military authorities waiting and in full uniform with their medals, cocked hats, etc. and it was amusing to see the self importance of each and all as they paddled about in the wet and snow directing the harnessing of the horses. Lord L. gave the *Commissaire* at Lomza a snuff box as he would not take any other reward though we had turned him out of the house and occupied it as our own.

Sunday 19th. We continued our journey through a long hard day. The roads were dreadful and in the worst possible state there being too much snow for wheels, not enough for sledges, and in some places the snow drifts were tremendous. In addition to the fright and jolting we had jibbing horses and all sorts of delays and misfortunes. The country seemed desolate and wretched and the ravages of waste and war were evident in the ruined and roofless burnt cottages. The people looked poor and squalid, a quantity of beggars and Jews and miserable objects. In a Russian ballet I saw some Polish soldiers in beautiful light blue and silver uniforms with large, white, expanded wings like a swan's and I was told this was the dress of the Polish Royal or Noble Guard formerly. Seeing some light blue soldiers I asked the Mayor who was standing by the carriage side, *"si c'était des soldats Polonais?" "Madame, il n'en existe pas"*, was the reply.

We reached the next post to Warsaw at four o'clock in the morning and were met by an escort of dragoons which Prince Paskevich had sent to conduct us to our abode. We were informed that, by the Emperor's orders, the *Palais Brühl*, formerly inhabited by the Grand Duke Constantine, had been prepared for our reception.[10]

We proceeded, crossed the Vistula on a bridge of boats, a beautiful moon illumined the old town on the opposite rising bank,

138

and we drove to the ancient palace which we found lighted up from one end to the other and Marshal Paskevich's staff waiting for us.

After being up two nights (one passed in open kibitkas exposed to snow and rain), at five o'clock in the morning we were hardly fit to be seen and, having established us in our magnificent and comfortable residence, ordered our supper and requested we would give our own directions, they left us and at past seven we retired to bed requesting the illuminations might not be continued, and Lord L. sent away the sentinels and begged to decline all military honours, guards, aides de camp, etc.

CHAPTER X

A Conquered Country, a Subdued Kingdom

ON THE FOLLOWING DAY I was so tired that I was obliged to lie in bed all day and decline a dinner and *soirée* at the Princess of Warsaw's.[1] The people seemed to have no idea of fatigue and were surprised at my being knocked up, and a young Prince Ouronsov who had been named as Lord Londonderry's aide de camp came at ten o'clock to Seaham and said he had been twice already; as we had all had four good hours' sleep what could we want more. He was extremely rejoiced at being liberated and set off for St. Petersburg two nights afterwards to catch the last gaieties of the carnival. Prince Paskevich called on Lord L. with his guard of Cossacks and Mussulmans galloping after him. Lord L. immediately returned the visit according to etiquette and dined there that day. General Agerovsky came to see me and Prince Rosciolovsky whom I thought stouter than ever.

Tuesday 21st. I remained at home all the morning and at half past five went to dinner at the Governor's. I found the Princess *sans toilette et sans cérémonie*—no other lady and about thirty men to whom I was introduced. In the evening there was a ball but, it being Lent here according to the Old Style, the Polish ladies made some difficulties about dancing though the Archbishop promised them absolution. The dancing at times flagged but the scene was very gay and pretty.

Wednesday 22nd. I begged to be allowed to dine quietly at home and I had visits all day, and at nine o'clock we went to a concert at the Governor's. Being a small party it was in his own *cabinet de travail*, a large and fanciful room picturesquely decorated with trophies and marks of his victories, partitioned by columns, and in one corner stood the tent used by the Emperor during the whole of the Turkish war and presented by him to the Marshal. Sabres, scimitars, richly embroidered housings from the Shah of Persia covered the walls—medals, amber pipes, prints, pictures, models—all sorts of interesting and characteristic things adorned this room. It is a curious fact and serves to prove that good and evil are more equally balanced than we in hours of joy or grief imagine, that on the day which saw Warsaw fall before Paskevich and when this conquest placed him at the very summit of fame and military glory, on that day his son, a noble boy, died at Moscow, and, as the poor Princess said, she heard of the triumph when absorbed in misery and reckless of bliss or woe. Mademoiselle Karl, a German, Madame Crescini and others sang, and the Russian *chantres* of the Prince's Greek chapel gave us some beautiful national airs.

Thursday 23rd. The Prince arranged to give Lord L. a great review at Bielany forest about five versts from Warsaw, and in summer a very pretty spot. From twelve to fourteen thousand men composed the garrison. At twelve o'clock he called for Lord L. in his Russian equipage, an open *calèche* with a long bearded Russian driving four horses abreast and his escort of Cossacks and Mus-sulmans galloping round him. The Princess came for me in a chariot-and-four *à l'Anglaise,* the coachman in boots and leathers driving four in hand, outriders and English horses. When we arrived at the wood the gentlemen mounted their steeds and we drove about a ploughed field expecting every moment to be over-turned. At last the Prince finding we did not appear sent aides de camp to bring us into the middle of the whole *mêlée* and explain to me the plan and scene. There was a village which the troops from Warsaw came out to reconnoitre, and finding unoccupied, entered. The solid squares of infantry succeeded by light cavalry slowly emerging from the forest followed the attacking party. The General commanding the opposing forces being hid by sandy hills and having concealed his strength till nearly the whole of the infantry was in possession of the village now charged and I never saw so beautiful a *coup d'oeil.* The regiment of Mussulmans, the only one in Europe and formed by Paskevich from the provinces he has conquered and entirely composed of picturesque, handsome looking men of the highest birth, each dressed in every colour of the rainbow, their beautiful barbs and Arab steeds dancing and pawing came first and nothing can exceed the beauty of this extraordinary regiment. Then came the wild Cossacks of the Don and those of the line, the

141

heavy cuirassier hussars in the brightest apple green. The charge was repeated, the Circassians looking like a garden of tulips, all their bright colours floating in the air. The infantry attempted to retreat from the village and the combat began, a regular scene of action, only the bullets and the killed and wounded wanting. The firing, the artillery, the wild music, the smoke, the savage cries, yells, howls and inspiring songs as they dashed to a fresh charge were very exciting. I felt like a child that claps its little hands with pleasure at what it sees.

The infantry, however, retreated without confusion but were met before they reached Warsaw and a pitched battle then took place. A blinding snow storm came on and I saw no more. The cold had been tremendous. Several of the Mussulmans with *chevalresque galanterie* formed *en escort* to conduct me from the field of battle. A Prince Andronicus, one of the handsomest men I ever saw, with raven hair and eyes, a son of the Shah of Persia, who wanted to give me his golden Arab, docile as a dog and wild as the desert steed, a poet who gave me verses, and three more composed this guard of honour. We all went to a small *quinquette* or summer *cabaret* where dinner was prepared and we were joined by Princess Radziwill, Princess Jablonovska,[2] Countess Potocka and other Polish ladies who had not been at the review. The troops bivouacked outside round immense fires of blazing logs, the wild horses and Arab steeds neighing at their pickets. Bread and brandy were given out, the men grouped themselves about and, notwith-standing the snow, began dancing and singing. The wildness of the scene, the singular beauty of the dresses and costumes, the thickly falling snow, and night closing round formed such a striking picture that I never longed so to draw, to place before the eyes of others a scene I shall never forget.

Boards were laid down and with these and many helping hands and arms I stepped from sledge to sledge and saw the whole. We then had a very merry dinner with beautiful music and when Lord L. rose and gave the health of the Emperor of Russia and *la belle armée Russe* there was a burst of enthusiasm. We then returned to Warsaw, made a hurried *toilette* and went to a beautiful ball given us by Madame Fuhrmann, wife of the Minister of the Interior.[3]

Friday 24th. A tremendous fall of snow prevented my going, as arranged, to the fortress. Count Agerovsky came to see me and talked of the Emperor Alexander. He had been his aide de camp twenty two years and truly worshipped him. He was not with the Emperor at the time of his death having been sent *en mission* to Warsaw where he was to meet him and accompany him back to St. Petersburg. He had never heard of his master's illness, and hearing some great misfortune had occurred and that the Grand Duke Constantine, then the Rey [Viceroy] of Poland and residing at the Palace Brühl, *s'était enfermé et qu'on n'ose pas approcher*, concluded, of course, that news of the death of the Empress had arrived as she was known to be in delicate health and the poor Emperor had conducted her with the greatest care and attention to the south of his Empire meaning to place her near the Sea of Azov. He entreated *au nom du Ciel* that the Grand Duke would see him but for an instant. He admitted him and exclaimed, *"Un grand malheur ! mon frère est mort"*. Poor Agerovsky was overpowered— his friend, his benefactor, the object of his worship was gone, *"et depuis cette heure mon sort est changé, mon avenir obscurci"*.

He was sent for to ⟨Taganrog⟩ and with the other aides de camp had the sad duty of accompanying the body of their Imperial master from the shores of Azov through the interior of Russia to St. Petersburg. The *cortège* went *au pas*, and at every church they passed the priests performed a *service mortuaire* and this lasted above two months and left an impression he was long before he could overcome. He said the Emperor had confided many things to him but had never mentioned the change of the succession; that it was, however, the Empress Mother and himself who had set Constantine aside and, on his marrying the Princess Lowitz had forced him to sign his exclusion.[4] This was never known till Alexander's death but by the three brothers and their mother who knew that Constantine *"aurait fait le malheur à la Russie"*. I asked how the Grand Duke came to relinquish the throne so easily, *"parce qu'il était poltron et il savait qu'on l'aurait égorgé comme son père"*. He added, *"Que de scènes j'ai vu dans cette appartement, lui qui fumait et jurait contre les Polonais, sa femme, ange de douceur, Polonaise elle même, essayait de le calmer et l'adoucir"*. He escaped from Warsaw at the time of the insurrection and died of the cholera on his way to St. Petersburg and the Princess did not long survive him. Her heart was broken. I had many visitors and heard much conversation on Poland. They said that the folly and weakness of the Grand Duke

143

had brought about the revolution. The Emperor Nicholas has left them their language, their religion, their money, their customs, but has been obliged to reform their army which, in its then state, was literally putting *un rasoir dans les mains d'un fou.*

Paskevich told me a curious fact: that when he was sent to command the army before Warsaw he came to Riga in the *Ischora*, the Emperor's yacht, and had he been twenty four hours later he must have been delayed twenty one days as the cholera had declared itself and rendered quarantine imperative. On how slight a thread fate sometimes hangs and how many destinies and matters of moment depend on a trifle! In the evening we went to the theatre with the Prince and Princess. A national ballet was given and the mazurka danced. It is most animated, stirring music and graceful action, but the Polish salutation of kissing the feet of their superiors struck me as very slavish and cringing.

Saturday 25th. There was to have been a great manoeuvre to show us the activity and extraordinary feats of charging, riding, firing backwards, etc. of the Cossacks and the Mussulmans but the snow fell heavily and the weather was so bad it was put off and at three o'clock the Princess took me to Lazienka, a beautiful *château de plaisance* four versts from Warsaw.[5] It was built by Stanislaus Poniatovsky and is literally on a lake.[6] Covered with snow as it was in the end of February was certainly not the best moment for seeing it, but on a hot summer's day it must be lovely. The theatre is in the open air on a little island, the actors arriving in boots [boats] and, as I am told, the scene is quite unique when a fête is given there.[7] The inside of the palace combines comfort and beauty. It is small and like an English country house, the drawing rooms below, the bedrooms above. There are three salons and a large hall of beautiful proportions where we dined about one hundred and fifty persons, the immense orange trees coming through the table. In about half an hour, as if by magic, this was entirely cleared, lighted up and prepared for dancing. The illuminations outside were beautiful notwithstanding the snow on the ground. Polonaises, waltzes, quadrilles, mazurkas, cotillons were all kept up in rapid succession and it was impossible to see a prettier or a gayer fête.

I found the Princess an extremely kind, amiable person and the Prince an agreeable man, but though I sat by him every day at dinner and danced all the polonaises with him he talked but little;

144

yet when he did after long intervals of silence and absence, was very agreeable.

Sunday 26th. I received visits from all the principal Polish ladies and, *entre autres*, a very pretty person, Countess Potocka. She was of low birth but had been educated by Count François, a clever man and a great collector of antiquities. She gave me a very curious old illuminated *livre d'heures*. We dined quietly at home for I really was quite knocked up by the succession of reviews, fêtes, dinners, concerts and balls, and being obliged to dance a great deal added to my fatigue.

The centre of the Brühl Palace was a square, round which the whole suite of apartments communicated but there was a door on one side of my bedroom that seemed to lead to some small room in a wing. The morning after my arrival I heard singing there. I jumped up and tried the door which was open on my side but bolted on the other and, thinking it rather unpleasant, I went back to bed, and calling my maid desired her to cover the door with a sheet while I got up and dressed to go and discover who my neighbour was and get the key. She returned saying it was the new Archbishop and that nobody dared ask him for the key. I insisted and he refused to give it thinking it an insult I should suppose he could want to come into my room. At last, after a great piece of work, I obtained it and with the key and the sheet the door was pretty safe. Whether it was the holy man or his servant I know not, but the noise began there early in the morning and puffs of smoke came in all day and neither open windows not burnt pastilles overcame the poisonous smell. Every time I entered my room my exclamation, "Heavens, what a smell!", was responded to by my maid by, "Yes, it *is* the Archbishop". I have omitted to observe that notwithstanding our remonstrances our table was kept by the Emperor whose servants attended us, and three carriages were placed at our orders, a state chariot-and-four for me, another for Lord L. and a *calèche* for Seaham. The large plate glasses in the Russian carriages are very handsome. The chariots have a single large one in front. In availing ourselves of all the distinction and kind attention shown us we endeavoured to be as discreet and delicate as possible but it was rather embarrassing.

In the evening there was a great ball at the Marshal's for me to take leave of the Polish ladies. We were to have set out the next morning but the Princess so urged our stay for me to have a quiet day that we delayed our departure but, as usual, I never had one moment's rest from early dawn.

[The] 27th. The Prince came to me bringing the beautiful, spirited oil sketches he had painted for me of the Mussulmans firing and of a wild Cossack charging while standing lashed to his horse. He also brought me two blue silk books with the Russian airs I had admired and the polonaise we so often had walked. The latter was dedicated to me and *Souvenir de Varsovie* written upon it in gold letters.

He then asked me to show him my jewels which he admired extremely and I begged him to write a line for me. I thought his vanity was touched by his autograph being placed among those of great men and sovereigns.

Some of the Circassians then came to take leave of me. They spoke little French generally except the poet who brought me his verses and their translation and the young Persian again offered his barb. At twelve o'clock I went with General Gorchakov[8] by appointment to see the far famed citadel which has been constructed within the last three years. Even to an ignorant female eye this is wonderful though seen by me covered with snow and to the greatest possible disadvantage. The enormous size (for it is like an immense town and the barracks form regular squares), the height, the wonderful strength and the Vistula rolling on one side at the bottom of its ramparts show what a stupendous work has been accomplished. But whatever the Russians undertake is on a scale so colossal that the mind is bewildered in contemplating the details—no medium between actual barbarism and this sort of wondrous conception and execution. For example, there is no road except a wild track over trunks of trees or, if it is attempted to make one at all it is a magnificent work without a rise for hundreds of miles, four times as wide and as fine as our much vaunted English North Road and with handsome stone bridges and cast iron rails wherever necessary. There is wisdom in this. The doctrine we hear from our childhood is to do little but to do it well. With these Russians it is *tout ou rien* and as their vast empire becomes civilized, cultivated and peopled, though they will have much to do they will never have to improve upon or to undo what they have already done.

This citadel must answer its purpose of keeping the Poles in submission for it evidently can annihilate Warsaw and sweep the

146

whole country round at a moment's notice. The legends say that the town takes its name from two lovers, the man's name being Var and the lady's Savie and that they were united one day by the reigning Duke of the province when *à la chasse*. Others say that a man and his wife of these names settled close to the Vistula and that their cottage was the beginning of Warsaw which is a gloomy, desolate looking old town without any fine buildings.

Poland, like so many other things in this world, is interesting in the vague obscurity of distance but when seen near all one's illusions and *beau idéal* are destroyed. I asked for the far famed beauties—I saw none. The Polish women are generally short and defective in shape. Instead of the tall, handsome Poles one has heard of, the streets are crowded with dirty old Jews. Allowing for the ravages of war and its attendant train of horrors, burning, exile and slaughter, still the nation must have degenerated since the days when it gave heroes and heroines for romance and chivalry. Lord Byron's lines on Greece are ever in our mind, while in Poland:

> "Clime of the unforgotten brave
> Whose land from plain to mountain cave
> Was freedom's home or glory's grave,
> Shrine of the mighty, can it be
> That this is all remains of thee?"[9]

This was my constant feeling. I went from the citadel to the field of battle which is a little out of the town, a flat plain, an old church where the Poles took refuge. Here Paskevich was wounded. The engagement lasted two days. There were about forty thousand Poles, he having taken advantage of the absence of fifteen thousand who were expected as a reinforcement. General Gorchakov told me the chief had been pardoned and was living in Warsaw. I asked if that was prudent. "*Mais, Madame, voilà nos précautions*", he said pointing to the citadel. "Yes", said I, "that is all very fine, but surely it is better not to have recourse to that but to be prudent and amiable *avec vos radicaux, par exemple*?" The Russians and Poles cordially hate each other. The latter seem a vain, cringing, demoralized people and one does not see how good feeling is to be restored. Poland is to Russia very much what Ireland is to England, a conquered country, a subdued kingdom that can never forget it was once independent but is always internally agitating and bringing down misery and forging for itself fresh chains. General Gorchakov talked feelingly of the misery and the ravages of war as we passed some roofless cottages. He said in the middle of the first day's battle a woman had come to him imploring him to save her life and that she was starving. Soon after he had placed her in safety and directed that she should be fed she came to him again to desire he would fetch her fur cloak from some distant cottage exposed to the whole fire! He said how wretched was the *journalier* life of an officer, the dulness of being shut up in a fortress, the uncertainties and hardships of campaigning. *"Ah, Madame, c'est une triste vie et celui qui vous dit qu'il aime la guerre, ment."* Napoleon, when asked, *"si pendant sa première campagne (qui était sa plus belle) il n'était pas l'homme le plus hereux du monde"*, replied, *"Non, au contraire, car les succès de la veille n'empêchaient pas les inquiétudes du lendemain"*.

I then called on Madame Paskevich who gave me many curious details about the habits and customs of the Georgians and Armenians. She had lived among these people while Paskevich formed the Mussulman regiment. All the family are present at the *accouchement* of the women and open house is kept for a month. There is one singular part in their marriage ceremonies which is that the priest seals a piece of silk round the bride's neck which is broken by the bridegroom. The funerals, like the *accouchements*, require six weeks' feasting. The widow is chief mourner, tearing her hair, scratching her face, shrieking and relating all the virtues of the deceased. The Princess showed me all the house and pointed out to me some fine vases which the King of Prussia had sent her after the review at Kalisz.[10] She gave me a painted glass cup, showed me a quantity of fine jewels and many curious things, amongst them a silver basket she was taking to the Empress. They were to go to St. Petersburg soon and to be lodged in the Palace. Indeed, I was told that a Field Marshal always is so. She finished by saying as I went away, *"A présent, chère, vous viendrez dîner à l'heure qui vous convient, nous serons seuls dans le cabinet du Prince. Après cela nous irons pour un petit moment au théâtre, je vous reconduirai chez vous, je vous déshabillerai, et je vous embrasserai en nous disant adieu"*. I made many speeches of gratitude for all the kindness and distinction they had shown us but intreated her not to think of performing the last named service for that I would take leave of her at the theatre.

148

Paskevich's answer to all my thanks was, "*Madame, j'obéis les ordres de mon maître et je le fais avec plaisir*".

I went home to pack up and prepare for the next day's journey. I found General Agerovsky who had come to take leave of me. "*Voilà*", he said, "*vous avez demandé le maréchal d'écrire pour vous mais comme vous ne m'avez rien dit j'ai écrit sans que vous me demandez; vous n'en voulez pas, eh bien, c'est égal, je veux vous les lire.*" "And what on earth is your name", said I, seeing an A at the bottom of the sheet. "*Adam, comme le premier homme; allons, je vous apporte aussi une coiffure Arabe, Perse, ce que vous voulez*", producing a sort of high cap and shawl of white cloth peculiarly cut and all in one. "*Tenez voilà, ce que vos amis les Mussulmans portent, mettez votre jolie petite tête la dedans et voyagez en cela; cela tient chaude et vous serez très bien. Adieu, vous partez, ayant tourné la tête à toute le régiment et des Mussulmans ainsi qu'aux Chrétiens et vous n'y penserez pas après demain.*" We dined with the Prince and Princess of Warsaw and their family and a curious antiquity of the place, an old *ci-devant* Chamberlain of King Stanislaus Poniatovsky. I examined all the things in the Marshal's room where he dined. He gave me one of the medals struck for his first victories, the Russian eagle towering over the Persian lion; also a beautiful model in cast iron of the great column in the middle of the principal square in the citadel erected to the memory of the Emperor Alexander.

We then went to the theatre where a national ballet was given. After this was over and I was taking leave, "*Nous nous allons chez vous prendre le thé et finir d'emballer*", said the Princess. I was very much tired. However we all four went to the *Palais Brühl* and there sat for some time talking. At last they took an affectionate leave and on Tuesday 27th [*recte* 28th] we left Warsaw.

CHAPTER XI

Old Friends at Berlin

THE CHAUSSÉE is excellent to Kalisz and with our *feldjaeger* and all previous orders given we got on very fast. The suburbs of Warsaw are miserable and we passed the scene of action where the burnt, ruined cottages show the destruction of war. The country looked flat, desolate and uncultivated; the people seemed poor and wretched. The snow fell fast and thick and all around was dreary. Not an object met the eye that wandered over the great plains except the very high white crosses seen at intervals all over Poland. We passed the night at Kutno in a commissariat house said to be better than the posthouse. I thought nothing worse could exist. There is literally not a vestige of an inn in Poland that a human being can enter. This was a government building, a small cottage with three excessively dirty holes for all the party.

Wednesday 28th [*recte* March 1st]. We were well driven and, notwithstanding the very deep snow and the heavy fall all day, we reached Kalisz early. We were received by a colonel whose life seemed to have been one of singular vicissitude. He said as *Gouverneur du Palatinat* he had the Emperor's commands to receive us. He was a Pole and had been aide de camp to *Maréchal* Ney.[1] Afterwards he became aide de camp to the Grand Duke Constantine whom he remained with till his death. After this he removed to Berlin where he married and lived four years and now was allowed to wear the uniform as the Emperor's aide de camp though employed in the civil service. He told us that the building where we were received on arriving had formerly been a convent but that now the archives were kept there and that the Emperor had reserved for himself apartments which he had occupied during the reviews and which were prepared for us. This town was greatly added to at that time— houses, ballrooms rapidly rose up and many royal persons lodged. It is the frontier town and here our friend the *feldjaeger* was to have left but being as desirous to go to Berlin himself as we were to take him I had asked permission to do so from Paskevich who immediately granted it. We had an excellent dinner and very comfortable rooms and the next morning, Thursday March 2nd, we entered Prussia. The snow was tremendously deep, the roads dreadful and no *chaussée* and after toiling on for fifteen hours we were obliged to stop at Trebnitz, a horrible place within two hours of Breslau which we only reached next day, Friday March 3rd, at eleven o'clock a.m.; and notwithstanding the snow, the thaw and a sea of black mud, I walked about this curious old town. Its narrow streets, old buildings, high houses, gable ends, etc. reminded me of Bruges but it is larger, dirtier and older. The statue of Blücher is fine and its motto touching: "My God, my King, the Fatherland and the fine Silesian Army".[2] There are here some very curious ancient buildings and old churches but we went away very early next morning and I had not time to see much.

Saturday, March 4th. We had a long fatiguing day, half way to Berlin through deep snow, the tedious miles and German driving forming a sad and wearing contrast with the short versts and swift little Russian horses.

We found from Breslau an excellent *chaussée* and a better country.

Sunday 5th. We started at six and had a long wearisome day through snow. We passed Frankfurt on the Oder, a clean, fine town, and noticed a church with a beautiful, old, painted glass window, and we arrived at Berlin after twelve o'clock at night. The Duke of Cumberland had taken rooms for us at the *Hôtel de Petersbourg* and we found them ready, and a six weeks' collection of letters.[3]

Monday 6th. The Duke of Cumberland came to see me, the Duke of Cambridge,[4] etc. and notwithstanding I was fatigued and ill I was obliged to go to Court at six o'clock to be presented to the King[5] and the Princesses. There was a German play and a French *vaudeville* after which we went to supper at little tables and when this was over there was dancing, and I, more dead than alive, asked permission to retire. The rooms were the private ones of the Princess von Liegnitz, a good natured, unaffected person, to whom the King is married *de la main gauche*.[6] I thought them small, dirty and ill lighted. Lord L. had dined at the Duke of Cumberland's.

The hours at Berlin are insupportable. The King dines at half past one, the Princes at two, the Duke of Cumberland at four, but

151

the whole town is *sur pied* when one is in one's first sleep and the King himself rises at five. Nothing is more true than the proverb, *"Il faut hurler avec les loups"*, for if you keep your own different hours you find yourself entirely *dépaysée*. For example, if you dine at six or seven, visits would disturb you and you could not go to *soirées* that begin at seven or eight.

Tuesday 7th. We dined at home and Lord L. went to a concert at the Duchess of Cumberland's.[7] I was too ill to stir.

Wednesday 8th. Lord L. dined with the King.

Thursday 9th [We dined] with the Prince Royal who is married to a daughter of the King of Bavaria.[8] They are good natured, amiable people and have no children.

Friday 10th. We dined with Prince William, a most agreeable person and married to a charming young Princess, daughter of the Duchess of Saxe Weimar and niece to the Emperor of Russia.[9] She is excessively pretty, *pétillante d'esprit et remplie de talent*. I was obliged to decline all invitations, and Doctor Graefe, the famous physician patronized by the Duke and Duchess of Cumberland ordered repose and complete quiet.

Saturday 11th. Lord L. dined out. I had constant visits. Lord William Russell was very good natured and attentive and lent me a comfortable sofa.[10] Monsieur Bresson, the French Minister, I found a most agreeable and distinguished man.[11] Monsieur Ribeaupierre, the Russian, the two Counts Redern, the Duke of Cumberland, etc. were my daily visitors either morning or evening.

Berlin is a beautiful capital, so clean and regularly built, wide streets, fine large stone buildings, etc. and the perfect symmetry of the whole is very striking. Not a house can be built without permission and according to the general plan. There is a very clever architect and they have good stone.[12] Altogether I believe it is as fine a town as can be seen though it always struck me as dull and heavy. Perhaps my living on the wrong side of the street made me see things *en noir*, for though I seldom care for aspect still in my case was verified the Italian proverb, *"dove non viene il sole entra il medico"*.

Sunday 12th. I went out for the first time to see the Duchess of Cumberland, and Lord L. dined again with the King.

Monday 13th. We dined with the Duke and Duchess of Cumberland. Indeed, they most kindly invited us to do so whenever we were not better engaged. It was a very nice house, a small party, and I saw poor Prince George whose state really makes one's heart ache. To see so fine a creature, blind and led about, bearing this heavy calamity with angelic sweetness and resignation and appearing cheerful before his parents, is quite heartrending.[13] He is so amiable that everyone adores him.

Tuesday, March 14th. We dined at two o'clock at Princess Charles's. She is a sister of the Princess William and likewise pretty but less animated.[14] Prince Charles was absent in St. Petersburg. The King dined there, also the Duke and Duchess of Mecklenburg-Strelitz,[15] but that antediluvian hour spoilt all. To be full dressed at two o'clock in the day to dine is a penance nothing can make up for. There was a concert and supper at the Prince Royal's but I was too tired to go.

Wednesday, March 15th. There was a reception at Court similar to the former one, a German play, French *vaudevilles*, supper and dancing. I thought the whole very dull.

The town is undeniably handsome, large, clean, regularly built, wide streets and handsome buildings. The shops are not good. Except those of the *fer de Berlin* which I think frightful in ornaments and not handsomer than bronze in larger things, and the canvas work which is done in quantities, I found nothing particular. I went to the china manufactory reckoned the first almost in Europe and the painting is certainly beautiful but I saw nothing very remarkable.

Friday, March 17th. I remained quietly at home.

Saturday 18th. We dined at Prince Albert's who has a fine palace with a beautiful double staircase of cast iron, extremely light. He is very young looking and married to a daughter of the King of Holland.[16] The suite of rooms is very fine and there were between fifty and sixty people to dinner. The whole thing was most magnificent, the service, plate, glass, porcelain, etc., but the cold was intense and the barbarous hour as usual spoilt all. A military band plays at these royal dinners. The Prussian princes have about twenty thousand pounds a year, no taxes, and a magnificent palace built for each.

Monday 20th. I went to a great dinner at Lord William Russell's. The house is very pretty. The Duke of Cumberland and all the *corps diplomatique* dined there. I had a long conversation with

Monsieur Ribeaupierre. He described the Crimea to me as lovely, *"La Suisse portée sur les bords de la mer"*, with the climate of Paradise and Eastern vegetation. He said Odessa was a most extraordinary place and seemed as if created by a magical wand. He found there an Italian opera and when he arrived a box had been given him and one of the principal inhabitants of the town came in true Italian fashion *le trouver dans sa loge* and remarked to him, *"Monsieur, vous ne croiriez pas qu'ici dans cette place où j'ai l'honneur de vous présenter mes hommages il y a trente ans que je tuais des bécasses"*. The staircases in Berlin are enough to kill anyone; they are not heated and the wind from the street rushes up them.

Tuesday 21st. We had a great dinner at the French Ambassador's, Monsieur Bresson, who negotiated the marriage of the Duke of Orleans.[17] There was an immense party in a very fine house and I envied him a noble Persian greyhound with long silky hair. It was the largest and most beautiful beast I ever saw.

Wednesday 22nd. We dined with the Russian Minister. There was an immense number of people but the house was dreadfully cold and I got a chill and was so ill I was obliged to go home and send an excuse to a great dinner at the Duke of Cumberland's, Thursday 23rd, and Lord L. went alone.

Good Friday 23rd [*recte* 24th]. Prince Wittgenstein came to us by order of the King to request we would delay our departure.[18] We had ordered and arranged everything for going on Tuesday but in consequence of this order we settled to delay till Thursday.

Sunday 26th, Easter Day. I was still ill. Lord L. and Seaham went to church at the Duke of Cumberland's and Lord L. dined with the King.

Tuesday 28th. I was so much worse that another doctor was called in, a Dr. Gaspard, who had studied in Edinburgh and was recommended by Lady William Russell,[19] upon which the famous physician, Dr. Graefe, wrote a very important epistle and chose to be affronted. The King sent me a beautiful *cadeau*, a porcelain *jatte* of a new shape, and Prince Wittgenstein called to explain that this was expressly for me and a fine vase with the King's picture was finishing for Lord L.

Wednesday 29th. [There was] another *soirée* at the King's beginning at six o'clock, the same routine as the former ones. I thanked him and expressed my gratitude for his kindness though I felt it was on account of his old friendship for Lord L. He was very civil in his expressions, regretted our departure, the state of my health, etc. and soon after we all went into the little theatre where the German and French pieces were given and a ballet. This is the King's *manie* in his old age. He never misses the theatre and when the representation is *chez lui* he gives the actresses their dresses. They sup there and he takes every opportunity he can find to trot out and have a little talk with them. I was too ill to stay supper.

Thursday 30th. I went to the *Musée* which is a beautiful Grecian building, very large and supported by columns. The lower part is devoted to casts and statues which are remarkably well arranged on pedestals of grey marble, and the *salles* are supported by columns of red scagliola.[20] There are two immense *baignoires* of granite, a fine jasper vase and a bath of Siberian verd-antique. The two latter are presents from Russia. In the court before the building is a granite building of immense size; above stairs is a very large collection of paintings remarkably well arranged. The rooms are lofty but not large, the particular school is designated over every door, and a list of the pictures in each room is fixed at the entrance.

I was too ill to see all this in detail as it deserves. I saw the famed Carlo Dolce St. John. The head, the hand, the expression, all except the intensely blue sky, struck me with admiration. There are four fine Rembrandts, one beautifully painted head of a Cardinal, the white hair, the keen eye with the spectacles and the wrinkled face seemed starting from the canvas.

Friday 30th [*recte* 31*st*]. We went to the china manufactory and I found I had not been shown the finest things when there before. It is an immense establishment and at this moment surpasses all others, the painting being superior to that of Vienna and the clay to that of Dresden. Of all this, however, I had no means of judging, first from my ignorance and secondly, my want of strength to see half. I climbed up endless stairs, however, and was rewarded by seeing a room full of beautiful vases. I then paid some visits of adieu and dined, a family party, at Lady William Russell's. In the evening we went to the theatre to see the *Sylphide*.[21] The ballets of Berlin are even more famed than those of Paris owing to the King's known passion for the theatre, the ample space and means; but I had heard so much of *Ondine, Robinson Crusoe, Fernand Cortez* and their *spectacles* that I was greatly disappointed.[22] The exterior of the theatre is fine but the interior is cold, dirty, dark and not very large, and this old ballet was not better given than at St. Petersburg or London.[23] The King was in a private side box. The large state one in the middle of the house was lighted up and occupied by the Prince and Princess Royal and several of the Royal Family. The common boxes are small, uncomfortable and extremely dirty. From the theatre we went to the Duke of Cumberland's where supper was served. The Prince and Princess Royal, *Prince de Solms*,[24] etc. were there and I returned home very tired.

Saturday, April 1st. We left Berlin after a *séjour* of four weeks. Seaham went to Stade in Hanover to study German for a couple of months. I asked the King to give me an autograph which he kindly sent me by the Princess von Liegnitz. A beautiful palace was building for Prince William. The furniture was not all finished and they had not moved into it.[25] The Princess showed it to Lord L. and Seaham but I was too ill to go. On our way out of Berlin we stopped to see some Arabian horses that were for sale and we arrived at Potsdam in about four hours. Whilst our dinner was preparing we walked to the old palace which forms a large square.[26] Upstairs are the rooms of Frederick the Great, and every remembrance of him is carefully preserved—the table where he wrote and of which the once light but now dirty blue velvet has had a bright square patch put in to replace the piece Napoleon carried off as a souvenir of this great man; his musical instruments and books, his library, his own works filling one whole shelf, even the torn, faded, queer, old silk shade for his eyes, all are preserved. The furniture has been untouched for ninety years. We then saw the modern suite where Napoleon lived and which is used by the King. There is nothing very remarkable here with the exception of some interesting pictures and some fine vases from the china manufactory at Berlin. The late Queen's rooms remain untouched, and all the white muslin draperies and hangings are become completely black.[27] There is a custom in Berlin of giving china eggs at Easter. On the Sunday the Duchess of Cumberland sent me two and this is an universal practice. In the King's room these eggs were hung in festoons round, probably the collection of years. We were unable to see the new palace which is out of the town.[28] Our inn was not particularly good, our dinner very bad and the charges exorbitant.

Sunday, April 2nd. We proceeded to Herzberg, a clean little

town, where we were far better off and for half the expense of Potsdam. There is a famous *ébéniste* here who makes beautiful parquets. From Herzberg we proceeded [on] Monday, April 3rd. The road was hilly and heavy and the German driving very slow. At Moritzburg, the last relay, is a fine royal *chasse* and a curious old palace with a piece of water and stiff cut trees and avenues. Here the King comes in November for two months to hunt. The descent into the valley where Dresden lies presents a fine view and the entrance over the great bridge is very striking with the old domed church on one side and the fine cathedral on the other. The environs of Dresden are beautiful in summer. The town is very old with high houses, narrow streets, etc.[29]

We drove to *l'Hôtel de France* where our rooms were ordered and a good dinner prepared. In the evening Mr. Forbes, the Minister, paid us a visit.[30]

Tuesday 4th. We went round some old china shops. We saw nothing very extraordinary and were wearied with climbing up three pair of stairs to the different *magasins*.

Wednesday 5th. Lord L. dined with the King.

Thursday 6th. At twelve o'clock we went to the far famed gallery which is not heated and the pictures are spoiling from damp and want of care and they are lost for want of arrangement.[31] There are several large *salles* filled and out of an immense quantity of endless mass of confusion some of the finest are the famous Raphael, six Corregios, his first and latest works and his much esteemed Magdalen, a lovely picture, some Paul Veroneses, and many beautiful specimens of the Dutch school. I talked with Mr. Evans, an English artist whom I found copying the Raphaels and Corregios for Mr. Liddell. The poor man seemed half dead with cold.[32]

We then went to the porcelain *fabrique* which we found is only a depot from the one at Meissen and not, as I had imagined, a separate manufactory.[33]

At three o'clock we went to the Jewel Chamber.[34] It is a very tiresome arrangement in Dresden that to see anything tickets must be obtained a day previously and an hour fixed for the purpose. This treasure is in eight rooms in the *rez de chaussée* of the Palace. The first contains beautiful carvings in bronze; the second curious carvings in ivory of great beauty and immense value; then old elaborate *ciselures en bois*; one room filled with agate, onyx, lapis, bloodstone, crystal *de roche* and all sorts of precious things in the shape of cups, vases, etc., a *pietra dura* table, an immense enamel picture, etc. Another room is filled with old plate of all shapes and forms, some embossed, some encrusted and adorned with jewels, and a small chamber with all sorts of toys, ornaments, etc. made in enamel and rubies and diamonds to employ masses of imperfect and deformed pearl; lastly, a room lined with *armoires* filled with diamonds of immense value and size. There was a large green diamond pointed out to us. However it is quite in vain to attempt description or details of this unique collection of which the riches, beauty and extent are unrivalled.

In cases of emergency large sums of money have been advanced by Holland as loans upon the jewels. The old man who showed the whole to us told us that while in his charge this had been done five times but they were redeemed as soon as possible. He showed us what the Queen had sent for to wear that evening at the concert which they were good enough to give for my presentation. We then returned home, dined and made our *toilettes*. I was carried up two pair of very high stairs and was afterwards informed this was quite unnecessary as there is a small cabinet in which one may deposit oneself and be screwed up and down scarcely conscious of the movement. The rooms were not fine nor very large but extremely hot.

The Queen is a daughter of the King of Bavaria.[35] She is tall, pleasing and agreeable though plain. She has no children but her sister, married to the King's brother, has several.[36] The Princess Jean is so like her twin sister the Princess Royal of Prussia that it would be impossible seeing them together and dressed alike to distinguish the one from the other. The Queen's twin sister is the Archduchess Sophia of Austria.[37] I was seated between the King and Queen who were very kind, but however grateful and flattered I might feel I cannot say I was amused. As I entered the concert room the old *Grande Maîtresse* bustled up to me: "*Madame la Marquise, soyez assez bonne pour vous mettre à la gauche de la Reine, à la droite du Roi.*" The consequence of which was my standing for a moment *ébahie*, till the signs of the King and Queen made me comprehend I was to climb into and deposit myself in a large armchair between them. This I did and the concert began and lasted long. Violins accompanied bad voices and for two hours I expected every moment to faint away. Between every fresh piece

158

were lamentations for Madame Schröder who is their best singer and was absent.[38]

The Princess Augusta of Saxony, sister to the King, seemed agreeable and good natured. She had lost her voice from cold and could hardly speak. She is now no longer young. She never would marry and refused Napoleon, the late Emperor of Austria, the King of Bavaria and several others.[39]

Friday, April 7th. We went to dine with the English Minister. There was a party of twelve, an excellent dinner, a very pretty house, beautiful old china, and everything in the best possible taste. We were obliged to accept a *soirée* next day at Monsieur de Zeschau's, the Minister,[40] and a dinner at the Russian Minister's.

Saturday 8th. The various interruptions of *marchands* bringing old lace, old tapestry, old china, old pictures, etc. [continued] all day. Even now, ransacked and rummaged as it has been by hordes of English and travellers from every country, there is no place where so many curiosities may be picked up cheaply.

We went to the *soirée* and next day we dined with Monsieur Schroeder, the Russian Minister, and there met the handsome Madame Gouriev, daughter to the celebrated Madame Narishkin to whom the Emperor Alexander was attached.[41] The house was handsome but rather cold and comfortless. The satin chairs and sofas were pinned to the walls and there was not a table, except the one for dinner, in any of the rooms.

We returned to our inn and almost immediately Monsieur Schroeder was announced. We were rather surprised but found afterwards this attention is considered the highest compliment that can be paid, and it is only to those to whom he wishes to show marked civility that the master of the house comes to see they are not poisoned but quite well and to express his hope that nothing has disagreed with them.

I had asked the King and Queen for their autographs and they very amiably sent them to me by the Minister for Foreign Affairs. I was very sorry to leave Dresden which deserves a longer *séjour*.

CHAPTER XII

Return to England

ON MONDAY 10TH we left Dresden at eight o'clock in the morning. To Meissen is three posts and in summer must be a beautiful drive through the valley of the Elbe, vines covering the steep sides on the right hand, and on the left the river which the road follows in picturesque windings. Meissen is a very old town. The entrance over an ancient bridge with a large and ruined castle perched like an eagle's nest on a hanging rock above is very striking. It was cold and bleak weather with deep snow and all this was of course seen to disadvantage and at its most unfavourable moment. The old castle is turned into a china manufactory and is almost inaccessible.[1] However we tried a ⟨⟩ and wound round and round the ascent till we reached "the summit of the tower crowned hill". There was little to see except a few old pieces for sale called *les doubles*, for these good people only value the modern and part with the old as soon as they have copied it. I thought the charges immense and, though a royal *fabrique* with fixed prices, the man tried to cheat which so disgusted and enraged me I would not even take what I had intended though he cried after me that I should have it for what I pleased. We then proceeded through a long toiling day, bad roads, worse driving, incessant snow and arrived at Leipzig at eleven o'clock at night worn to death where we were greeted with the agreeable intelligence that there was not a corner to be had at any of the inns on account of the fair[2] but that what they called an *appartement* consisting of two small dirty garrets at the top of a narrow sort of ladder stairs was prepared for us and our supper would be sent from the inn two streets off. All this was not better on trial than it appeared in perspective and we did not fare well or enjoy much comfort.

Tuesday 11th. We started very early. The town was in a great bustle—stalls, *magasins* without end. Their fair lasts above three

160

weeks. The productions of every country are here collected exhibiting a scene of great wealth and traffic. We had not time and I had not health or strength to explore over the exposed, much less the hidden, treasures, and after a weary long day we arrived at Weimar, an old dismal town where we found a cold, noisy inn and a bad supper.

Wishing to avoid the fatigue and worry of presentation and delay at this little Court we left early next morning, Wednesday 12th, and proceeded by Erfurt to Gotha and though the distance was only six German miles we were above eight hours accomplishing it. The whole of this journey was *au pas*, the roads so hilly and bad, the driving so slow and the snow so deep it was up to the carriage windows. At Gotha we equally *esquivéd* Court and passed unknown.

These little powers always exact more ceremony and etiquette while they have so much less of interest to offer than great ones, and they make up in form what they want in reality. The inn here was good, at least clean. All German cooking is poisonous and, next to the driving, most trying to the patience of the traveller.

Thursday 13th. We set out very early which was a fortunate precaution for all the ills we suffered on former days were increased on this. More snow, steeper hills, worse driving and we were five hours reaching Eisenach, a distance of three posts. From this place, however, an improvement was perceptible. The snow diminished, we got on faster and reached Fulde, an old town where the Bishop's Palace has been transferred [transformed] into a cold, comfortless inn. Here we passed the night and [on] Friday 14th proceeded to Frankfurt. We found our letters and took possession of very fine apartments at *l'Hôtel de Russie* meaning to rest a day and continue our journey to Paris.

Saturday 15th. We went to the famous shop here for Bohemian glass the beauty of which is indescribable, so bright and brilliant and of every shade and shape and colour. Here we made some purchases. At the workshops I did not find the tapestry or canvas embroidery as good or as cheap as at Berlin. I was taken very ill with spasms and remained for above a week in wretched suffering. It then became a question of taking me to England up the Rhine and from Rotterdam as most expeditious and avoiding all carriage motion and for this purpose we moved to Mainz about four hours' drive from Frankfurt. Here I literally went on board a steamer which was very large and nice and clean but the weather being so cold and [there being] no possibility of making a fire in the state cabin, after much consultation, it was decided we should go on by easy journeys to Paris. Monsieur Bresson had advised our taking the Nancy road as the best and most picturesque. However, the Metz line being the shortest we were induced to try it. The *chaussée* was tolerably good but through an ugly country and bad inns. We reached Paris in safety the ⟨ ⟩ and found it so full that not a room was vacant at any hotel.

We stayed a week in a wretched lodging in the *Rue d'Algar* and then moved for three weeks to *l'Hôtel Meurice* which was dirty and noisy. I dined once at the Tuileries, where I found the Queen[3] greatly altered, and once at a grand entertainment given us by the Russian Ambassador;[4] but with these exceptions I did not go into society and we returned to England the end of May after an absence of ten months.

Notes

CHAPTER I *pp.* 20–25

1. A travelling carriage very popular from 1824 until about 1840. It had a straight body with a single folding hood and was hung on C springs.
2. The *Lakenhalle* or Cloth Hall, built 1200–1334. It was completely destroyed in 1914, but rebuilt on the old lines in 1933–34.
3. Sir George Hamilton Seymour (1797–1880), the Envoy Extraordinary to the Belgian Court, had previously been Private Secretary to Lord Castlereagh.
4. A four-wheeled carriage with a separate hooded seat behind, detached from the body of the vehicle. It originated in Berlin about 1670. Perhaps the railway carriage resembled one, hence the word's use here.
5. The King of the Belgians, Leopold I, had been elected to the throne only with the help of an ultimatum to the Belgian Congress by the Five Powers. Louis Philippe, King of the French, had hoped to establish his younger son on the Belgian throne but was forced to accept Leopold as King, largely because of British opposition to French influence in Belgium.
6. Sir Edward Cromwell Disbrowe, Envoy Extraordinary and Minister Plenipotentiary to the Netherlands, 1836–51.
7. The *Mauritshuis*, built for Count John Maurice of Nassau in 1633–44, housed the Royal Gallery from 1821 and served as a museum until 1875. It still maintains a fine gallery of paintings, but the other collections are now housed in various museums throughout the Netherlands.
8. This model is now in the *Rijksmuseum*, Amsterdam. In an old catalogue it is said to have taken twenty-five years of work and to have cost thirty thousand D.fl.

CHAPTER II *pp.* 26–33

1. Sir Henry Watkin Williams Wynn (1783–1856), Envoy Extraordinary and Minister Plenipotentiary at Copenhagen, 1825–53.
2. Landgrave Charles of Hesse (b. 1744), the father of Queen Marie of Denmark, died on 17 August 1836.
3. More correctly Baron de Talleyrand, the French Minister at Copenhagen. He was a relative of the more famous Talleyrand and had been

Minister in Switzerland and Italy. See Lord Londonderry's *Recollections of a Tour in the North of Europe in 1836–37* (London, 1838), p. 37, hereafter cited as *Recollections*.

4. Jean de Krabbe-Carisius, Head of the Department of Foreign Affairs and not "Prime Minister" as stated here.

5. King Frederick VI (b. 1768) succeeded to the throne in 1808.

6. *Vor Frue Kirke*, the cathedral church of Copenhagen, was almost entirely destroyed in the bombardment of 1807. It was restored in the years 1811–29 and the Danish sculptor, Bertel Thorwaldsen (1770–1844), was commissioned to make a series of statues of Christ and the Apostles. These were not completed until 1838 and, of the statues of the Apostles, only that of St. Paul was executed by Thorwaldsen himself.

7. The *Nationalmuseet* (National Museum of Danish Life and Antiquities) contains one of the oldest and largest collections in Europe. The idea of a museum developed out of a Royal Commission of 1807 and the prehistoric collections were opened in 1820.

8. Charlottenborg is a huge building dating from about 1672. It was given by King Frederick V to the Academy of Arts.

9. Some of the paintings from the Royal Collection are now in the *Kunstmuseet* (Fine Arts Museum), including Rubens' *Judgment of Solomon*.

10. The present Palace of Christiansborg was designed by Thorvald Jørgensen and built in 1907–16. It replaced an earlier building of 1803–28 which was destroyed by fire in 1884.

11. An imitation stone, not unlike marble, which is composed of plaster mixed with glue.

12. The *Slotskirke*, a classical building by C. F. Hansen, dedicated in 1826.

13. Presumably *Frederiks Kirke*, begun in 1749 for King Frederick V. The original intention was to construct the church entirely of marble but work was suspended in 1770 because of lack of funds which probably accounts for the impression that it had been destroyed. The building was not completed until 1894.

14. The Castle of Rosenborg, an irregular building in Gothic style, was built in 1610–17. It continues to house the majority of the *objets d'art* mentioned here.

15. One of the principal European orders of knighthood. It was founded by King Christian I in 1462, although it did not become a regular institution until 1693.

16. Anne of Denmark, the wife of King James I of England and VI of Scotland. Christian IV was her brother.

17. The Castle of Frederiksborg was built in the Italian style between 1699 and 1730 for King Frederick IV. It is now a military academy.

18. Caroline Matilda (1751–75), daughter of Frederick, Prince of Wales. She married King Christian V of Denmark in 1766, but the marriage was dissolved in 1772.
19. *The Prisoner of Chillon* (1816) by Lord Byron.
20. Later King Christian VIII (1786–1848). He succeeded King Frederick VI in 1839.
21. The Castle of Kronenborg was built towards the end of the sixteenth century but it was extensively restored after a fire in 1637.
22. The falls at Trollhättan on the Göta are six in number, at a point where the river descends one hundred and eight feet in the course of nearly a mile.
23. The length of artificial work on the Göta canal is fifty-four miles and it has fifty-eight locks. It was built between 1810 and 1832 under the direction of Thomas Telford.

CHAPTER III *pp.* 34–45
1. John Arthur Douglas Bloomfield, later 2nd Baron Bloomfield (1802–79). Secretary of the British Legation at Stockholm, 1826–39.
2. Eugénie Bernardine Désirée Clary (1777–1860), who had married Bernadotte (see below) in 1798. Her father was a banker.
3. Charles XIV (*né* Jean Baptiste Jules Bernadotte), King of Sweden and Norway (1763–1844). His father, Henri Bernadotte, had been Procurator at Pau.
4. Later Oscar I, King of Sweden and Norway (1799–1859). The son of Charles XIV, he married Joséphine Beauharnais, daughter of the Duke Eugène of Leuchtenberg in 1823.
5. The Palace of Drottningholm with its fine park and formal gardens was originally built at the end of the sixteenth century. The existing building, by Nicodemus Tessin and his son, dates from the second half of the seventeenth century.
6. The Queen must in fact have been about twenty-one when she married. See *n.* 2 above.
7. The Palace was designed by Nicodemus Tessin the younger (d. 1728), although not completed until 1754. The building is in the Italian Renaissance style but many ornamental details were added in the restoration of 1901.
8. Christopher Hughes (1786–1845), American chargé d'affaires at Stockholm, 1830–42.
9. Anne Louise Germaine Necker, Baronne de Staël Holstein (1766–1817). Her writings caused offence to Napoleon and she gained the respect of the rest of Europe by her stubborn resistance to his methods.
10. Count Loewenhjelm was a senior member of the Swedish Council of State.

11. Gustavus III (1746–92) was shot in the back at a midnight masquerade at the Stockholm Opera House on 16 March 1792.

12. Although Hughes was appointed Secretary of the American Legation as early as 1816, he had in fact served in the Netherlands before his appointment as chargé d'affaires at Stockholm in 1830. See also above p. 165, n. 8.

13. Count Wetterstedt had been Minister of Foreign Affairs in the Swedish Council of State.

14. A member of the Council of State and Commander of the Army.

15. The approach to St. Petersburg was considerably improved by the construction of a canal through the shallows in 1875–85.

CHAPTER IV *pp.* 46–57

1. Now the Gorny Institute. It was built in 1803–07 and modelled on the Temple of Poseidon at Paestum. See also pp. 99–100.

2. The statue, by the French sculptor, Etienne Maurice Falconet, was erected by Catherine the Great in 1782.

3. The column was erected in 1832 as a monument to Tsar Alexander I. It could hardly be described as small, rising as it does above Palace Square to a height of one hundred and sixty feet.

4. Built in 1704 but much altered in 1823, it continues to house naval departments of the government.

5. John George Lambton, 1st Earl of Durham (1792–1840). Ambassador Extraordinary to Russia, 1835–37.

6. Count Karl Robert Nesselrode (1780–1862), the Russian Minister of Foreign Affairs. He had been at the Congress of Verona in October 1822.

7. Baron Philippe de Brunnow (1797–1875). At this time Brunnow was *Premier Rédacteur* in the Ministry of Foreign Affairs. He too had been at Verona.

8. The Winter Palace was built in 1754–62 and the part of the Palace where the great collection of paintings was kept was called "the Hermitage". They were placed there in 1775 and a few years later a new wing was added, but there was a disastrous fire in 1837 which destroyed most of the furniture and interior decoration. The present Hermitage was erected in 1840–52.

9. The collection of the ex-Empress Joséphine, wife of Napoleon I, was acquired by Tsar Alexander I in 1814.

10. Antonio Canova (1757–1822), an Italian sculptor particularly admired in Russia. A number of his works such as *The Dancing Girl* and *The Three Graces* can be seen in the Hermitage.

11. A reference to the original building, completed in the year of Elizabeth's death (1762). She was the daughter of Peter the Great.

12. Prince Peter Volkonsky was the most senior officer of the Imperial Court.

13. George Dawe (1781–1829), an English painter and engraver commissioned by Tsar Alexander I to paint a series of portraits of the principal Russian officers who fought against Napoleon I.

14. The King of Prussia is presumably Frederick William III who reigned 1797–1840. The Grand Duke Constantine was the Tsarevich, but renounced his claim to the succession in 1823 (see *Intro.*, p. 10). Both Prince Grigory Potemkin and Count Alexander Suvarov were Russian field marshals.

15. The Academy of Arts was built during the period 1756–88 and occupies a large area on Vasilyevsky Island. It is now a State University for Painting, Sculpture and Architecture and the art gallery has been divided between the Hermitage and the Russian Museum.

16. Now the Russian National Museum. It was built in 1819–25 by direction of Tsar Alexander I, for his younger brother, the Grand Duke Michael. The Museum was opened in 1898.

17. Now the City Museum or "Pioneer's Palace". Originally built for Count A. G. Rasumovsky, favourite of the Empress Elizabeth, in 1742–53, it was used as a residence by the Imperial family after 1866. The Museum was founded there in 1919.

18. Alexander Nevsky *Lavra* was built in 1710–16 in honour of the Grand Duke of that name (1218–53). It is the former seat of the Metropolitan.

19. Wife of the Grand Duke Michael and sister-in-law of Tsar Nicholas I.

20. The building of the Great Palace was begun in 1715, and considerably enlarged about 1750. It was completely destroyed in the Second World War, but has since been reconstructed.

21. The Palace of *Mon Plaisir*, originally modelled on a Dutch brick house. Peter the Great (1672–1725) lived there during the construction of the Great Palace.

22. Dorothy von Benkendorf, Princess Lieven (1784–1857) was the wife of Prince Christopher Lieven, the former Russian Ambassador in London who had been recalled in 1834 to become Governor and Tutor to the Tsarevich. Although the couple returned to Russia together, they soon separated and Princess Lieven went to reside in Paris.

23. The Alexander Palace was built in 1792–96 for the future Tsar Alexander I. After the revolution of 1905 it became almost the permanent residence of the Imperial family.

24. See *Intro.*, p. 9.

25. Grand Duke Nicholas (b. 1831) and Grand Duke Michael (b. 1832).

26. Tsar Alexander I died at Taganrog on 1 December 1825. Count Tchernischev was Minister of War at the time of the Londonderrys' visit.

27. See *Intro.*, p. 9.
28. The English Farm was established by Tsar Alexander I after a visit to England; the Arsenal was also commenced under the direction of Alexander but it was greatly added to by Nicholas. See *Recollections* pp. 136–8.
29. A fine variety of inlaid mosaic, in which hard and expensive stones are used in relief.
30. Grand Duchess Catherine (d. 1819).
31. The former Princess Maria Louisa of Baden, who adopted the names Elizabeth Fedorovna when she married in 1793.

CHAPTER V *pp.* 58–78
1. A unit of measure equal to about two-thirds of an English mile.
2. A battle fought on 29 and 30 August 1813, in which the French were defeated by a combined force of Russians, Prussians and Austrians.
3. See *Intro.*, p. 13.
4. Much of the Kremlin, which had been built over a period of centuries, was destroyed in the burning of Moscow in September 1812.
5. The so-called "Queen of Bells" dates from the eighteenth century and is decorated with bas-reliefs by Bartolomeo Rastrelli. It fell from its special roof in a fire of 1737 and buried itself deeply in the ground. In 1836 it was put on the pedestal which holds it to this day.
6. Prince Alexander Golitsin was the Director General of Posts.
7. Count Peter Tolstoy, President of the Second Department (military affairs).
8. The present Grand Kremlin Palace was not built until 1838–49. It stands on the site of the old palace built in 1753 for the Empress Elizabeth.
9. Sir Thomas Lawrence (1769–1830) probably painted this portrait in 1818 when he went to Aix-la-Chapelle to paint the sovereigns and diplomatists gathered there.
10. Charles XII, King of Sweden (1682–1718) invaded the Ukraine in 1709 but his army was totally defeated by the Russians at Poltava in July.
11. The Cathedral of the Assumption built 1467–79, the Cathedral of the Annunciation built 1482–90, and the Cathedral of the Archangel Michael built 1505–09. The coronations of the Tsars took place in the first, while the Cathedral of the Archangel Michael was the burying place of the Tsars before Peter the Great.
12. The Allies occupied Paris on 31 March 1814.
13. An opera in three acts by Ferdinand Hérold, first produced at Paris in 1832.
14. The first Bolshoi Theatre was built in the years 1821–24 but was destroyed by fire in 1853. The present theatre dates from 1856.

15. Founded by the Empress Catherine II in 1764. The premises described here, built in 1823–25, are now the headquarters of the Academy of Medical Sciences.

16. This palace was built in 1798–1802 for a rich mine owner and was only later acquired by the Golitsin family. A hospital, now known as the *Medsantrud*, was installed there as early as 1876.

17. The droshky is the Russian version of a low carriage with four wheels.

18. The Troitse-Sergievskaya Monastery was built about 1422 on the site of the earlier wooden church established by St. Sergius. It is situated in the town of Zagorsk, forty-four miles from Moscow.

19. A reference to events in 1608–09 when the Monastery withstood a lengthy siege by the Poles.

20. Count Tolstoy's aide de camp. See *Recollections* p. 183.

21. The Theological Seminary founded in 1744 was transformed into an Academy in 1814.

22. Levshin Platon (1737–1812), Archimandrite of the *Troitse* Monastery. He became Archbishop of Tver in 1770 and Metropolitan of Moscow in 1787.

23. The great bell, in a tower three hundred and twenty feet high, weighs sixty-four tons.

24. The Cadets' School was founded in 1824. The buildings now house the Red Army School.

25. An opera by Giacomo Meyerbeer (1791–1863), first produced at Paris in 1831.

26. Built in 1796–1801 and situated in Lenin Avenue, it is now considered one of the finest buildings in Moscow.

27. Prince Léon Radziwill (b. 1808), the Tsar's aide de camp.

28. The Cathedral of St. Basil was commenced under the direction of Tsar Ivan IV ("the Terrible") in 1554 to commemorate the conquest of Kazan. With its cluster of towers and cupolas, it is one of the most striking buildings in Moscow.

29. The Saviour's Gate is the principal entrance to the Kremlin and, until the Revolution, passers-by were obliged to acknowledge the icon of Christ above the gate. It was designed by Solario and Mario Ruffo and dates from 1491, although the upper part is of seventeenth-century workmanship.

30. Now the House of Unions. The building was erected in 1786 as a club for the nobility. The Column Room described here, the marble of which is real, is now used for concerts and public meetings.

31. This building, which dates from 1804–07, now houses the Tuberculosis Institute.

32. The former Alexander Institute, built in 1805, is situated at No. 4 Samotyochnaya Street.

33. Princess Sophia Dorothea of Württemberg, second wife of Tsar

Paul I (1754–1801) who succeeded to the throne in 1796. On her marriage she adopted the Russian names Maria Fedorovna.

34. See above p. 168, *n*. 31.

35. The Maly Theatre, which resembles the *Comédie Française*, was redesigned in 1838–40 shortly after the Londonderrys' visit.

CHAPTER VI *pp*. 79–95

1. The Field of Mars was originally a marsh which was transformed into a parade ground by Tsar Peter the Great. It is now a pleasure garden.

2. A light low-hooded carriage, known as a calash in English.

3. Now the Little Opera House in Brodsky Street. It was built between 1831 and 1833.

4. Wife of the Austrian Ambassador, Count Antoine Apponyi.

5. Her husband was Prince Kyril Narishkin, the *Grand-Maréchal* of the Imperial Court.

6. In the Great Flood of 1824, the River Neva rose by almost fourteen feet and the whole city was inundated. The flood is commemorated in Pushkin's epic poem *The Bronze Horseman*.

7. Angelica Catalani (1780–1849), Maria Caradori-Allan (1800–65), Henriette Sontag (1806–54), Marie Malibran (1808–36) and Giulia Grisi (1811–67) were all famous sopranos of the early nineteenth century.

8. Prince Alexander Menshikov (1787–1869), Navy Minister at this time

9. Julia, daughter of General Sir John Floyd, who married Sir Robert Peel in 1820.

10. Better known as Lady Conyngham, the mistress of King George IV. Her husband Henry, Baron Conyngham of Mount Charles, was created Marquess Conyngham in 1816 and acted as Lord Steward of the Household for almost the whole reign of the King.

11. Amable Guillaume Prosper Brugière, Baron de Barante (1782–1866), a well-known French statesman and historian. He was appointed French Ambassador to Russia in 1835.

12. Princess Theresa, daughter of the Grand Duke Charles of Mecklenburg-Strelitz. She married Prince Charles Alexander of Thurn and Taxis in 1789.

13. Both the Duchess of Cumberland and Queen Louise of Prussia were daughters of the Grand Duke Charles. Princess Frederica Caroline married Ernest Augustus, Duke of Cumberland and Princess Louise married King Frederick William III of Prussia. The Empress Alexandra was, of course, the daughter of Frederick William and Queen Louise.

14. Princess Maria Theresa (b. 1794), the wife of Prince Paul Esterhazy.

15. Frances Susan Lambton (d. 1840), sister of the 1st Earl of Durham. The widow of the Hon. Frederick Howard, she married General the Hon. H. F. C. Cavendish in 1819.

16. Adelaide, the daughter of Duke Charles of Saxe-Meiningen, who married the future King William IV in 1818.

17. Illegitimate sons of William IV by Mrs. Jordan.

18. Princess Victoria Mary Louise, daughter of Duke Francis Frederick Antony of Saxe-Coburg-Saalfeld and widow of Edward Augustus, Duke of Kent and Strathearn.

19. The "new" arsenal built in 1808, situated at No. 3 Liteyny Prospect.

20. A peace treaty between Russia and Turkey, signed on 14 September 1829. The Sultan at this time was Mahmud II (1785–1839).

21. This palace was built in 1782–86 in a style somewhere between baroque and classical. It was badly damaged in the Second World War but has since been restored.

22. Wife of Count Ivan Voronzov-Dashkov, the *Grand-Maître des Cérémonies* at the Imperial Court.

23. Sir James Wylie (1768–1854) had been appointed a physician to the Imperial Court as early as 1798. He became physician-in-ordinary to Tsar Alexander I in 1814. See also below, pp. 93–94.

24. The two centres of conspiracy were the Northern Society in St. Petersburg and the more radical Southern Society based in Tulchin. Although aware of the plots against him, Alexander failed to take any action.

25. This sonnet was almost certainly written by Henry Thomas Liddell, later 1st Earl of Ravensworth (1797–1878). See also *Intro.*, p. 15.

CHAPTER VII *pp.* 96–115

1. Now the Pushkin Theatre in Ostrovsky Square. It was built between 1828 and 1832 in the Empire style.

2. *La Révolte au Sérail*, a ballet in three acts with choreography by Filippo Taglioni (1778–1871).

3. Charles X, King of France (1757–1836) died at Goritz on 6 November.

4. A small species of sturgeon found in the Black and Caspian Seas. It is very highly regarded in Russia and is used in the best quality caviar.

5. The Bolshoi Theatre, built at the end of the eighteenth century, was reconstructed in 1836. It re-opened with the first performance of Glinka's *Life for the Tsar*, an event regarded as a landmark in the history of Russian music. In 1889 the building was given to the Russian Musical Society for the use of the Conservatory.

6. On the Neva embankment and now known as the Red Fleet Quay.

7. Edward Law, 1st Earl of Ellenborough (1790–1871). His first wife was Octavia Stewart (d. 1819), Lord Londonderry's sister.

8. See above p. 166, *n.* 1.

9. A card game invented during the last quarter of the eighteenth century. It is said to have originated at Boston (Mass.) during a siege by the British, but it enjoyed its greatest popularity in French society. A variation of the game is sometimes known as Russian Boston.

10. Louise Le Brun (1755–1842), a French portrait painter.

11. He was in fact *Grand-Maître des Cérémonies*.

12. More correctly Prince (Kyril) Narishkin.

13. Count, later Prince, Alexis Orlov (1787–1862), at this time a member of the Tsar's Council. Orlov was Commander of the Cavalry Regiment of the Life Guards on the occasion of the rebellion of 1825.

14. The name adopted by the Cossacks as a title for their head who was virtually an independent prince under Polish suzerainty. When the Cossacks came under Russian rule in 1654 the position lost its influence and the title was vested in a member of the Imperial family, usually the Tsarevich.

15. Don Carlos (1788–1855) was the second surviving son of King Charles IV of Spain and claimed the succession on his brother's death in 1833. The latter, however, had suspended the Salic law by the Pragmatic Sanction and declared his daughter heir to the throne. The Carlist party was regarded as the supporter of absolutism and divine right.

16. Prince Ivan Gagarin was one of two *Grands-Maîtres* at the Imperial Court.

17. The fortress of St. Peter and St. Paul was constructed between 1703 and 1740 and is situated on the island opposite the Winter Palace.

18. The mint, founded in 1742, stands within the walls of the fortress. The present building, however, was erected at the beginning of the nineteenth century.

19. The Peter and Paul Basilica is situated in the centre of the fortress and contains a mausoleum where all the Tsars from Peter I to Alexander III, with the exception of Peter II, are buried. The present Basilica dates from 1750 when the earlier building of 1713–21 was largely rebuilt after a fire.

20. A great review of Russian troops, at which Frederick William III of Prussia had been present, was held upon the plain of Vertus near Châlons on 10 September 1815.

21. See above p. 167, *n.* 14.

22. Frederick Augustus II, King of Saxony (1797–1854).

23. Grand Duchess Marie, see *Intro.*, p. 10.

24. Probably Prince Peter of Oldenburg (b. 1812) who was a lieutenant-general in Russian service.

25. Prince Frederick Charles Alexander of Prussia (b. 1801), the fourth child of the King.

26. Founded by Tsar Peter the Great in 1698.

27. One of the most distinguished European orders of chivalry, founded in 1701 by Elector Frederick I.

28. The Württemberg Minister at this time was Prince Henry of Hohenlohe-Kirchberg. The name "Leuchenfelles" does not appear in contemporary lists of the diplomatic corps.

29. The King narrowly escaped death on 27 December 1836 when a pistol-shot grazed his chest while his carriage was crossing the *Quai des Tuileries*.

30. Wife of a member of the Tsar's Council.

CHAPTER VIII *pp.* 116–128

1. The Feast of the Epiphany (6 January) was set aside throughout the Empire for blessing the waters, a ceremony closely associated with the Orthodox Church.

2. It was the usual practice for foreign princesses who married into the Imperial family to adopt Russian names.

3. For a fuller description see *Recollections*, p. 222 *et seq.*

4. The Marble Palace was built between 1768 and 1785 as a present from the Empress Catherine II to Count Orlov. It has a façade of pink and blue marble and now contains some government offices and a branch of the Lenin Museum.

5. This house was originally built in the Dutch style in 1703. Under the direction of Empress Catherine II, however, the wooden walls were covered with stone.

6. This Cathedral was completed in 1811 with a colonnade inspired by St. Peter's, Rome, of which it is an ugly imitation. The trophies of the Napoleonic Wars can still be seen there.

7. Mikhail Larinovich Golenishchev-Kutusov, Prince of Smolensk (1745–1813), the Russian Field-Marshal responsible for the pursuit of Napoleon on his retreat from Moscow.

8. Louis Nicholas Davout, Duke of Auerstädt and Prince of Eckmühl (1770–1823), a French general of the Napoleonic period.

9. The Smolny Convent was built in the baroque style between 1744 and 1757. A boarding school for the daughters of the nobility was attached to it under the direction of the Empress Catherine II.

10. The territory of the Kalmuck Tartars bordering on the Caspian Sea.

11. Built between 1783 and 1789 for Prince Grigory Potemkin (1739–91). In 1787 Potemkin received the title Prince of the Tauride in recognition of his conquest of the Crimea, hence the name of the palace. It was the seat of the Duma from 1906–17.

12. See above p. 165, *n.* 4.

13. A son of the Crown Prince of Persia accompanied the embassy which was sent to St. Petersburg after the murder of the Russian envoy at Teheran in 1828.

14. Queen Louise of Prussia visited St. Petersburg with King Frederick William III in 1808.

15. See above p. 171, *n.* 16.

CHAPTER IX *pp.* 129–139
1. John Ralphe Milbanke. Secretary of the British Embassy, 1835–38, and Minister Plenipotentiary *ad interim,* 1837–38.
2. See *Intro.,* p. 10.
3. See *Intro.,* p. 10.
4. Ivan Fedorovich Paskevich, Count of Erivan, Prince of Warsaw (1782–1856). In 1831 he was given the command of the Russian army sent to crush the Polish revolt and made Viceroy.
5. As above p. 165, *n.* 19.
6. See above p. 172, *n.* 24.
7. Strictly speaking the anchar tree. "Upas" is the Javanese word applied to the poison obtained from the gum of the tree.
8. A carriage much employed for winter travel in Russia, usually in the form of a sledge with a cover or hood.
9. This was not part of Finland at all but Estonia. Earlier travellers often made this mistake possibly because of the linguistic affinities of Finnish and Estonian.
10. Built for Count Heinrich von Brühl (1700–63), the palace was used by Constantine while Viceroy of Poland, 1815–30.

CHAPTER X *pp.* 140–149
1. The wife of Paskevich.
2. Princess Pauline Constance, Countess Mniszek, wife of Prince Antoine Jablonovsky whom she married in 1818.
3. Fuhrmann was in fact a member of the Council of Administration and Director of the Treasury Commission.
4. After his morganatic second marriage to Johanna Grudzinska in 1820 Constantine renounced his claim to the succession in a manifesto not opened until Alexander's death in 1825. This inevitably led to a period of confusion before Nicholas ascended the throne. See also *Intro.,* p. 10.
5. The Lazienka Park was laid out between 1764 and 1794 and the construction of the Palace commenced in 1775. It was damaged by fire in 1944 but a large part of it has been rebuilt.
6. Stanislaus II, King of Poland (1732–98).
7. The theatre was established in 1790 and is a copy of the ancient theatre at Herculaneum.
8. Mikhail Dmitrievich Gorchakov (1795–1861), later Prince Gorchakov. He played an important part in the defeat of the Polish insurrection of 1831 and was appointed Military Governor of Warsaw in 1846.

9. *The Giaour, a Fragment of a Turkish Tale* (1813).
10. A treaty between Russia and Prussia was signed at Kalisz, about 147 miles from Warsaw, in 1813. It was also the scene of a review of Russian and Prussian troops in 1835.

CHAPTER XI *pp.* 150–159

1. Michel Ney, Duke of Elchingen, Prince of the Moskowa, Marshal of France (1769–1815).
2. Gebhard Leberecht von Blücher (1742–1819), who commanded the Prussian army at Waterloo.
3. Ernest Augustus, Duke of Cumberland, later King of Hanover (1771–1851). He was the fifth son of George III and a personal friend of Lord Londonderry.
4. Adolphus Frederick, Duke of Cambridge (1774–1850), seventh son of George III.
5. Frederick William III.
6. A reference to the King's morganatic second marriage (1824) with the Countess Auguste von Harrach whom he created Princess Von Liegnitz.
7. See above p. 170, *n.* 13.
8. Frederick William (1795–1861), the eldest son of Frederick William III, married Princess Elizabeth Louise, the daughter of King Maximilian Joseph of Bavaria in 1823. He succeeded his father as King Frederick William IV in 1840.
9. William Louis (1797–1888), Frederick William III's second son, married his second wife, Princess Louise Augusta, the daughter of the Grand Duke Frederick of Saxe-Weimar, in 1829. He succeeded his brother as King William I in 1861 and became German Emperor in 1871.
10. Lord George William Russell (1790–1846), son of John Russell, 6th Duke of Bedford. British Ambassador at Berlin, 1835–41.
11. Count Charles Bresson (1798–1847).
12. Presumably a reference to the neo-classical architect Karl Friedrich Schinkel (1781–1841) who had a profound influence on the architecture of Berlin.
13. The only son of the Duke of Cumberland and later King George V of Hanover (1819–78). He lost the sight of one eye as a child and the other by an accident in 1833.
14. Prince Charles (see above p. 172, *n.* 25) married Marie Louise Alexandrine, daughter of the Grand Duke Frederick of Saxe-Weimar in 1827.
15. George Frederick Charles, Duke of Mecklenburg-Strelitz (b. 1779). His wife was Marie, the daughter of the Landgrave Frederick of Hesse-Cassel.

16. Prince (Frederick Henry) Albert (b. 1809), another son of King Frederick William III, married Princess Frederica Louise Charlotte, daughter of King William I of the Netherlands, in 1830.

17. Ferdinand Philippe, Duke of Orleans (1810–42), son of Louis Philippe. He did not in fact marry Princess Helen Louise, daughter of Grand Duke Frederick Louis of Mecklenburg-Schwerin, until 30 May 1837.

18. Prince William of Sayn-Wittgenstein-Hohenstein (b. 1770), Great Chamberlain at the Prussian Court.

19. Elizabeth Anne Rawdon, daughter of the Hon. John Theophilus Rawdon. She married Lord William Russell in 1817.

20. The museum in the *Lustgarten* was built by Schinkel and opened in 1830. The collection of paintings was kept there until the construction of the Kaiser Friedrich Museum in 1904 and is now housed in the *Gemäldegalerie* of the Dahlem Museum.

21. A ballet in two acts with choreography by Filippo Taglioni and music by Jean Schneitzhoeffer. It was first produced at Paris in 1832.

22. *Ondine,* usually referred to as *Undine* and *Fernand Cortez* or *La Conquête du Mexique* are both operas by composers with close associations with Berlin. The former is the work of Gasparo Spontini and was first produced at Paris in 1809; the latter is the last opera of Ernst Hoffman and was first produced at Berlin in 1816. We have been unable to identify *Robinson Crusoe.*

23. The *Königliche Hofoper,* predecessor of the present *Staatsoper,* was built in 1740–43 with an exterior resembling a Corinthian temple. It was converted into a galleried theatre by Carl Langhans in 1788 and altered again by his son in 1844 after a fire.

24. Probably Prince Bernard (b. 1800), a major in Prussian service and son of Prince William of Solms-Braunfels.

25. The former *Palais Kaiser Wilhelms I* in the *Unter den Linden* was severely damaged in the Second World War but has been restored for the use of the Humboldt University.

26. The *Stadtschloss,* begun in 1661 and greatly enlarged, 1745–51.

27. Queen Louise. See above p. 89.

28. Built at enormous expense under the direction of Frederick the Great between 1763 and 1769, the palace is now a teachers' training college.

29. Many of Dresden's most famous buildings were destroyed by bombing in 1945. The two churches referred to here are the *Frauenkirche* and the *Hofkirche,* both of which were severely damaged. The latter has been restored and the former has been included in reconstruction plans. The Great Bridge (*Augustusbrücke*) of 1727–31 was an earlier casualty, having been demolished in 1906 and replaced by a wider bridge.

30. The Hon. Francis Reginald Forbes, the British Minister at Dresden.

31. The gallery was founded by King Augustus I of Saxony (1750–1827). The collection, including Raphael's *Madonna di San Sisto,* is now

176

housed in the Semper Gallery which was destroyed in 1945 and re-opened in 1960.

32. Richard Evans (1784–1871), the British portrait painter and copyist.
33. Meissen china was frequently referred to as Dresden although the factory was not moved there until 1863.
34. The Green Vault (*Grünegewölbe*) of the Royal Palace contained a famous collection of precious stones, pearls, and works of art in gold, silver, ivory, amber, etc.
35. Queen Maria, daughter of King Maximilian Joseph of Bavaria. She married Frederick Augustus II in 1833 and was his second wife.
36. The King's brother, Prince Jean, married Princess Amelia Augusta of Bavaria in 1822. Her twin sister was Princess Elizabeth Louise of Prussia.
37. Princess Sophia of Bavaria. She married the Archduke Francis of Austria in 1824.
38. Wilhelmine Schröder-Devrient (1804–60), a German operatic singer particularly popular at Dresden.
39. Not in fact the King's sister but his cousin Princess (Maria) Augusta. She was born in 1782 and was the daughter of King Augustus I.
40. Minister of Foreign Affairs and Minister of Finance.
41. Marie Narishkin (1779–1854), mistress of Tsar Alexander I.

CHAPTER XII *pp.* 160–162
1. The Royal Porcelain Factory was housed in the *Albrechtsburg* until 1860.
2. One of Europe's most famous fairs which is thought to have been founded as a market about 1170.
3. Maria Amelia (b. 1782), the daughter of King Ferdinand IV of Naples (and I of the Two Sicilies). She married Louis Philippe in 1809.
4. Count Pahlen.

Select Index of Persons and Places

180

Frederica Louise Charlotte of the Netherlands, Princess of Prussia, 153, 176
Frederick II (the Great), King of Prussia, 62, 156, 176
Frederick VI, King of Denmark, 26–30, 34, 164–5
Frederick, Prince of Hesse-Cassel, 9
Frederick Augustus II, King of Saxony, 110, 157–9, 172, 177
Frederick Charles Alexander, Prince of Prussia, 110–11, 113, 116–17, 124, 153, 172, 175
Frederick William III, King of Prussia, 9, 49, 56, 89, 101, 109–10, 148, 151–7, 167, 170, 172–3, 175–6
Frederick William, Prince Royal of Prussia (later King Frederick William IV), 152–3, 156, 175
Frederiksborg, 29, 164
Fuhrmann, Madame, 142
Fuhrmann, Monsieur, 174
Fulde, 161

Gagarin, Prince Ivan, 106, 172
Gascoyne-Cecil, Frances Mary, 6
Gaspard, Dr., 154
Gatchina, 9, 12
George III, King of England, 26, 62, 175
George IV, King of England, 30, 90, 100, 124, 170
George, Prince (later King George V of Hanover), 153, 175
Germany, 26
Ghent, 20
Golenishchev-Kutusov, Mikhail Larinovich, Prince of Smolensk, 120, 173
Golitsin, Prince (founder of Golitsin Hospital), 71
Golitsin, Prince Alexander, 60, 168
Golitsin, Prince Dimitri, 60, 71, 88, 100
Golitsin, Prince Serge, 64–5, 71–4, 77, 104, 106, 131–2
Golovkin, Count, 91
Gorchakov, General Mikhail Dmitrievich (later Prince Gorchakov), 146–8, 174
Göteborg, 8, 17, 31–2
Gotha, 161
Gouriev, Count, 61
Gouriev, Madame, 159
Graefe, Dr., 152, 154
Gravelines, 20
Greece, 17, 147
Grisi, Giulia, 87, 170
Grudzinska, Johanna, Princess Lowitz, 143, 174
Gudevich, Countess, 66, 70, 76
Gustavus III, King of Sweden, 40, 43, 62, 166

Haarlem, 19
Hague, The, 15, 19, 22–3, 80
Halmstad, 31
Hälsingborg, 30–2
Hamburg, 7, 24
Hanover, 24–5, 156
Hare, Anne, Lady Ennismore, 4
Harrach, Countess von, see Liegnitz, Princess von
Heeckeren, Baron, 91

Hélène, Grand Duchess of Russia, 10, 52, 88, 90, 102, 107, 126, 129–33, 167
Helsingör, 30
Herculaneum, 36, 114, 174
Herzberg, 156–7
Hesse, Charles, Landgrave of, 26, 163
Hesse, Princess of, see Marie
Hesse-Cassel, Landgrave of, see Frederick
Hesse-Cassel, Prince of, see Frederick
Hogarth, William, 100
Holland, 22–5, 27, 158
Holstein, 25
Howard, Frances Susan, see Cavendish, Frances Susan
Howard, Madame, 13, 59
Hughes, Christopher, 37, 40, 165–6

Ireland, 11, 22, 58, 147
Italy, 17, 123, 164
Ivan IV (the Terrible), Tsar of Russia, 75, 169

Jablonovska, Princess, 142, 174
Jargivo, 80
Jean, Prince of Saxony, 158, 177
Jean, Princess (wife of above), see Amelia Augusta
Joséphine, Princess Royal of Sweden (née Beauharnais), 36, 39, 165
Joukovsky, Basil, 9

Kalinovsky, Olga, 9
Kalisz, 148, 150, 175
Karl, Mademoiselle, 141
Kaunas (Kovno), 136
Keitsev, Madame, 113
Kent and Strathearn, Duchess of, 90, 171
Victoria Mary Louise of Saxe-Coburg-Saalfeld
Kiel, 15, 24–5
Kiev, 66, 69
Kindener, Madame, 89, 106
Kingisepp (Yamburg), 134
Kisselov, General, 61, 91, 99, 104, 133
Klaypeda (Memel), 135
Klin, 59
Kohl, J. G., 13
Kotchoubey, Princess, 121
Krabbe-Carisius, Jean de, 26, 29, 164
Kronenborg, 30, 165
Kronshtadt, 37, 44–6, 52, 85
Kutno, 150
Kutusov, Marshal, see Golenishchev-Kutusov

Lambsdorff, General de, 8
Lambton, Frances Susan, see Cavendish, Frances Susan
Lambton, John George, 1st Earl of Durham, 46, 51–3, 80, 83, 85, 89, 91–2, 96–8, 124, 126, 129, 131, 133, 166, 171
Lambton, Louisa Elizabeth, Countess of Durham, 53, 97, 107
Laval, Countess, 118
Laval, Monsieur, 112
Law, Edward, 1st Earl of Ellenborough, 99, 171
Law, Mr., 99
Lawrence, Sir Thomas, 61, 168

Le Brun, Louise, 100, 172
Leipzig, 160
Leningrad, 19
Leopold I, King of the Belgians, 22, 163
Leuchenfelles, Monsieur de, 112, 173
Leuchtenberg, Duke of, *see* Beauharnais, Eugène
Liddell, Henry Thomas (later Earl of Ravensworth), 15–16, 95, 157, 171
Lieberman, Monsieur de, 108
Liegnitz, Princess von (previously Countess von Harrach), 151, 156, 175
Lieven, Madame de, 8
Lieven, Prince Christopher, 98, 104, 124, 131, 167
Lieven, Princess, *see* Benkendorf, Dorothy von
Loewenhjelm, Count, 39, 41, 165
Loewenhjelm, Countess, 39
Loftus, Lord Augustus, 14
Lomza, 137–8
London, 1, 2, 4–5, 7, 11, 17–19, 24, 41, 70, 114, 156, 167
Londonderry, Marchioness of, *see* Vane-Tempest-Stewart, Edith
Londonderry, Marchioness of, *see* Vane-Tempest-Stewart, Frances Anne
Londonderry, Marquesses of, *see* Stewart, Charles William, 3rd Marquess; Stewart, Robert, 1st Marquess; Stewart, Robert, 2nd Marquess; Vane, George Henry, 5th Marquess
Long Newton, 1
Louis XIV, King of France, 62, 105
Louis XVIII, King of France, 107, 122
Louis Philippe, King of the French, 14–15, 22, 105, 112, 122, 163, 173, 176–7
Louise, Queen of Prussia, 89, 114, 125, 156, 170, 173, 176
Louvain, 19
Lowitz, Princess, *see* Grudzinska, Johanna
Lübeck, 24
Lutzerode, Baron (Monsieur) de, 105
Lyall, Dr. Robert, 11
Lyon, Miss, 8
Lyons, 38, 65

McDonnell, Anne Catherine, Countess of Antrim, 1, 3–4
Mahmud II, Sultan of Turkey, 61, 90, 171
Mainz, 161
Malibran, Marie, 87, 170
Maria, Queen of Saxony, 158–9, 177
Maria Amelia, Queen of the French, 14–15, 162, 177
Maria Fedorovna, Empress of Russia (Empress Mother), 12, 49, 62, 65, 74, 76–7, 90, 94, 102, 114, 121, 143, 169–70
Maria Louisa, Princess of Baden, *see* Elizabeth Fedorovna, Empress of Russia
Marie, Grand Duchess of Russia, 9, 86, 104–5, 111, 131
Marie, Princess of Hesse, 9
Marie, Queen of Denmark, 26, 28, 163
Marie Louise Alexandrine of Saxe-Weimar, Princess Charles of Prussia, 153, 175

Mariestad, 32
Marijampole, 137
Matilda, Queen of Denmark, *see* Caroline Matilda
Maximilian, Duke of Leuchtenberg, 9
Maximilian Joseph, King of Bavaria, 152, 158–9, 175, 177
Mecklenburg-Strelitz, Marie, Duchess of, 153, 175
Mecklenburg-Strelitz, George Frederick Charles (Grand) Duke of, 153, 175
Mednoye, 79
Meissen, 157, 160
Melnitsa, 72
Melrose, 137
Menshikov, Prince Alexander, 87–8, 91, 108, 170
Metternich, Prince Charles, 5
Metz, 14, 162
Miatlev, Madame, 113, 121, 124, 128
Michael, Grand Duke of Russia (b. 1798), 8, 10, 51, 88, 90, 97, 130, 167
Michael, Grand Duke of Russia (b. 1832), 9, 54, 117, 167
Milbanke, John Ralph, 129
Milbanke, Sir Ralph, 5
Moore, Sir John, 2
Mornay, Count Charles de, 36–7, 40, 42
Moritzburg, 157
Morocco, Emperor of, 37
Moscow, 8, 10, 12–13, 16–17, 19, 23, 47, 53, 57–60, 62–6, 69, 71–3, 75–6, 78–81, 85–6, 90, 96, 101, 105, 120, 136, 141, 168–9, 173
Mount Charles, Lady, *see* Conyngham, Lady Elizabeth
Mount Stewart, 2
Müller, Christian, 19
Muller, Eugénie, 122
Murillo, Bartolomé, 47, 65

Nacka, 39, 41, 43
Nancy, 120, 162
Naples, 63, 84, 98
Napoleon I, Emperor of France, 38–9, 62, 65–6, 105, 120, 122, 148, 156, 159, 165–7, 173
Narishkin, Prince Kyril (Monsieur), 101, 170, 172
Narishkin, Madame, 84, 91
Narishkin, Marie, 159, 177
Narva, 134
Neboulsin, Monsieur, 60, 70
Nelson, Horatio, 1st Viscount Nelson, 28
Nesselrode, Count Karl Robert, 47, 51, 53, 65, 92, 104, 106, 108, 121, 131, 166
Nesselrode, Count (son of above), 60, 92
Nesselrode, Countess (Madame), 52–3, 83–4, 91, 101–2, 107, 109, 128, 132
Netherlands, 2, 163, 166
Neva, The, 45, 48, 84–5, 99, 113, 116, 118, 133, 170–1
Nevsky, Alexander, Grand Duke, 51, 167
Ney, Michel, Duke of Elchingen, Prince of the Moskowa, 150, 175
Nicholas I, Tsar of Russia, 8–11, 16, 19, 23, 37, 42, 48–54, 61–3, 71–7, 80–2, 84–90, 93–4, 97–8, 100–106, 108, 110–13, 116–17, 121, 123–5, 128–33, 140, 142, 144–5, 150, 152

182